ENVIRONMENTAL
CORRECTIONS

For those who have inspired us in so many ways,
this book is dedicated to
Isaac Ervine by Lacey Schaefer
Paula Dubeck by Francis T. Cullen
and
Milton Heumann by John E. Eck

Lacey Schaefer
Griffith University

Francis T. Cullen
University of Cincinnati

John E. Eck
University of Cincinnati

ENVIRONMENTAL CORRECTIONS

A New Paradigm for Supervising
Offenders in the Community

Los Angeles | London | New Delhi
Singapore | Washington DC

Los Angeles | London | New Delhi
Singapore | Washington DC

FOR INFORMATION:

SAGE Publications, Inc.
2455 Teller Road
Thousand Oaks, California 91320
E-mail: order@sagepub.com

SAGE Publications Ltd.
1 Oliver's Yard
55 City Road
London EC1Y 1SP
United Kingdom

SAGE Publications India Pvt. Ltd.
B 1/I 1 Mohan Cooperative Industrial Area
Mathura Road, New Delhi 110 044
India

SAGE Publications Asia-Pacific Pte. Ltd.
3 Church Street
#10-04 Samsung Hub
Singapore 049483

Acquisitions Editor: Jerry Westby
Editorial Assistant: Laura Kirkhuff
Production Editor: Libby Larson
Copy Editor: Kris Bergstad
Typesetter: C&M Digitals (P) Ltd.
Proofreader: Allison Syring
Indexer: Will Ragsdale
Cover Designer: Scott Van Atta
Marketing Manager: Liz Thornton

Copyright © 2016 by SAGE Publications, Inc.

Printed in the United States of America

Library of Congress Cataloging-in-Publication Data

Schaefer, Lacey, author.

Environmental corrections: a new paradigm for supervising offenders in the community / Lacey Schaefer, Francis T. Cullen, John E. Eck.

pages cm
Includes bibliographical references and index.

ISBN 978-1-5063-2328-2 (pbk. : alk. paper)

1. Police supervision. 2. Criminals—Rehabilitation. 3. Crime prevention. 4. Community-based corrections. 5. Criminology. I. Cullen, Francis T., author. II. Eck, John E., author. III. Title.

HV9275.S26 2016
364.6'8—dc23   2015029664

This book is printed on acid-free paper.

15 16 17 18 19 10 9 8 7 6 5 4 3 2 1

Brief Contents

Contents

Preface

For a criminal act to occur, two elements must be present: a motivated offender and a crime opportunity. This simple, almost commonsensical criminological principle has profound—but until now largely unrecognized—implications for correctional practice. It means that to reduce the likelihood that offenders under community supervision will commit a crime, probation and parole officers have two potential targets for intervention: lessen offenders' motivation to break the law or lessen offenders' access to opportunities to break the law. These two intervention strategies are complementary, not mutually exclusive. In fact, correctional rehabilitation should involve efforts to help supervisees relinquish their desire to offend and to avoid opportunities to offend.

Until now, community supervision has focused mainly on only one element of the criminal act: offender motivation or what is sometimes called "criminal propensity." Treatment programs—such as cognitive-behavioral therapy that seeks to correct "thinking errors"—try to cure probationers and parolees of the desire to re-offend. Another, more punitive approach is to try to scare supervisees straight—to threaten them with revocation and a stay in prison if they do not resist their criminal urges. The opportunity element of the crime act, however, is either neglected or addressed only in a general way. In this regard, offenders are given a document listing out "conditions" of probation or parole, which may say that they cannot associate with known felons or perhaps must obey a curfew. A blunt approach at opportunity reduction is at times employed: incapacitate offenders by placing them under home confinement with electronic monitoring.

Environmental Corrections proposes to rectify this imbalance in the attention given to opportunity and thus to provide a *new paradigm* for supervising offenders in the community. Let us hasten to say that this model is not a rejection of the long-standing correctional focus on rehabilitation; in fact, we argue that there are points at which the traditional treatment approach and the new opportunity approach intersect and become reinforcing (e.g., teaching offenders not to have thinking errors about criminal opportunity). Still, once the element of opportunity is taken seriously, it becomes apparent that probation and parole officers could engage in a variety of innovative practices that have the potential to reduce their supervisees' recidivism. In this approach, the guiding practice question becomes the following: What can officers do to make it less likely that offenders on their caseload will have access to the opportunity to commit a crime? *Environmental Corrections* calls attention to this crucial question and tries to provide answers to it.

Importantly, this new paradigm disavows a get tough, punitive approach to supervision. In virtually any supervision model, some punishment is inevitable, given that non-compliance must evoke meaningful consequences. But this caveat aside, the paradigm of environmental corrections rejects the idea that threatening, yelling at, belittling, and other harsh supervision methods are capable of effecting enduring behavioral change in offenders. These practices border on being unethical—and at times clearly cross the line of ethical correctional conduct—and they simply do not work. Rather, the goal in the model being proposed is to have officers first assess how specific criminal opportunities underlie their supervisees' past involvement in crime and then to design individualized supervision plans that channel offenders away from these criminogenic situations. In a way, this approach mirrors the current best practices in correctional rehabilitation where the criminogenic needs of offenders are assessed and then treatments that address or are "responsive" to these propensities are prescribed. The key difference, of course, is that environmental corrections applies this approach to the opportunity element rather than to the motivational element of the criminal act.

Some readers might wonder why we call this new paradigm *environmental corrections*. Within the field of criminology, there is the same imbalance in the focus on what causes crime as there is within corrections. Nearly all major criminological theories try to explain why some individuals are more likely than others to be motivated to offend. Could it be that they grew up in a disorganized neighborhood where a criminal culture was learned? Could it be that they were blocked from economic advancement that placed them under strain? Or might they lack the self-control or strong social bonds to keep their criminal desires in check? By contrast, criminologists traditionally have paid far less attention to the opportunity element of the criminal act. Still, some scholars did so—such as Lawrence Cohen and Marcus Felson who argued that beyond a "motivated offender," crime was contingent on opportunity. In their well-known routine activity theory, they identified two components that comprised opportunity, arguing that a crime could not take place unless an "attractive target" was present and "capable guardianship" was absent.

Over the years, interest in how opportunity is implicated in crime has increased considerably. Various lines of inquiry have coalesced into a criminological school known as *environmental criminology*. More recently, some scholars have argued that the perspective should be relabeled as *crime science*. This proposed name reflects the scholars' applied interest in using knowledge about criminal opportunity to reduce criminal acts. Their primary focus is less on reducing the number of people with criminal motivation and more on reducing the number of crimes that occur (thus the term "crime" science). For this reason, crime science has little interest in offender rehabilitation but a substantial interest in situational crime prevention. In this approach, a criminal act can be stopped by analyzing a situation and removing the opportunity to offend—such as by making a target less attractive or by providing guardianship that did not exist.

The paradigm of *environmental corrections* thus builds directly on the rich insights and applied focus of *environmental criminology*. Environmental criminology has called attention to the neglect of the role that opportunity plays in crime. In the same way, environmental corrections now hopes to alert the correctional community to how efforts to reduce offenders' access to opportunity while under supervision may prevent them from recidivating and improve public safety.

The invention of the concept of environmental corrections was a serendipitous event—in a sense, a matter of opportunity! Shortly after John Eck joined the criminal justice faculty at the University of Cincinnati, Frank Cullen dropped by his office to engage in a welcoming chat. Cullen was a traditional criminologist who studied criminal motivation and how it could be diminished by correctional rehabilitation. Eck was an environmental criminologist who thought that everything that Cullen did was irrelevant because it had little to do with reducing crime. But as the conversation proceeded, it shifted from an exchange of mutual (but humorous) disrespect to the growing discovery that their two orientations were not fully at odds. In fact, it became obvious in the course of that meeting that their two specialized interests—Eck's in *environmental* criminology and Cullen's in *correctional* rehabilitation—might be merged in an exciting way to form the new paradigm of *environmental corrections*. Shortly thereafter, they recruited Christopher Lowenkamp to coauthor an article by this title that appeared in *Federal Probation*. We wish to note our debt to Chris for his insights on how our ideas might translate into correctional practice.

For the next decade, Cullen and Eck discussed embarking on a book project, but sufficient impetus did not take hold until another serendipitous event occurred: the arrival of Lacey Schaefer to the criminal justice doctoral program at the University of Cincinnati. The details are of no special interest, but the intersection in time and space of the three of us created the opportunity for *Environmental Corrections* to be pursued in earnest. The delay in writing this book has been fortuitous. Our collaboration, of course, would not have been possible. But another consideration is relevant. Since the original article appeared, many advances have been made both in environmental criminology and in correctional rehabilitation. Our book thus reflects the increasingly rich scholarly literature that has developed in recent years.

Writing this book has been an intensely collaborative enterprise, but we also realize that we have benefited from the support of many others outside our authorship trinity—only some of whom we can list here. On a broad level, we are fortunate to have had our intellectual home in the School of Criminal Justice at the University of Cincinnati. The School not only is a vibrant scholarly community but also is one of the few academic departments that values and recruits multiple faculty members in the areas of corrections and environmental criminology. It is this "cognitive environment," to borrow Robert K. Merton's term, that nourished the ideas and relationships that made *Environmental Criminology* possible.

As the book was in progress and then finalized, Lacey Schaefer changed not only her academic home but also her continent, moving to Australia where she worked first at the University of Queensland before accepting her current position at Griffith University. Lorraine Mazerolle was instrumental in supporting Lacey's transcontinental transition and merits heartfelt gratitude. Thanks must also go to colleagues at the Australian Research Council's Centre of Excellence in Policing and Security, the Institute for Social Science Research, and the School of Social Science at the University of Queensland.

Environmental Corrections also would not have been possible without the abiding support we have received from Jerry Westby, our editor at SAGE. Jerry has a keen eye for new developments and the courage to pursue projects that are different. We are grateful for his faith in us and in our ideas. We also are grateful that Jerry has arranged for us to work with a wonderful staff at SAGE. We must express our special appreciation to Kristin Bergstad, Laura Kirkhuff, Libby Larson, and Terra Schultz.

Jerry must be credited as well with recruiting an excellent set of reviewers. We thank them for their detailed evaluations and for helping to sharpen our arguments. We are pleased to acknowledge their contributions:

Chima O. Ahanotu
Texas A&M University-Commerce

Elizabeth Perkins
Morehead State University

Jon A. Cooper
Indiana University of Pennsylvania

Deirdre M. Warren
Kent State University at Stark

Adam J. McKee
University of Arkansas at Monticello

Richard P. Wiebe
Fitchburg State University

Randy Myers
Old Dominion University

Finally, we have benefited in untold ways from those close to us who support us in our careers and in our pathways through life. Lacey Schaefer dedicates this book to her son Isaac, who inspires her to hope for a future with less crime and more justice. Frank Cullen wants to celebrate Paula Dubeck, his fellow sociologist and partner in every sense of the word for more than thirty years. John Eck wishes to express his appreciation to Milton Heumann, who was instrumental in inspiring his interest in the study and improvement of criminal justice agencies.

Lacey Schaefer
Francis T. Cullen
John E. Eck

1

Why Offender Supervision Does Not Work

Over the past four decades, mass incarceration has been the elephant in the room of corrections. During this period, state and federal prison populations increased dramatically, from under 200,000 to over 1.5 million. When jail populations are included, the daily count of incarcerated Americans reaches more than 2.2 million—or 1 in every 108 adults in the nation (Glaze & Herberman, 2013; Pew Center on the States, 2008a). Understandably, a rich body of work has arisen to account for this seemingly intractable willingness to place fellow citizens behind bars (see, e.g., Clear & Frost, 2014; Garland, 2001; Gottschalk, 2006; Pratt, 2009; Tonry, 2004).

Another critical correctional development, however, has been overshadowed by this concentrated focus on mass imprisonment: the rise of *mass community supervision of offenders* (Clear, 1992). Thus, in 1980, about 1.34 million offenders were on probation (1.1 million) or parole (220,438). By 2012, this figure had ballooned to almost 5 million Americans. The probation population had increased by almost 3 million offenders to 3,942,800, whereas the parole population had increased by over 620,000 offenders to 851,200. In concrete terms, this means that on any given day, 1 in every 50 adults in the United States is under some form of community supervision (Glaze & Herberman, 2013).

The question that arises is whether supervision matters—that is, in the parlance of the day, whether it "works" to reduce recidivism. This issue matters because of the sheer number of offenders whose lives will be touched by correctional control, and whose criminal habits can be affected by this system (McNeill & Weaver, 2010). Further, due to the ongoing financial crisis, states are looking for opportunities to trim their budgets. Criminal justice expenditures have not been immune, and state prison populations declined for the first time in 38 years in 2009 (Pew Center on the States, 2010). With limited resources available, state officials are now looking to probation and parole to supervise offenders either diverted or released early from prison. In short, the policy and practical salience of community corrections is likely to rise in the time ahead.

Some evidence exists that in terms of recidivism, probation is as effective as a custodial sanction as incarceration (Cullen, Jonson, & Nagin, 2011; Nagin, Cullen, & Jonson, 2009). Although not plentiful, other research finds that compared to being free in the community, probation supervision diminishes criminal participation (MacKenzie, Browning, Skroban, & Smith, 1999). Even so, evidence has been slow to come indicating that beyond the mere fact of being on probation, specific supervision strategies or styles regularly produce lower recidivism rates (recent exceptions may include intensive monitoring leading to higher rates of technical violations or procedural justice supervision orientations having positive intermediate outcomes for offenders; Paparozzi & Gendreau, 2005; Petersilia & Turner, 1993; Skeem & Manchak, 2008).

In traditional discussions, it is proposed that officers perform two functions—the delivery of treatment and the exercise of control—either of which might be used to reduce offender recidivism. There is increasing knowledge about "what works" when it comes to offender treatment (Andrews & Bonta, 2010). The challenge for corrections is implementing such evidence-based practice in the field and, in particular, how to use probation and parole supervision as a conduit for treatment delivery. A growing body of research has uncovered several effective rehabilitative strategies for offenders supervised in the community (Craig, Dixon, & Gannon, 2013; Cullen & Gilbert, 2013; Gleicher, Manchak, & Cullen, 2013), and many of these treatments are being applied in the field with early evaluations of success (Bonta et al., 2011; Luong & Wormith, 2011; Robinson et al., 2012).

Our primary concern here, however, is with the other side of offender supervision: control. Specifically, how can the control orientation of probation and parole be enhanced to improve offender outcomes? Traditionally, in this control role, officers are expected to exercise what amounts to a policing function. Their job is to watch offenders and, if they break prescribed rules—whether criminal laws or conditions of supervision—to revoke their community status and send the wayward to prison. The policing or control function works best when the mere threat of punishment evokes compliance. This proposed outcome is based on the notion of specific deterrence: that threats or the application of sanctions scares offenders straight, either in the short term or, after a stay in prison, in the long term. Such policing is supposed to be most effective when it is intensive, and when officers have small caseloads so they can apply close surveillance to offenders. Unfortunately, studies show that vague, deterrence-oriented intensive supervision does not work (see, e.g., Cullen, Wright, & Applegate, 1996; MacKenzie, 2006; Petersilia & Turner, 1993).

Given this stubborn reality, what might officers do differently? Answering this question—how to prevent recidivism among supervisees—leads us to consider why criminal acts occur. The simple but revealing answer is that two conditions must be present: An individual must have the *propensity* to offend and must have the *opportunity* to offend. The factors that underlie the propensity to recidivate have been researched (Andrews & Bonta, 2010; Gendreau, Little, & Goggin, 1996).

These risk factors, sometimes called "criminogenic needs," are what should be targeted for treatment intervention. Thus, one answer to what we should do differently is to use evidence-based treatment to reduce an individual's propensity to commit crime.

By contrast, relatively little is known about what officers might do to "knife off" the crime opportunities of probationers and parolees (Cullen, Eck, & Lowenkamp, 2002). Nonetheless, there is an extensive body of theory and research, drawn from the field of "environmental criminology" (sometimes called "crime science") regarding opportunity reduction. This at times falls under the umbrella of "situational crime prevention." Importantly, this perspective eschews legal deterrence, whose application is often uncertain and occurs far after a crime might be committed, in favor of strategies that steer offenders away from criminal opportunities or that block them from availing themselves of opportunities that might exist.

Thus, a second answer to what we should do differently is to use the insights of *environmental criminology* to create a supervision style that seeks to reduce offenders' access to opportunities needed to engage in crime. Importantly, this approach is not anti-propensity or anti-treatment. Propensity matters, and efforts should be made to use treatment programs to blunt it. But simultaneously, probation and parole officers should be equipped with the conceptual knowledge and practical technology to work with offenders to reduce their access to crime opportunities. In this sense, *the control function of supervision should be transformed from a deterrence orientation to an opportunity-reduction orientation*. The purpose of this book is to explore how this might be accomplished.

In so doing, we follow this roadmap. The current chapter reviews four topics. First, a brief discussion is provided of the invention of probation and parole, with a special interest in the treatment and control functions of the officers' role. This discussion will include an assessment of the role of current-day officers. Second, evidence is presented on the limited effectiveness of offender supervision. This will focus on rates of recidivism and technical violations. Third, the analysis will consider the effectiveness of offender treatment. A case will be made that much supervision either brokers inappropriate services or provides no services whatsoever. By way of contrast, an effort will be made to outline what effective offender supervision should involve. This analysis will be based on the principles of effective correctional intervention. Fourth, research will be reviewed that demonstrates the ineffectiveness of deterrence-oriented offender supervision. In particular, evaluations of control-based intensive supervision programs will be examined. This discussion will furnish a rationale for moving away from this approach toward supervision that is focused on *opportunity reduction*.

In this regard, the remainder of this volume articulates what such a paradigm shift in offender supervision would entail. Thus, Chapter 2 introduces the field of environmental criminology, exploring how it leads to practical programs to reduce crime. Chapter 3 uses this information to outline a new strategy for supervising offenders that is based on opportunity reduction. Chapter 4 seeks to present assessment technology that can be used by probation and parole officers to discern where, when, why, and with whom offenders commit crimes and to use this information to target the intervention at reducing criminal opportunities. Chapter 5 argues that the line between treatment and control may be largely artificial, asserting that cognitive-behavioral therapy can be expanded to develop opportunity-reduction elements. Chapter 6 explores how probation and parole can rely on the police to further limit supervisees' crime opportunities. Finally, Chapter 7 makes a broader case for moving beyond current, failed methods of supervising offenders and embracing a new vision to assist offenders resist the seductions of crime.

The Invention of Probation and Parole: Treatment and Control

From their inception, probation and parole supervisors have faced the challenge of competing goals. Often cited as the father of probation, John Augustus encountered this frustration, struggling to reconcile an offender's prospect of change with the person's known history of offending. As is still common today, Augustus selected individuals whom he believed would be amenable to rehabilitation, and would require little in the way of crime prevention (Dressler, 1962). Through the mid-1800s, Augustus earned bail (probationary release) for nearly 2,000 offenders and was held accountable by the court for their outcomes. Upon advising the judge of the offenders' progress, Augustus was required to demonstrate that the offenders had earned their freedom and did not require a prison sentence; this was achieved by showcasing the positive changes the offenders had undergone (such as gaining employment or reducing antisocial influences), and the diminished threat to public safety born from scrupulous supervision (Augustus, 1852/1972).

The emergence of parole experienced similar strains, having to balance conflicting ideas about what produces desistance: treatment or control. Observed in Alexander Maconochie's experiment with a mark system on Norfolk Island, as well as with Sir Walter Crofton's Irish ticket of leave system, offenders could progressively lease their liberty following a period of incapacitation (Barnes & Teeters, 1959; Eriksson, 1976; Hughes, 1987). Given their behavioral history, offenders were subjected to rigorous discipline in an effort to suppress further criminal acts. Yet at the same time, in order to prepare the offenders for an unsupervised life, treatment was required, and the gradual return to society included prosocial activities expected of an upstanding citizen. As seen in the Elmira Reformatory system, discretionary release from prison (under an indeterminate sentence) resulted from prosocial institutional behavior. This reformation was believed to be instigated by both individualized remedies for an offender's shortcomings and corporal punishment for misbehavior (Brockway, 1926; Pisciotta, 1994; Wines, 1919).

These innovations in corrections occurred following the Age of Enlightenment, which ushered in the Classical School of criminology. These theories, based largely on the humanitarian writings of Cesare Beccaria (1764/1963) and Jeremy Bentham (1789/1948), promoted a new philosophy of punishment that moved away from retribution and toward deterrence. According to this utilitarian framework, humans operate according to a rational consideration of the potential costs and benefits of a potential action; the outcome of this hedonistic calculus can be influenced by the threat of punishment, particularly when such pains are certain, swift, and severe. These ideas were countered, however, by the introduction of the Positivist School of criminological theory, wherein various biological, psychological, and sociological factors are identified as the origination of criminal behavior. These two dominant approaches to understanding (and thus controlling) criminality are inherently at odds; one emphasizes threats of punishment and the general reduction of the benefits of crime, while the other advocates for a reversal of criminogenic variables. Hindsight reveals that the pendulum of correctional theory has swung from conservative to liberal orientations, guided by cultural contexts; at some points in history, Classical theories have reigned supreme, whereas at others, Positivist theories have been favored (Cullen & Gilbert, 1982; Cullen & Jonson, 2012; Rothman, 1980; Taxman, Henderson, & Lerch, 2010).

For generations, the promotion of individualized intervention dominated correctional theory (Blomberg & Lucken, 2010). Treatments sought to distinguish those factors that promoted crime within each offender, and then present reform tailored to the individual (Rothman, 1980). Yet the use of indeterminate sentences, in which offenders could earn their freedom by showing evidence of their reform and desistance from crime, was flawed for two central reasons. First, a medical model (in which criminality is "diagnosed" and "fixed") is reliable only insofar as expertise is available and put to use, which correctional interventions of the time were lacking. Next, the assumption that practitioners would employ their newfound discretion toward the goals of reformation was shortsighted. The discovery of these shortcomings brought ideological challenges from contrasting political interests (Cullen & Gilbert, 1982), which influence the crisis in correctional philosophies seen still today. The correctional revolution of the 1970s was greatly influenced by the surrounding social turmoil, as a public atmosphere of distrust caused most to scrutinize the ability of the state to manage offenders (Rothman, 1980). As if almost historically fated, Martinson's (1974) scathing critique of rehabilitative programming provided the necessary ammunition for both political parties to confirm what they had already believed (Cullen & Gendreau, 2001; Cullen & Jonson, 2012). Despite the methodological flaws within his study (and later contradictory findings), Martinson's mantra of "nothing works" was propelled into public rhetoric.

Although there was unity in the demand for reform, conservative and liberal representatives diverged on why reorganization was needed, and how best to achieve change (Cullen & Gilbert, 1982). As a result of this disagreement, offender supervision practices still suffer from ideological *and* practical schisms. The social chaos present within the 1960s led conservatives to demand "law and order." Many believed that claims of rehabilitation were an insincere charade by which offenders would be coddled, and this lenient handling of dangerous offenders was jeopardizing public safety. To remedy this dilemma, they called for an increase in sanction certainty (determinate sentences) and severity (tough-on-crime initiatives) to deter offenders. Contrarily, the liberal minded believed that rehabilitation promoted injustice, insofar as the state could not be trusted to employ its discretion responsibly. In their calls for reform, liberals maintained their promotion of offender treatment, but through the safeguard of determinate sentencing (with shorter terms and additional legal protections). If rehabilitation was to be embraced, it must be through the medical model's adage: Above all, do no harm.

These two directions created a virtual impasse. The resulting crisis in corrections, coupled with increasing offender populations and associated costs, required a solution. As with the attack on rehabilitation (Cullen & Gilbert, 1982), support from opposing political parties birthed dramatic and swift change (Cullen & Jonson, 2012). Conservatives desired punitive programs that spared expenses, while liberals aspired to divert offenders from the evils of incarceration (Cullen et al., 1996). Consequently, the 1980s experienced a surge in a reliance on community-based punishments. Community control programs were campaigned as commonsensical (Cullen, Blevins, Trager, & Gendreau, 2005), meeting the desires of each political party. These sanctions were intertwined with two competing value systems: an increase in monitoring and control (combined with the threat of imprisonment for failure to comply), coupled with aimless but undamaging treatment.

It is debatable whether either of these strategies is capable of independently decreasing re-offending (MacKenzie, 2006), as discussed in the subsequent section. In any event, it is important to note that these two conflicting tactics have produced significant role strain for offender supervisors. Probation and parole officers have long embodied different styles of supervision, producing a number of role typologies. Of principal concern are the punitive or law enforcement officer and the welfare or therapeutic officer (Allen, Carlson, & Parks, 1979; Ohlin, Piven, & Pappenfort, 1956). The embodiment of one of these frameworks (to the logical sacrifice of the other) may be the consequence of an officer's personality, the clientele being supervised, the political culture of the time or place, or the aims of the organizing agency (Bonta, Rugge, Scott, Bourgon, & Yessine, 2008). Over the past few decades, an important shift has occurred, in which these two incongruous functions have melded together (Feeley & Simon, 1992).

Unfortunately, this role conflict may not easily be resolved. Many passionate arguments have been forwarded in favor of sacrificing one goal of supervision to save the other (Taxman et al., 2010). That is, the treatment model should be sacrificed to focus on control (Barkdull, 1976), or the law enforcement stance should be eliminated to emphasize rehabilitation (Stanley, 1976). Regardless, the task of supervising offenders under community corrections must be completed, whether officers are under strain or not. Caseload management (especially meticulous recordkeeping) is a bureaucratic necessity (West & Seiter, 2004). Particularly in an era of increased populations with decreased resources, probation and parole officers are required to be efficient as opposed to effective (Feeley & Simon, 1992). Contemporarily, the dominant supervision style is the synthetic or combined model, in which surveillance and social services are at play simultaneously (Klockars, 1972; McCleary, 1978; Skeem & Manchak, 2008; Taxman, 2011).

Consequently, offender supervision has reached a period of stagnation. Officers must balance two seemingly incompatible goals—treatment and control—often forcing them to choose one to the detriment of the other. Furthermore, the day-to-day functions of the organizing agency leave officers in the position of passive brokers simply trying to meet the overwhelming demand (Solomon, Waul, Van Ness, & Travis, 2004; Turner, 2010). These factors undoubtedly influence the efficacy of offender supervision. The persistent juggle of rehabilitation, social service brokerage, enforcement, and case management encountered by probation and parole officers has produced an atmosphere of atheoretical community corrections. As a result of trying to be everything to everyone, it is of little surprise that current eclectic models of offender supervision are ineffective.

The Limited Effectiveness of Offender Supervision

Although offender supervision was not previously perfected, there is little doubt that the addition of 3.5 million community corrections clients over the last 30 years has hamstrung efforts to effectively supervise offenders in the community (Glaze & Bonczar, 2011). As Feeley and Simon's (1992) classic piece on the new penology has demonstrated, population growth has contributed to pivotal changes in correctional rhetoric, goals, and strategies. Former expressions of clinical diagnosis and retributive justice have been replaced by the colder, calculating idioms of probability and risk. This has resulted in de-emphasizing individualized approaches to offender monitoring and welfare. In essence, previous objectives of management and rehabilitation have been replaced by a systemic requirement: efficient control. In an attempt to balance competing approaches, offender supervisors have largely regressed into *bureaucrats*—hardly the stance required in community corrections *interventions* (MacKenzie, 2006; West & Seiter, 2004).

Official statistics demonstrate the product of such a stalemate in correctional philosophies (see Glaze & Bonczar, 2011). In 2010, 65% of probationers were recorded as successfully having completed their term of supervision. Among parolees, only half were successfully discharged, with 33% being reincarcerated while under community supervision. Within three years of release from prison, two thirds of parolees are re-arrested for a new offense, with more than half of these returning to prison due to a technical violation of the conditions of their supervision (Langan & Levin, 2002). Among those offenders released from prison in 2005, nearly 50% had a probation or parole violation or committed a new crime that led to imprisonment within just three years (Durose, Cooper, & Snyder, 2014). The re-arrest rate for property offenders is particularly telling, with about three quarters being arrested for a new offense. Given this failure rate, some studies have simply concluded that community supervision does not help to reduce the re-arrest rates of offenders at all (Solomon, Kachnowski, & Bhati, 2005; cf. MacKenzie & Li, 2002).

This is not to say that there are no benefits accrued from community corrections; yet, the central goal most highly demanded—unambiguous recidivism reduction—is not being achieved at an acceptable level (for a discussion of the difficulties in operationalizing and measuring recidivism, see Maltz, 1984). Despite variation in the motivation of such requests, whether practical or political, there is an expectation that offenders supervised in the community will desist, no matter the impetus (Boone & Fulton, 1996). There is certainly considerable controversy regarding how to meet this goal, often divided along party lines, which mimics the impasse in guiding strategies experienced by community corrections officers. In essence, the voracious debate surrounding whether public safety can be enhanced best by controlling offenders or by rehabilitating offenders seems inherent to discussions about supervision. Worse yet, it is often presented as intractable. Reasonable consideration births the realization that these two competing and "incompatible" demands are both necessary, but insufficient; the crime prevention strategies of surveillance and treatment cannot be sacrificed one for the other.

As street-level policymakers (Lipsky, 1980), the actions taken by probation and parole officers in their routine work implicate certain correctional philosophies. Community corrections can no longer tolerate practices in which the selected model of offender supervision is an afterthought, a byproduct of bureaucracy, or purely incidental to aimless decisions already made. The lack of a cohesive and directive theory of effective probation and parole is a disgrace. Community corrections officers are in a prime position to be agents of offender change, and while small discoveries of "best practices" in offender supervision are emerging, the absence of a guiding framework has undesirable consequences for offenders and their communities. Consequently, a paradigm shift in community corrections is required.

The "organized skepticism" generally observed in social science research and public policy (Cullen & Gendreau, 2001; Merton, 1973) is peculiarly absent from probation and parole practice. As empiricists, criminologists must scrutinize the validity of the available evidence, and should be particularly cynical when long-held maxims are replaced by sudden shifts in ideology (Engel & Atkisson, 2010). Yet after multiple generations of experimenting with deterrent and rehabilitative correctional philosophies, the evidence is conclusive: The current product of offender supervision, a hodgepodge of dispassionate and half-hearted exercises of control and treatment, *does not work*. The strong influence on correctional practice previously exercised by the rehabilitative ideal and the tough-on-crime movement has faded, making this the ripest time for innovation. The unproductive standards in probation and parole have been allowed to dominate practice (and resulting outcomes) for too long—something new must be done.

The unconvinced and ideologically allegiant may point to the isolated and limited efforts in community corrections that have achieved positive outcomes. Indeed, there is a growing base of knowledge, grounded in research evidence, that indicates that certain practices *can* reduce crime. But these are often aimless in their impact without an organizing theme to promote the use of the larger strategy in which the one effective practice ought to be embedded. More often, techniques employed under the guise of deterrence or rehabilitation theories are awfully conceptualized, implemented, and exercised (Gendreau, Goggin, & Smith, 1999; Latessa, Cullen, & Gendreau, 2002; Lowenkamp, Latessa, & Smith, 2006; Rhine, Mawhorr, & Parks, 2006). Both control and treatment are necessary tactics for effective offender supervision, and must (and can) be used in conjunction with one another. Yet to complement one another, each must first be a worthy contributor to probation and parole practice independently. As it currently stands though, neither approach, alone or in combination with the other, is suited to significantly and consistently reduce recidivism.

Why Treatment Does Not Work

The fall and reemergence of the rehabilitative ideal is a curious story, with vivid implications for community corrections practices. The way in which the "nothing works" hysteria framed subsequent debates over the efficacy of rehabilitation has been largely unreasonable. For generations, scholars have unfairly categorized highly variant programs into one subsuming pigeon hole, measuring their success only by bottom-line, dichotomized measures of recidivism (Boone & Fulton, 1996). Yet despite these unproductive tendencies, limited treatment efforts persisted. Simultaneously, new analytic techniques made a synthesizing evaluation of these interventions possible. Over the past two decades, several meta-analyses have indicated that, although many rehabilitative efforts were null to modest in impact, others showed promise that they *could be* highly effective. Across studies, a clear pattern emerged, demonstrating that "interventions that are based on social learning or behavioral principles, are structured rather than nondirective, seek to build human capital in offenders, and use more than one treatment modality to address the multiple problems that offenders may be experiencing" generate the most success at reducing recidivism (Cullen, 2002, p. 266). Given the heterogeneity observed in treatment effects, a new goal emerged, beyond "proving" that rehabilitation did not work. Specifically, researchers sought to unpack the black box of treatment, uncovering those variables that moderate the influence of programming on outcomes (Bonta et al., 2008).

This alteration in the discipline's tone led to the theory of effective correctional intervention, in which the factors known to provide successful treatment were identified (Andrews, 1995; Andrews & Bonta, 2010; Cullen, 2002; Gendreau, 1996). The three components of this paradigm include an empirically guided psychology of criminal conduct, technology that ensures that the theory is implemented with integrity, and three principles that contribute to reduced recidivism (Cullen & Smith, 2011). In particular, effective rehabilitation programs correspond with the risk, need, and responsivity principles. First, interventions ought to target high-risk offenders, which will be recognized through the use of standardized assessment instrumentation (as opposed to the less reliable clinical appraisals of risk). Next, treatment must evaluate the offender's criminogenic needs. Empirical research must identify and interventions must address those dynamic risk factors that contribute to the individual's criminality. Finally, the third principle demonstrates that only those approaches that are receptive to offenders and their risk factors ought to be used. As such, "treatment programs should be delivered in a manner that facilitates the learning of new prosocial skills by the offender" (Gendreau, 1996, p. 123), both generally (in terms of the treatment modality, with cognitive-behavioral techniques as the gold standard) and specifically (in reference to the capabilities of the individual).

As an increasing number of programs have begun to incorporate these principles, additional factors have demonstrated their influence on the effectiveness of treatment (Andrews, 1995). Specifically, a social psychological understanding of criminal conduct has revealed multiple treatment specifications that are aligned with the contingencies of learning theories of behavioral conditioning (Andrews & Bonta, 2010; Spiegler & Guevremont, 2009; Van Voorhis, Braswell, & Lester, 2009). Individualized treatment, therapeutic integrity, community settings, aftercare, social support, and quality program development and implementation will all be strongly related to successful programs (Gendreau, Cullen, & Bonta, 1994; Harper & Chitty, 2005). With an increase in the knowledge of effective correctional interventions also comes information on what consistently will *not* work to reduce re-offending. As Andrews (1995) notes, criminal sanctioning without accompanying treatment cannot be expected to diminish criminal behavior. Gendreau (1996) elaborates, citing how efforts to "punish smarter" remain replete with failure. Simply, programs that emphasize punishment fail to alter those characteristics believed to birth criminal behavior, and are consequently doomed to be unsuccessful (Cullen & Gendreau, 2000; Cullen, Pratt, Micelli, & Moon, 2002; Latessa et al., 2002; MacKenzie, 2006).

Thinking about face validity alone, the theory of effective correctional intervention can logically reduce recidivism. Rather than relying upon an implicit supposition that has no criminological underpinnings, the theory advanced in the coming chapters attempts to redress the *known* factors that sustain criminal conduct (Andrews & Bonta, 2010). Those programs that conform to the risk, need, and responsivity principles consistently achieve reductions in recidivism of around 25% to 50% compared to those offenders not receiving treatment (possibly higher, depending on the control group; Cullen, 2002; Cullen & Gendreau, 2000; Lipsey, 1999). Given this noteworthy accomplishment (and the unfortunate number of programs that do not subscribe to the principles of effective correctional intervention), future efforts must work toward technology transfer and theory fidelity (Cullen & Jonson, 2011). Future "professional ideologies" for offender supervisors ought to allow evidence-based corrections to provide information on how best to combat recidivism, striving for program integrity and motivated application. Provided the strong impact rehabilitation *can have* on reducing re-offending, failure to incorporate these principles ought to be considered professional malpractice (Cullen, Myer, & Latessa, 2009; Latessa et al., 2002).

And indeed, that is precisely what is noted in contemporary probation and parole organizations. We do know what works, yet recidivism rates persist largely unaltered. Three prospective explanations for this exist. First, it is possible that policymakers and practitioners are simply unaware of the principles and their corresponding techniques that are known to limit re-offending. Second, it is possible that relevant parties are aware, and choose to ignore them; reasons for this may relate to political pressure, tradition or professional pride, perceived resource limitations, disagreement over ideology, or anecdotal evidence to the contrary. Third, it is possible that probation and parole agencies are knowledgeable of the standards of effective intervention, but implement them poorly (Lowenkamp, Latessa,

& Smith, 2006). Whatever the case may be, it is clear that with our burgeoning understanding of how to successfully treat offenders, the current way of doing business is unacceptable.

In response to this charge, many practitioners would passionately insist that they *do* treat their offenders, but the desired results are not achieved. This is often blamed on the offender population, the lack of resources, and poor interagency cooperation. It is here that the central shortcoming of existing treatment efforts in community corrections becomes clear: These "treatment" attempts *will not work* if they are not aligned with the principles of effective correctional intervention; that is, community corrections services being delivered without adherence to these principles *cannot* reduce recidivism (Andrews, Zinger, et al., 1990; Gendreau et al., 1994). Examining these principles in turn, we can see where existing probation and parole treatment often falls short.

First, the risk principle maintains that treatment ought to be targeted at high-risk offenders. Clearly, offenders at greater susceptibilities of recidivating require a more intensive intervention than those less likely to re-offend (Baird, 2009; Lipsey & Wilson, 1998). Furthermore, when low-risk offenders receive concentrated attention, rates of recidivism often increase (Latessa & Lowenkamp, 2006). This is due to three primary reasons: exposure to stable criminal associates (and the learning/reinforcement that accompanies these associations), disruption of the prosocial factors that cause them to be low-risk, and risk of victimization by more predatory offenders (Lowenkamp & Latessa, 2004). Importantly, to faithfully abide by the risk principle, proper assessment and classification processes must be integrated into offender supervision practices. The assessment of risk must be systematized and actuarial in nature (Bonta, Wallace-Capretta, & Rooney, 2000; Latessa & Holsinger, 1998), and the classification of offenders must be generally allegiant to the determinations of risk revealed by these assessments. Moreover, offenders' level of risk should be determined prior to the delivery of services, and should be reassessed periodically to make reclassification decisions as necessary.

Within current probation and parole practices, a number of divergences from the standards of the risk principle are noted. Most notably, offenders are often indiscriminately grouped together, with little (or no) regard to their level of risk. Even aside from objective recidivism risk, approximations of risk (such as offense history, offense severity, and treatment/sanction history) are often likewise ignored in the allocation of caseloads and assignment to program participation (Petersilia, 2003). Despite the fact that treatment programs are in short supply, offenders are typically enrolled equally irrespective of the degree of intervention they actually require. The neglect of actuarial risk assessments is also problematic. A number of practitioners abide by the alleged infallibility of their clinical judgment, with little use of validated instruments (Latessa, 1999). And while many agencies use intake assessments, these often are unquantifiable, are unreliable and have not been validated, may not be properly scored, or target only concrete needs unrelated to criminogenic risk (Latessa & Holsinger, 1998). Further, in the rare organizations in which re-offending risk estimations are calculated, the information is often not properly employed (Burke, 2004). The distribution of cases to supervising officers can be determined by multiple characteristics (e.g., randomly, even number of cases among agents, by demographics or tangible needs unrelated to offending), though seldom is client allocation the result of risk assessments. In summary, failing to assess and classify offenders by level and type of risk will make it difficult to produce positive desistance-related outcomes (Lowenkamp, Latessa, & Holsinger, 2006). To not follow appropriate assessment and classification processes is nothing short of "correctional quackery" (Latessa et al., 2002).

Next, the need principle establishes that if criminal recidivism is to be reduced, the instigators or contributors of criminality must first be minimized (Andrews, 1989). This logical assertion also implies that reduced criminogenic needs are a desirable intermediate goal; that is, continued criminality can be prevented in the long term only if the characteristics causing the individual's offending are altered, making their periodic measurement worthwhile (Andrews, Bonta, & Hoge, 1990; Gendreau, 1996). The known causes of crime, consistently demonstrated by hundreds of empirical studies, include antisocial attitudes, antisocial associates, an antisocial personality pattern, and a history of antisocial behavior (note that this final risk factor is not dynamic, and therefore cannot be changed by corrections authorities; Andrews & Bonta, 2010). If probation and parole authorities desire to reduce recidivism, then supervising officers must address these dynamic criminogenic needs in their clients; a failure to do so cannot practically limit re-offending (Bonta et al., 2008; Dowden & Andrews, 1999). Notably, in order to target the causes of offending, agents must accurately assess the actual criminogenic needs of their clients. Moreover, there must be legitimate follow-through on the factors determined to contribute to recidivism risk. Contemporary fourth-generation assessments incorporate both risk and needs (Andrews & Bonta, 2010; see also Chapter 4 later in this volume); by thoroughly investigating the criminogenic needs of offenders upon intake and periodically through their supervision, the level of risk can be measured and adjusted as needed.

Unfortunately, however, existing community corrections efforts frequently fail to assess and target *criminogenic* needs. As Harland asserts, "For a field that by almost anyone's definition is so centrally involved in the management of risk and in responding to criminogenic needs of offenders, the continuing neglect or inadequate appreciation of the importance of this area in so many correctional agencies is little short of astounding" (1996, p. xvi). Frankly, the majority of programs do not adequately assess offender risks and address criminogenic needs (Matthews, Jones Hubbard, & Latessa, 2001). When offender risks and needs *are* assessed, they often indicate static factors (i.e., those incapable of being changed), or indicate concrete needs that are, at best, only indirectly related to offending (e.g., housing stability). This is not to say that officers cannot use information about an individual's history of victimization or unemployment, but this leaves unaddressed the underlying roots of criminality (Bonta et al., 2008).

Emphasizing service brokerage, or providing atheoretical or nondirective treatment, is not good enough (Latessa, 1999). Indeed, probation and parole agencies often coordinate "treatment" for their clients, but it is unrelated to criminological knowledge (notably misguided programs include pet therapy, cosmetic surgery, yoga/meditation, and control- or punishment-oriented interventions). Yet the research is clear: When rehabilitative programming does not operate in accordance with the need principle (that is, the precise causes of offending are being addressed), recidivism cannot be substantially affected (Andrews, Zinger, et al., 1990; Antonowicz & Ross, 1994). So much so, in fact, that addressing an offender's criminogenic needs is a necessary step toward safeguarding public safety (Crowe, 1998). The stark majority of community corrections programs do not explicitly measure and target for change those characteristics that cause the individual's crime; as such, they are designed to fail (Cullen, 2002).

Third, the responsivity principle conveys that the mode of treatment delivery must be sensitive to the learning styles and abilities of the individual client and offenders in general. Once we attend to measuring risk and needs associated with the chance of recidivism, we are naturally led to inquire about the techniques that can bring about change (Gendreau, 1996). Overall, cognitive-behavioral techniques are the most conducive to offender rehabilitation (Cullen, 2002). Quality probation and parole officers will match offenders not only to program intensity by their level of assessed risk, and not only to the rehabilitative interventions aimed at altering their criminogenic needs, but also to those services and supervisors that are most likely to produce modifications for that individual offender (Gendreau, 1996; Latessa, 1999; Smith, Gendreau, & Swartz, 2009). When possible, responsivity should be taken under consideration in the development of community corrections programs; if nothing else, referrals to services and treatments must be highly individualized, as a one-size-fits-all approach is bound to be ineffective (Cullen & Gendreau, 2000; Latessa & Holsinger, 1998). Identifying barriers to desistance can be achieved through thoughtful assessments, and referrals must be based upon the information gained therein (Andrews & Bonta, 2010; Van Voorhis et al., 2009; Ward, Melser, & Yates, 2007).

Again, existing community supervision practices leave much to be desired in the address of offender responsivity. Sadly, the majority of probation and parole programs do not adequately assess the strengths and weaknesses of offenders that may facilitate or hamper prosocial change, they do not use effective treatment models, and staff are not trained in evidence-based behavioral strategies (Matthews et al., 2001). Too often, a blanket approach to offender treatment is considered acceptable, with little thought provided to whether the service or program is conducive to the offender's personality or capabilities (DeMichele, 2007). Further, as offender motivation is a responsivity variable in correctional treatment (McMurran, 2009), probation and parole cases must be attentively allocated to thoughtfully matched officers as opposed to undirected caseload assignment (Bonta et al., 2000; Taxman & Thanner, 2006). Given the incredible diversity observed in offender populations, it is foolish to assume that a generic one-size-fits-all approach would be adequate. Simply, for treatment to be effective, it must be tailored to the offender, considering temperament, learning style, motivation, culture, and demographics (Clawson & Guevara, 2011; Harper & Chitty, 2005). There are a number of principles that should be consistently used with offenders, because research repeatedly demonstrates that they are effective; that said, each offender is different, and the intervention must be reflective of those individual characteristics. Unfortunately, very rarely do probation and parole offices customize an offender's case plan so that it takes into account risk, need, or responsivity considerations (Taxman, Yancey, & Bilanin, 2006).

Finally, there are a host of other guidelines that when used in conjunction with the risk, need, and responsivity principles, produce dramatic reductions in recidivism. Primary examples include knowledgeable and accountable staff, the use of community aftercare, multimodal interventions, enhancing motivation for change, firm but fair program contingencies, interpersonally sensitive and constructive relations, and advocacy (Andrews & Bonta, 2010; Cullen, & Gendreau, 2000; Gendreau et al., 1994; MacKenzie, 2006; Taxman, 1999). Perhaps most important, quality probation and parole programs embody the principles of core correctional practice: anti-criminal modeling, effective reinforcement and disapproval, problem-solving techniques, structured learning procedures for skill-building, effective use of authority, cognitive self-change, relationship practice, and motivational interviewing (Clawson & Guevara, 2011; Gendreau, Smith, & French, 2006). Of this litany of best practices, many can be achieved through the development of a multifaceted intervention built on a sound conceptual model, followed by quality implementation and periodic evaluation and adjustment (Antonowicz & Ross, 1994; Latessa & Lowenkamp, 2006; Lipsey, 2009).

Not surprisingly, the majority of these supplemental principles are not followed in average probation and parole programs. Therapeutic integrity is often low, and the typical emphasis on case management or law enforcement fails to promote (and sometimes discourages) long-term behavioral change (Taxman, 1999). Standard programs commit many of the same mistakes, producing unsavory outcomes for offenders and their communities (Latessa & Holsinger, 1998; Solomon et al., 2005). Such common shortcomings include atheoretical strategies, using techniques not based on the "what works" research, interventions that are too short or do not occupy a significant percentage of offenders' time with structured programs, poor staff outcomes (high turnover, improper training, poor clinical supervision, no assessment), employing inappropriate performance measures, minimal evaluation, and too few rewards with too many punishers (and these sanctions are used improperly).

Consistently, the clinically relevant and psychologically informed principles of effective intervention yield the strongest reductions in recidivism (Dowden, Antonowicz, & Andrews, 2000). However, probation and parole strategies rarely implement or adhere to these evidence-based best practices due to a number of political and professional barriers (Gendreau, Goggin, & Fulton, 2000). The overwhelming majority of community corrections interventions rely on some form of so-called treatment; these strategies are more appropriately categorized as service brokerage, as they are passive methods of service referral, as opposed to a directive and salient intervention aimed at substantial cognitive and behavioral prosocial change (Solomon et al., 2005; Solomon et al., 2008; Taxman, 1999). Rehabilitation is a necessary ingredient to recidivism reduction. Treatment within probation and parole supervision can be highly effective, though the way it is currently being executed requires substantial redesign.

Why Control Does Not Work

Much like probation and parole programs ignoring best practices in offender treatment, mechanisms of community correctional control are often likewise devoid of research-driven principles of effective intervention. It is important to note that while quality community corrections programs require a strong rehabilitation component, it would be foolish to assume that the inclusion of treatment equates to the exclusion of control. As discussed previously, both approaches are necessary for successful outcomes. Offenders, who have a demonstrable pattern of breaking the law, must be appropriately monitored to ensure that past actions do not all but guarantee similar future actions. Yet without an intervention that addresses the underlying causes of crime, it is unreasonable to believe that offending would cease under the presence of control. In the proceeding section, the reader will note that this balance of responsibilities is generally absent from control-oriented probation and parole strategies. Though they are compatible, there is a misconception that the law enforcement nature of much community corrections work makes offender treatment impossible. However, not only do these surveillance- or punitive-intensive programs fall short due to the omission of a behavioral intervention, but the actual way in which offender control is practiced is misguided.

To begin, effective probation and parole strategies must be based on a clear and valid criminological theory (Latessa, 1999; Latessa & Holsinger, 1998; MacKenzie, 2006; Moore, Gray, Roberts, Taylor, & Merrington, 2006). Whether the aim is early intervention, crime prevention, or crime reduction, it is illogical to anticipate that the desired goal could be met without a solid understanding of why people offend in the first place. Above all, then, accurate criminological theories are necessary. Though appearance should not take precedence over efficacy when enacting policy (Cullen et al., 2009), deterrence theory has often informed criminal justice strategies because of its inherently intuitive appeal (Cullen & Jonson, 2012). Simply, it seems a matter of common sense that offenders make cost-benefit calculations of the outcomes associated with crime. When the estimated rewards are expected to outweigh the perceived risks, they are likely to commit the criminal act under consideration. The key to crime prevention, according to those who ascribe to this theory, is to decrease the benefits of crime while increasing its costs. Rational choice theory underlies related policies, whereby sanction certainty, severity, and celerity (swiftness) ostensibly influence criminal decision making.

Although these ideas sound reasonable on the surface, they suffer from a few key paralyzing shortcomings. Some theorists have suggested that offenders do not have all information available when they make crime-related decisions. Rather, they suggest, people have bounded rationality or willpower that they use to make reasonable decisions given the information at hand (Jacobs & Wright, 2009; Jolls, Sunstein, & Thaler, 1998). However, even when we consider offender decision-making in light of this limited amount of information used in the cost-benefit analysis, it is clear that offenders often still behave irrationally (particularly if under the influence of an intoxicant, if suffering from a mental illness, or if judgment is clouded by extreme emotions). Manipulating the expected utility of crime may therefore be in vain. That the effect of punishment on re-offending is contingent upon numerous factors (beyond the two that rational choice theory would ascribe; Sherman, 1993) demonstrates the need for a more dynamic correctional philosophy, reflective of the individual differences between offenders (Cullen & Jonson, 2012).

Further, although the contributions of deterrence theory in its classical form ought not to be discounted, our ability to pragmatically or ethically apply it is questionable (Cullen, Pratt, et al., 2002). Principally, the criminal justice system cannot feasibly ensure that all crimes will elicit detection, prosecution, and punishment. As the contingency of sanctions upon offending weakens, crime statistically involves less risk. Next, for humanitarian purposes, the severity of punishments cannot be exercised far beyond current practices. Finally, constitutional rights afforded to offenders guarantee due process, thereby diminishing the swiftness with which sanctions are paired with crimes. Given the divergence between theory and application, an appreciable or consistent deterrent effect may not be possible. Because we cannot easily make certain criminal justice punishments any more certain, severe, or swift, we should rethink whether (or how) deterrence ought to guide offender supervision. This is especially evident when criminal justice policies are aimed at increasing the costs associated with crime rather than enhancing the rewards associated with conformity (Cullen, Pratt, et al., 2002). As they are frequently applied, control-oriented sanctions have had little influence in encouraging desistance, and have often worked in the opposite direction toward promoting recidivism (Taxman, 1999).

Yet this has not discouraged deterrence theory allegiants. How could an ineffective class of strategies become so popular? With the dust settling from the "nothing works" hysteria (Martinson, 1974), America required a new penal philosophy. A "crisis in corrections" was occurring, where two unrelenting forces demanded a new direction: an exponential increase in the prison population and the rising costs associated with the imprisonment binge. As with the attack on rehabilitation, both political parties advocated dramatic change (Cullen & Gilbert, 2013; Cullen & Jonson, 2012). Conservatives wanted to save money while not sacrificing punition, and liberals sponsored community corrections as a lesser evil than prison (Cullen & Jonson, 2012; Cullen et al., 1996). The product was a host of *intermediate* punishments. Despite being founded on ideals of offender assistance and service brokerage, probation and parole quickly became synonymous with the micromanaging of offenders (Lindner, 1994). Community control programs (including intensive supervision, electronic monitoring and home confinement, drug testing, and boot camps or shock incarceration) were campaigned as commonsensical (Cullen et al., 2005), falling along the continuum of sanction severity between prison and standard, uninvolved probation (Morris & Tonry, 1990). These sanctions were intertwined with deterrence theory, suggesting that an increase in monitoring and control, combined with the threat of imprisonment for failure to comply, would decrease re-offending. Increased foresight would have prompted the realization that expenditures and offender harm would be spared only if probationers and parolees were actually deterred; yet, emotionality and "common sense" were allowed to reign over logic and evidence.

For this reason, it is difficult to determine whether the movement toward intermediate sanctions was purely symbolic. When analyzing the substantive contributions of community control programs, several research dilemmas make conclusive evidence rare (Cullen et al., 1996). First, evaluation studies rarely have experimental designs, making selection biases probable. Next, there are outcome measures beyond bottom-line recidivism that may support the efficacy of a program, though these are frequently ignored. Finally, unsupportive results could be due to a lack of program integrity rather than a poorly specified logic model, given that researchers rarely measure what occurs inside the "black box" in their evaluations. Above all, however, assessments indicate that an increase in control does not translate into lower recidivism rates. When the methodological uncertainties in these evaluations are addressed, the results remain unsupportive of a deterrent effect of control-centered offender supervision (MacKenzie, 2000). In one particularly rigorous study, Petersilia and Turner (1993) concluded that an increase in surveillance did not diminish the frequency or severity of additional offenses among community corrections populations. As a result of intensive supervision, however, technical violations increased dramatically, often leading to revocation. Therefore, it seems that community control programs fail to resolve prison crowding, address fiscal concerns, or promote justice while preventing crime.

In the rare, successful offender control programs, the reduction in re-offending is attributable to the treatment-orientation of the sanction, rather than to the deterrence components (Cullen & Jonson, 2012). Control-intensive offender supervision has the prospect of efficacy, but this is only if probation and parole programs incentivized conformity as opposed to punishing deviance. Frankly, an individual's criminogenic risks do not remain at bay simply because the threat of punishment looms. Indeed, deterrence measures are among the *weakest* predictors of crime (Pratt & Cullen, 2005). If nothing else, the rationale—that if you watch offenders more closely you will observe them violating their supervision or breaking the law more often—is hard to deny. Offenders report that control-oriented programs are the most severe sanctions, not because of the decreased benefits of crime and the increased costs of crime, but because of the inconveniences resulting from having freedoms restricted (May & Wood, 2010). In fact, evidence indicates that offenders are more greatly deterred by informal social control (such as the pressure from family or the desire to keep a job) than by threats of severe, formal punishment (Piquero, 2003). Offenders are also more likely to comply with deterrent strategies when justifications for the supervision conditions are provided (Wood & Kemshall, 2007). Especially when the level of control is indiscriminately applied, regardless of the risk level of offenders, the results will be unbecoming (Carter, 2003; Gendreau et al., 1994). With all of these considerations in mind, the conclusion is stark: "For offenders who are already in the correctional system, there is just not much evidence that trying to punish them makes them less criminogenic" (Cullen & Jonson, 2012, p. 89).

As correctional populations have continued to climb, and the country's political culture has led to an unprecedented tough-on-crime movement, deterrence theory has lost face validity (Gibbons, 2000). Proponents argue that manipulating the environment so that the likelihood of detection is increased and pain is maximized will inhibit recidivism. This is all well and good: We demand that justice (retribution) be enacted for wrongdoing, and hopefully harsh punishments will protect public safety as crimes are prevented (deterrence). Yet while we like to apportion crime to personal responsibility (and offenders do have some degree of control over their destinies), probation and parole outcomes *are* shaped by community corrections strategies (MacKenzie, 2006; McCleary, 1978; Moore et al., 2006). Unfortunately, these control- or punishment-oriented philosophies promote re-offending, with harsher sentences and more scrupulous surveillance diminishing the likelihood of deterrence (MacKenzie, 2000; Pearson & Lipton, 1999; Solomon et al., 2005). Deterrence theory as it is currently applied as a probation and parole strategy is highly ineffective at reducing crime (Taxman, 1999). We require a new way of doing business, in which the goal of internal control (i.e., changing offenders' thought processes so that crime opportunities are avoided and resisted) supersedes the external pressure of punishment (Gendreau et al., 1994; Wood & Kemshall, 2007; Zimring & Hawkins, 1995). For community supervision to be effective, there must be a shift in collective thought. We must move away from the goal of trying to control offenders toward viewing probation and parole as a precise intervention of which control is a necessary component (Burke, 2004; Dickey & Klingele, 2004; Fulton, Stichman, Travis, & Latessa, 1997).

Conclusion: A New Paradigm for Offender Supervision

Despite these fairly consistent findings of what is known to work and what repeatedly fails, ineffective community corrections practices abound (Lipsey, 2009). In fact, offender supervision programs that have proven to be harmful have prospered (Cullen et al., 2009). If nothing else, there is an ambivalence between offender care and control (Worrall & Hoy, 2005). Historical momentum, political popularity, and the alleged rationality of traditional probation and parole strategies have produced "a socially constructed reality that is resistant to falsification" (Cullen et al., 2005, p. 55). Boot camps and intensive supervision are prime evidence that officials rarely incorporate evidence-based criteria into their decision making (Cullen et al., 2005; Cullen et al., 1996). Rather than investing correctional policy in common sense or political popularity (Cullen, Fisher, & Applegate, 2000), future efforts should seek to reverse the known conditions of crime causation (Engel & Atkisson, 2010).

This realization led to a proposed *environmental corrections*, in which probation and parole officers would aim to reduce offenders' opportunities for crime (Cullen, Eck, & Lowenkamp, 2002). Borrowing from the knowledge generated within environmental criminology, community supervision should seek to disrupt the routine activities that increase opportunities for offending, substituting prosocial, structured activities. These efforts produce the ideal community corrections intervention, in which the control aspects of deterrence would successfully merge with treatment efforts. Additionally, the principles of effective correctional intervention can be manipulated to complement place-based crime prevention tactics. Effective probation and parole programs must emphasize a *comprehensive* approach to crime control, in which offender accountability is balanced with offender assistance toward gaining prosocial outcomes (Evans, 2001; Fulton, Latessa, Stichman, & Travis, 1997; MacKenzie, 2006). Simply, we require an extensive shift away from risk control and toward risk reduction (Pierce-Danford & Guevara, 2010). This can only be accomplished when the fanatical obsession with surveillance and behavioral control is substituted with behavioral change objectives (Taxman & Byrne, 2001; Taxman, Young, & Byrne, 2003).

As established, current probation and parole operations have been managing an irreconcilable predicament: Community corrections caseloads are rising, but resources are diminishing. This crisis undoubtedly influences the way we assess practices—yet this still misses the heart of the matter: effectiveness. As the research evidence displayed above indicates, it is clear that offenders are not supervised in the best manner possible. This current state of affairs has prompted the realization that "the current practice of community supervision could be improved, perhaps dramatically, by adopting a new paradigm—a new way of thinking—about how best to supervise offenders on probation and parole" (Cullen, Eck, & Lowenkamp, 2002, p. 28). The "incompatible" goals of treatment and control have produced a period of stagnation in community corrections. Although somewhat discouraging, the promise of positive change is great; the lack of a clearly articulated goal provides policy-minded scholars a chance to reinvent offender supervision. Accordingly, in this volume, we propose a modest though unique conceptual framework (with corresponding recommendations for intervention techniques) that may improve existing probation and parole practices.

The main premise of this environmental corrections model of offender supervision is that effective interventions must be based on valid criminological theory and evidence-based best practices. Core insights from environmental criminology are borrowed, exploring the implications of theories and practices of opportunity reduction to probation and parole supervision. As the creators of this framework note, "The key aspect of environmental corrections is not its revolutionary character but its novel use of the insights of environmental criminology to illuminate how correctional supervision can lower recidivism by reducing offenders' opportunities to offend" (Cullen, Eck, & Lowenkamp, 2002, p. 30). The experiences of practitioners will be integral to the redesign of community corrections. By transforming probation and parole officers into problem solvers, sensitive to the context in which their clients' crime occurs, a specific intervention that can reasonably reduce recidivism can be developed.

The two ingredients to address for successful crime prevention are propensity and opportunity. As described by the principles of effective correctional intervention, re-offending likelihoods can be significantly reduced when certain conditions are met. Specifically, the focus must be on higher risk offenders, the known predictors of recidivism must be targeted for change, and cognitive-behavioral interventions within the context of multimodal programs should be delivered (applying a sufficient dosage of treatment combined with the provision of appropriate aftercare). As was also seen, the component of opportunity does not, and cannot, work when supervision conditions are premised on general deterrence (vague restrictions and prescriptions), when the amount of (rather than the nature of) supervision is changed, or when crude criminological understandings do not change propensity or restructure offending opportunities. It is the role of probation and parole officers to proactively intervene, determining how best to reduce their clients' access to criminal opportunities.

This reconceptualization of offender supervision will require thorough assessment, involve work with probationers and parolees, the recruitment of agents of informal social control, and the solicitation of community target guardians and place managers. This model emphasizes how "opportunity will be curtailed not only by threats of formal punishment for non-compliance, but more importantly by problem-solving officers who seek to expand informal social control over offenders, to increase the effort offenders must exert to access crime opportunities, and to work with offenders to restructure and fill their lives with prosocial routines" (Cullen, Eck, & Lowenkamp, 2002, p. 35). Practically, this new method of offender supervision identifies crime prevention options in the here and now, emphasizes the factors proximate and integral to offending, and ultimately identifies those elements amenable to manipulation. The following chapter explores in great detail precisely what environmental corrections is, describing how situational crime prevention and opportunity reduction can contribute to successful probation and parole outcomes.

2

Why Opportunity Matters

The research evidence is conclusive: Current probation and parole practices do not work. Criminogenic risks are not greatly reduced, offenders are not regularly deterred, and public safety is not reliably enhanced. Most agencies focus either on offender control or offender treatment (while ignoring the other). Moreover, as discussed in the previous chapter, neither is routinely performed well. Clearly, then, a new organizing framework is needed to create effective supervision strategies. We require an innovation in community corrections; one that targets the known causes of crime, both internal and external to the individual offender.

Determining what causes a person to be a criminal is a difficult, often controversial task. The explanations are varied, but do share one thing in common: There is no easy fix. Whether we blame biology or parents or education or neighborhoods, the problems are deeply rooted and not easily reversed. If it is the job of a probation or parole officer to reduce an individual's likelihood of committing crime (but, the officer cannot readily change the offender's biology or parents or education or neighborhood), then we may be foolish for expecting change at all.

However, we might achieve better outcomes by changing the way we look at the problem. Rather than thinking about what makes a person a criminal, we should ask what makes a crime occur (Clarke, 2010). Granted, part of that equation is the makeup of the offender, but to ignore the other pieces of the puzzle is misguided. This chapter proposes that by focusing on the *precipitators* of an offense (rather than the *characteristics* of an offender), the problem is more easily defined and managed. A precipitator is something that causes an event to happen, especially an event that happens suddenly. As presented in the discussion that follows, there are several crime precipitators that are known and can be addressed. We propose that if probation and parole authorities try to change these precipitators, offending among community-supervised offenders will be reduced.

These precipitators, though stemming from different sources, can be characterized as crime opportunities. When community corrections efforts focus exclusively on criminal propensity, the results are, at best, slow to come. Yet when we focus on opportunity, the situation is malleable. There are two components to opportunity that fall under the purview of probation and parole authorities. First, officers can work with offenders to provide services that change the ways that offenders perceive criminal opportunities. Second, officers can restructure the environment to limit the real opportunities for offending that their clients are actually exposed to. By addressing existing crime opportunities while also adjusting an offender's experience with those opportunities, the greatest impact will be achieved.

Thinking about these components graphically (as presented in Figure 2.1), there are two specific crime precipitators: cognitions and situations. Cognitions refer to the information people consider and the choices that individuals make; in the case of offenders, the decision to commit a crime will be influenced by their thoughts and values. As discussed at length in Chapter 5, there are a number of evidence-based best practices that can influence the way offenders think. Although part of offenders' belief systems may be out of reach (due to long-lasting socialization or stable neurology, for instance), the principles used in cognitive-behavioral interventions can recondition the way offenders interpret their environment. By providing appropriate reinforcers and punishers, probation and parole authorities can influence offenders to view crime opportunities as neutral stimuli or to actively avoid and resist chances to commit crime that appear tempting.

The other part of the crime opportunity equation is the immediate situation. Community corrections agents can manipulate an offender's surroundings to limit the opportunities that exist, or at least the chances to commit crime that their clients are exposed to. A wealth of research has uncovered the place-based instigators of crime. When the benefits of crime are reduced and the costs are increased within the context of a given situation, offenders are less likely to pursue available crime opportunities. That is, when an individual has less to gain and more to lose, the decision to commit a crime becomes less likely. Thus, community corrections agencies can limit offenders' access to situations that contain attractive chances to commit crime.

As depicted in Figure 2.1, offenders' cognitions and the situations in which they find themselves are reciprocating. Much of what offenders think (and thus, the decisions they make) is based on the environmental cues that the situation presents to them. For example, an offender may think about robbing a passerby only

Figure 2.1   Crime Precipitators

if it is night and there are no street lights around; otherwise (if it were daytime or the street was well lit), the offender would not begin to think about how he or she could easily get away with mugging someone. At the same time, the cognitions of offenders influence the situations they place themselves in. Whether criminally disposed or not, humans tend to create environments that are consistent with, or allow them to express, their beliefs and preferences. For instance, an offender who is antisocial tends to hang out with other individuals who are antisocial (a process called homophily). Or, an individual who condones violence will be more inclined to venture into a rival gang's territory. For this reason, it is absolutely necessary for community corrections solutions to address the whole problem—the internal and the external causes of crime. We need to limit the crime opportunities that offenders encounter, but obviously we cannot eliminate them all; therefore, we must also work to change the way they think about the crime opportunities they do come into contact with.

The final component of Figure 2.1 is the combination of these two crime precipitators. When cognitions and situations repeatedly converge, a routine develops. These routines can be described as patterns in crime, at both the individual level and the aggregate level. For individual offenders, their daily routines offer a point of influence for probation and parole authorities. By examining the routines of their clients, officers can tailor an intervention to the individual that disrupts that pattern by adjusting crime opportunities. For probationers and parolees at large, these routines create "hotspots" where opportunities for crime abound and are taken advantage of often. As discussed in Chapter 6, the police are in a prime position to disrupt these crime patterns, which will have a direct impact on the routines of community-supervised offenders.

To interrupt these routines, we must first know a great deal about crime opportunities. Community corrections officers and their partners must understand what features of the environment (physical, social, and experiential) make a crime more likely to occur, and how probationers and parolees interpret those cues. Fortunately, a highly effective framework for accomplishing this task exists. The crime science model is a problem-oriented approach that identifies and alters the explicit causes of crime. Using empirical research, the crime science model focuses on the offense rather than on offenders, with the exclusive goal of reducing opportunities for crime to occur. As explored in the following sections of this chapter, the solutions to crime problems proposed by crime science are fairly straightforward. This approach supposes that (1) we can identify the circumstances that cause crime, (2) we can change those circumstances, and (3) this will remove the opportunity for crime to occur. Probation and parole authorities are in a prime position to assess the circumstances that facilitate their supervisees' offending, and have the resources and tools available to change them. Naturally, then, by reducing or controlling the access to crime opportunities of probationers and parolees, the re-offending rate of community-supervised offenders should diminish.

Crime science may be particularly helpful in developing a framework for opportunity-reduction supervision. Crime science refers to studies and interventions aimed at understanding crime *in order to* prevent it, and compared to criminology, focuses on crime with the sole intention of reducing it. The crime science model has three overarching principles for crime reduction initiatives (taken from Wortley & Mazerolle, 2008) that each have clear applications to community corrections. First, criminal behavior is influenced by the immediate environment; rather than being a passive backdrop, the offender's surroundings can initiate and shape the course of crime. Second, crime is patterned according to criminogenic situations, concentrated around those environmental characteristics that facilitate offending. Third, targeting for change the criminogenic aspects of the environment will minimize the incidence of crime there.

Accordingly, the content of Chapter 2 is organized to highlight these different initiatives. First, the chapter begins with a thorough discussion of the precipitators of crime. Specifically, the contributions of crime science will be presented, exploring the ways in which this framework can effectively limit the criminognic opportunities encountered by probationers and parolees. The way offenders interpret these opportunities (the first circle in Figure 2.1) will be the matter of Chapter 5. Chapter 2 next examines the specific interventions that are produced by the crime science model (the second circle in Figure 2.1). The majority of these applications have been performed by police agencies with an emphasis on deterring a specific kind of crime (e.g., fights at a particular bar or retaliatory shootings among rival gangs). While Chapter 6 discusses ways in which police can assist probation and parole agents, the current chapter examines how the innovations from these police interventions can be applied to community corrections. By examining the routines of probation and parole clients, recommendations are made for how to reduce the crime opportunities offenders encounter.

Readers should note that Chapter 3 will specifically apply the advancements of crime science to offender supervision, only after first outlining the theory and current applications of crime science in the present chapter. Although the thrust of this book is on a novel practice of probation and parole, the relevance of opportunity reduction to offender supervision cannot fully be understood or appreciated without first outlining the evolution of the crime science model of crime prevention. As such, the discussion that follows traces the developments in crime science, allowing the reader to see the logical progression of ideas and crime prevention practices. Only then can we plot out the exact way that this model can improve offender supervision practices.

The Evolution of Crime Science

Although crime science has only recently become a coherent framework, its roots can be seen in early sociological explanations of crime from two centuries ago. Officially termed "environmental criminology" by C. Ray Jeffery in 1971, these theories explain patterns of crime by examining influences external to the individual offender. Although many scholars point to the origins of social disorganization theory (Burgess, 1916; Park & Burgess, 1925; Shaw & McKay, 1942), environmental criminology dates back further than the Chicago School of social theory. To name but a few pioneers, Balbi and Guerry (1829), Quetelet (1842), and Glyde (1856) each analyzed crime statistics, producing graphical representations of the spatial distribution of offenses. Importantly, these early empirical efforts demonstrated that crime does not occur at random. As popularly described by Harries (1974), macro-environments display that crime is higher in cities (and that offending is concentrated in the city center and radiates out toward the city suburbs), while micro-environments reveal that certain neighborhood characteristics are reliably associated with crime and disorder.

Although this criminological finding may seem like a truism to contemporary scholars, these early sociological theories of crime were a dramatic shift from the explanations for offending that had dominated the field for centuries. During the Age of Enlightenment in the 18th century, humanitarians and ethicists grew dissatisfied with the use of torture, corporal punishments, excessive violence, and executions used by the criminal justice system. Many of these forward-thinking theorists sought penal reform by emphasizing utilitarianism—the idea that the value of an action should be determined by its utility of maximizing benefit. Premised on the belief that humans have free will and are calculating animals, reformers argued that society can shape people's choices by manipulating the outcomes associated with their decisions. Rational choice theory stipulates that individuals will act in their best interest, a combination of trying to minimize pain while maximizing pleasure. Thus, the component parts of this cost-benefit analysis, or hedonistic calculus, can be altered to prevent crime. Recognizing this influence, philosophers Cesare Beccaria (1764/1963) and Jeremy Bentham (1789/1948) argued that potential offenders can be dissuaded from committing crime by reducing the benefits and increasing the costs that may result from that act. Deterrence theory states that, in particular, when punishment is quick, certain, and severe, the individual will be less likely to make the decision to commit a crime.

These ideas founded the Classical School of criminology. At the center of Classical theories is the volition of the actor; simply, offenders *choose* to commit crime, because crime pays—it is beneficial in some way, and those benefits outweigh the costs. Accordingly, preventing crime is a matter of adjusting the component parts of the criminal decision so that crime is not the most attractive choice (Clarke & Cornish, 1985). Yet after generations of popular support, rational choice and deterrence theories were trumped by the Positivist School of criminology. In contrast to the Classical theories that explain crime through the offender's will, Positivist theories argue that crime is *caused* and not chosen. Early Positivist explanations for crime were individual trait theories (such as biology or personality), while later theories emphasized sociological factors. Aside from the belief that crime is determined, Positivist theories are alike in their methods of investigation, preferring more objective empiricism and a results orientation to speculation. Following the Industrial Revolution and rapid American urbanization at the turn of the 20th century, scholars tended to agree that social influences cause crime. Different theories emerged as researchers made their case as to which social factors were most likely to produce crime.

As theories from the Positivist School of criminology were popularized, the Classical School ideas of rational choice and deterrence were largely dismissed by liberal academics. The calculations and choices of individual offenders were now largely ignored as these scholars shifted their attention toward identifying the external criminogenic conditions that were acting upon offenders and compelling them to break the law. So much so, in fact, that when responsibility for crime was placed with the people committing those crimes, these policies were accused of blaming victims of circumstance; it seemed unreasonable and harsh, after all, to find fault with offenders when some external force "made them do it." The majority of these explanations were sociological, and efforts to discover the structural causes of spatial crime patterns became the norm. The sociopolitical measures that were typically used as correlates of crime (such as poverty, demography and population mobility, or institutionalized racism) all ignored the role of the offender in the experience of a criminal act.

Moving beyond the loose association between place and crime, upcoming ecological theories required a "collective geographic imagination" in order to be taken seriously (Brantingham & Brantingham, 1981). By shifting analyses toward quantifying the influence of the physical world on the actions of the offender, environmental criminology became a field all its own. Rather than focusing on distant community characteristics seen in high-crime neighborhoods, environmental criminology explores the outcome of crime from the perspective of the offender. This is a faint yet vital distinction in the unit of analysis; environmental criminology began to remove itself from the social problems that impacted the individual, emphasizing instead the study of how the individual actively interacts with his or her environment. This important shift allowed environmental criminology to combine the best of two worlds: the incorporation of offender cognition from the Classical School and the reliance on empiricism in evaluating the situation from the Positivist School (see Figure 2.1).

In this new, merged perspective, the determinants of offending can still be located in the environment. After all, the stimuli that prompt a crime and the rewards/ punishments that reinforce a crime are largely external to the individual (Cornish & Clarke, 2008); however, these same stimuli and reinforcements are the considerations that influence the rational choice (the weighing of costs and benefits) to commit the crime. Thus, environmental criminology is an ideal approach to disrupting recidivism, given the significant association between the physical world and the offender's decision-making processes. The individual's relationship with his or her surroundings is substantially different here than in previous schools of criminological thought. The individual is not entirely free-willed or rational (Classical School) and the environment is no longer acting upon the offender (Positivist School); rather, the environment is interwoven into the *trajectory* of the individual's choices. Predispositions are still important, but certain environments will be more or less favorable to their expression. As Felson observes, "People make choices, but they cannot choose the choices available to them" (1986, p. 119).

Central to this reality is the concept of bounded rationality, first proposed within the field of economics. In an influential statement, Herbert Simon (1957) argued that there are three unavoidable conditions that constrain decision making: (1) the limited and unreliable nature of the information that is available regarding each choice and its consequences, (2) the limited ability to process infinitely large quantities of information, and (3) the limited amount of time available to reach a decision. When considering the influence of these limitations on decision making among offenders, the situation is of greater import than the offender. The process that offenders undergo in making their choice will be clouded by personal tools that are unknowable to the outside world (e.g., thinking shortcuts, heuristics, and cognitive scripts). And, as a result, deterrents will only work sometimes with some criminals (Cornish & Clarke, 1986). The goal for environmental criminologists, then, is to identify cues that trigger the decision-making process that a crime opportunity is available. By examining opportunity perception and resistance, the goal of cognitive-behavioral techniques is the adjustment of *situational* propensity (explored in greater depth in Chapter 5).

Thus, environmental criminology represents a pivotal movement away from solely rational choice or ecological explanations for crime, and toward the role of criminal opportunity (Brantingham & Brantingham, 1981). The most vivid example of the importance of opportunity can be noted in Cohen and Felson's (1979) routine activity theory. The theory stipulates that crime will occur when three conditions are present: a motivated offender, a suitable target, and the lack of a capable guardian. These three factors must converge in time and space. Importantly, the theory addresses how the activities of individuals will be more or less conducive to criminal opportunity. Moreover, the larger routines of society—the patterns that emerge from individuals' activities—can influence the availability and pursuit of crime opportunities, as well. Each of these three components contributes to an individual crime event.

First, there must be an individual motivated to commit a crime (or who can become motivated when an opportunity for crime presents itself). Although it is unclear who is included in this categorization (e.g., is motivation ubiquitous across all people?), viewing offender motivation as necessary but generally present has provided scholars a chance to focus their efforts on the lure of opportunity. If people are largely hedonistic (i.e., everyone wants to maximize their pleasure and minimize their pain), then people will largely respond the same way to a criminal opportunity. If, on the other hand, an individual is not motivated to exploit a chance to commit crime, then that person is not of concern for theorists or policymakers. In either case, routine activity theory demonstrates that the motivated offender is a necessary ingredient to a crime event, but means nothing without opportunity. Even if there were a large group of offenders intent on breaking the law, without the chance to do so, there would be no crime.

Second, for a crime to occur, a suitable target must be present. Cohen and Felson (1979) cleverly spoke of an attractive target to convey that some crimes (such as theft or vandalism) do not require a human victim. The activities of offenders may allow them to come into contact with a greater number of suitable targets. At a larger level, changes in technology have resulted in more portable, durable, and expensive goods (Clarke, 1999; Ekblom, 1997), and a shifting workforce has meant more people out of the house at more times of the day (Cohen & Felson, 1979). Thus, rates of certain types of crime have increased during certain time periods, reflecting the changes in the routine activities of society (Clarke & Eck, 2005).

Third, crime can occur when there is a lack of a capable guardian; stated differently, a crime cannot occur when there is someone or something to guard against it. Perhaps the most obvious guardian is the formal social control of police. More casually, family, friends, or neighborhood residents may prevent offenders from engaging in a crime. Beyond people, a guardian can include a number of safety measures, like a lock on a safe or a guard dog or a security camera. As with offenders and targets, changes in the way social life is structured have produced changes in guardianship (Ekblom, 2005; Felson & Boba, 2010; Reynald, 2011).

As outlined in the sections that follow, a number of crime prevention responses have been developed based upon each of these three elements of a crime event. It is important to note that all three factors are needed for crime to occur. As such, an increase in suitable targets or a decrease in capable guardians can by themselves lead to more crime, without any change to the motivation of potential offenders. More optimistically stated, this means that crime can be prevented by reducing access to targets or adding guardians, without needing to change an individual's criminal propensity. This realization has allowed criminology to move beyond aimless theorizing or distant social policy. The importance of opportunity has penetrated the study and practice of crime prevention, leading to a number of innovations that collectively form a solutions-oriented approach to deterring offending.

The reemergence of rational choice in criminology, as seen in the way motivation is influenced by opportunity, establishes offenders as active participants in the milieu of a criminal act. Rational choice matters to routine activity theory, because the offender's interpretation of a criminal opportunity depends on his or her evaluation of the benefits (targets) and the costs (guardianship) associated with that act. As such, if we want to manipulate the benefits and costs of crime, we must do more than alter the physical places where crime is likely to occur (after all, we cannot objectively prevent 100% of crime through place-based crime prevention). Rather, more well-rounded approaches to crime prevention policy aim to change the physical environment so that offenders interpret the opportunity (the costs and the benefits) differently. The goal is to design spaces and control their use in such a way so that any person entering the space does not receive a cue that crime is possible, tolerated, or invited.

As further explained by routine activity theory, the convergence of these three elements in space and time is impacted by the way community life is organized. As research into crime opportunities progressed, new ideas were created to explain the routines that account for crime patterns. To better understand the interplay of the circumstances that are conducive to crime, the crime problem triangle (see Figure 2.2) was developed to portray the conditions that can encourage or stymie crime opportunities. The innermost triangle, based on Cohen and Felson's (1979) routine activity theory, shows that crime will occur when an offender and a victim or target converge at a location. The addition of place has led to a number of problem-oriented crime prevention innovations (discussed in the following sections) that emphasize the role of opportunity reduction.

To enable the creation of solutions to recurring crime problems, Eck (2003) developed an external triangle to correspond with the elements of routine activity theory (see Figure 2.2), with each side representing a "controller" that can influence one of the inner conditions. First, "handlers" are people who prevent an offender from committing crime. Second, "guardians" make targets less vulnerable to victimization. Third, "managers" make places less attractive for crime and can influence the behavior of offenders and victims who occupy those spaces. Crime is more likely to occur when any of these controllers are absent or corrupt. Offender handlers, target guardians, and place managers each represent a point that can be manipulated for preventing crime or addressing repeat crime problems. A number of interventions have been developed and tested, establishing the importance of each of these controllers. As we discuss in following chapters, probation and parole authorities can capitalize on the expertise and influence of these different controllers in order to prevent re-offending among their clients. Specifically, as Chapters 3 and 4 outline, probation and parole officers can identify and work with these controllers to manipulate the elements of a crime event, thereby limiting the crime opportunities that community-supervised offenders are exposed to. As explored in Chapter 5, crime controllers can help offenders to identify and resist crime opportunities and make prosocial choices. And as Chapter 6 elaborates, the police are "super controllers" who have remarkable influence over the actions handlers, guardians, and managers take to prevent crime.

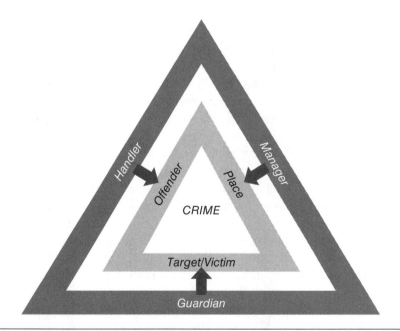

Figure 2.2   The Crime Problem Triangle

SOURCE: Clarke, R. V., & Eck., J. E. (2005). *Crime analysis for problem solvers in 60 small steps*. Washington, DC: Office of Community Oriented Policing Services, U.S. Department of Justice.

The insights of crime science are especially relevant for probation and parole practices. Under an opportunity-reduction supervision model, the role of the offender supervisor would be twofold, because there are two primary contributions to a criminal act (cognitions and situations, or, propensity and opportunity; see Figure 2.1). First, the probation or parole officer would uncover where the offender's motivation comes from, and then implement ways to change the offender so that criminal propensity is reduced (Clark, Walters, Gingerich, & Meltzer, 2006). Second, the probation or parole officer would determine what environmental cues the offender interprets as attractive chances to commit crime, and then manipulate the environment (or the offender's exposure to it) so that these opportunities are reduced. The following chapters outline what community supervision for offenders would look like according to an opportunity-reduction model of probation and parole. Yet first we use the remainder of this chapter to elaborate on the contributions of the crime science model. In order to establish what community corrections officers can do to reduce opportunities for offending, it is important to explore the crime science innovations that have revealed (1) why opportunity is important for crime prevention, (2) how we can best determine what criminal opportunities exist, and (3) how we can change those opportunities to reduce offending. These three categories of advances made by crime science—theory, method, and practice—are discussed in turn below.

INNOVATIONS IN THEORY

A common observation in policing research is that the goals of law enforcement often have to be sacrificed for allegiance to the means of law enforcement (Scott, Eck, Knutsson, & Goldstein, 2008). Standard police procedures emphasize random patrols and responses to (and later investigations of) reported crime; these daily routines can perhaps be detrimental to some larger end, such as the *proactive* prevention of crime. With this in mind, Herman Goldstein (1979, 1990) developed a new approach to policing, relying on an orientation that views crime as a problem in need of a solution. Problem-oriented policing addresses recurring crime problems as opposed to resolving individual crime incidents (Eck & Spelman, 1987a). By carefully examining a chronic crime place or population, the underlying conditions that give rise to the crime problem can be aptly determined, making way for the development of preventative solutions (Braga, 2002).

As an organizational framework, problem-oriented policing created a new way of thinking about crime. The police traditionally react to crime after the fact; contrarily, by viewing crime as the product of an equation, each of the contributions to the final outcome has to be uncovered, and these factors can be manipulated to avoid the outcome of crime. This has repositioned criminal justice agencies from enforcing punishments for violations of the law, to preventing the law being broken in the first place (Eck & Spelman, 1987b). However, in order to reduce crime, the constituent parts must first be understood. It would be unwise to devote crime prevention resources to anything that we do not believe is actually causing crime.

To understand what causes crime, the problem of interest must be analyzed in depth, gathering information from a variety of sources (Clarke & Eck, 2005). By emphasizing a specific crime problem in need of an unambiguous solution, generic prescriptions for crime prevention give way to specific actions that target the cause of the problem (Scott et al., 2008).

As the following subsections discuss, problem-oriented policing has ushered in a new way of doing business for crime prevention agencies. Crime is analyzed and responded to in novel ways under this framework. Yet it is important to note that this is more than just a topical fad. The entire way crime is thought about has been revolutionized. As previously demonstrated, environmental criminology ushered in ideas about how the individual interacts with his or her surroundings to create a crime event. Although criminology concerns itself with abstract and distant concepts (e.g., how poverty is related to crime), crime science aims to identify and alter more concrete and local factors (e.g., how street lights or security cameras are related to a reduction in crime). The task, then, is to determine what features in an offender's environment might lead to crime. Though an innocuous stimulus might provide a "cue for crime" to a psychopathic predator, the current mission is to discover environmental characteristics that the average offender would see as opportunities for crime. Put differently, uncovering the instigators of crime will here be an offense-centric (as opposed to offender-focused) approach.

One helpful framework is crime pattern theory, which argues that offenders, like all people, have relatively stable spatiotemporal movement patterns. That is, offenders generally have a routine that places them in certain places at certain times; hence, crime is most likely located around these normal activities. Crime data can be aggregated, and in many cases clear patterns emerge. Brantingham and Brantingham (1993) defined an offender's movement patterns as activity nodes (sites where crimes are concentrated), pathways (the traveled area between the nodes), and edge effects (perceptual or physical boundaries that distinguish between places). If, when, and where crime occurs will be influenced by the environments encountered during this patterned activity (see Figure 2.1: situation precipitators). It is important to note, however, that a triggering event must coincide with the individual's decision-making process that produces the outcome of crime (see Figure 2.1: cognition precipitators; Brantingham & Brantingham, 2008). As this process stabilizes after repeat occurrences, the characteristics that encourage crime among particular offenders become more predictable (see Figure 2.1: routines).

Crime pattern theory has led to a number of specific crime prevention applications, discussed in the subsections that follow. By emphasizing the role of opportunity, particularly how opportunities are perceived and acted upon by potential offenders, crime science theory has set itself apart from mainstream criminological theories by being action-oriented. For academics and practitioners alike, the logical consequence of crime science theories has been to identify the situational precipitators of crime. The approaches that have stemmed from these theoretical innovations have assumed a rational choice perspective, insofar as the decision to commit crime is a direct consequence of environmental cues. With previous theories, uncovering the circumstances that initiate a crime assumed that the process is involuntary, operating below consciousness for the offender. Although crime science acknowledges that offending is situation-specific, the offender's interpretation of the environment will vary. That is, crime prevention efforts must seek to alter situations that offenders encounter in their daily routines that they are likely to perceive as opportunities for crime (Wortley, 2008). Crime science theories have focused attention on the importance of criminal opportunity and the way these opportunities are routinely encountered (Clarke & Eck, 2005). As a result, the methods used to discover what these opportunities are and the interventions that have been used to reduce these opportunities have been radically altered.

INNOVATIONS IN METHOD

A prominent feature of crime science is the incorporation of scientific methods and practical responses to crime patterns. Rather than pursuing moralistic efforts that address the deficiencies of the offender, crime science views the offender's surroundings as the important ingredient in need of attention. As Clarke notes, "crime is an act, not merely a propensity, and it can only be explained in terms of the interaction between the disposition . . . and the situation that provides the opportunity for crime to occur" (2008, p. 178). Agents responsible for preventing or reducing crime will often have little information available regarding the personal characteristics of offenders (such as their mental health or family background). In the rare occasions when the factors causing a person's offending are known, there is often nothing that can be done with the resources available (e.g., a police captain can increase patrol in a high-crime neighborhood, but cannot mandate cognitive-behavioral therapy for offenders who congregate there).

The need for practical solutions to ongoing crime problems has created a reliance on the scientific method. As concern for positive outcomes grew, tools that assist in observable crime reductions were enthusiastically embraced. The scientific method, guided by crime science theory, reshaped the way crime is understood and addressed, creating a problem-solving or intelligence-led approach. Viewing crime as a problem, the solution must address the cause; and to design and implement the solution, the cause must be accurately identified. The technological revolution of the 1990s accelerated the use of crime science tools. Rather than relying on the subjective reports of beat cops or neighborhood residents, computer programs made the synthesis and analysis of quantitative crime data possible.

Data-led crime analysis can reveal the who, what, when, and where of a selected crime problem. With the advent of computer aided dispatch (CAD) and geographic information systems (GIS), the spatiotemporal dispersion of crime can be quantified, mapped out in black and white. Yet the introduction of these empirical efforts was not without debate. Specifically, there has remained a divide concerning the cause of crime patterns revealed through these methods (Anselin, Griffiths, & Tita, 2008). Are these crime concentrations a result of broad social, economic, or political influences? Or have these hotspots emerged due to some feature of the environment that brings together the readily motivated offender with an attractive target and no capable guardian? Though there is no easy answer in this debate, the query of concern is the *why* or the *how* of crime. It is not enough to demonstrate on a chart that crime is highest at a certain time of day near a certain street intersection. Rather, as these analyses have become more commonplace, agencies began to explore the precise context that produces the observed offending pattern.

New technologies have revolutionized place-based criminology by providing updated research methods and analytic tools. Yet merely summarizing crime data provides minimal insight into the context that encourages a crime problem. To solve a crime problem, an iterative process is required in which hypotheses are tested and retested, then modified and retested again (Weisel, 2003). An effective problem-solving effort must correctly appraise the cause of crime, then implement an intervention that alters those same causes (Goldstein, 1990; Scott, 2006). The use of the scientific method demands this process, and is thus hailed as a supreme crime-fighting tool.

However, readers should be aware of the lure of the undeserved "scientific aura" (Braga, 2002) often given to the methods used in crime reduction strategies; even the most advanced analytical capabilities have flaws (Harries, 1999). Our values must shift from the impression that our methodological and statistical techniques should be as complex as possible, to an insistence that our understanding of the crime problem be as thorough as possible (Townsley & Pease, 2003). More practically, an analysis of a crime problem will only be as accurate as the data collected (Maguire & Hopkins, 2003). In their classic article on law enforcement as problem solvers, Eck and Spelman (1987b) identify perhaps the largest issue with crime analysis: The results are used to allocate already existing policing resources. As such, "responses" to crime are determined before the problem is fully understood, and a blanket prescription for crime reduction is applied to substantially different problems. A successful intervention may not translate into further success across space or time (Ekblom, 1997). Indeed, as Braga describes, the tendency is for agencies to "blindly adopt these 'proven' responses rather than conducting the necessary problem analysis to determine whether the program fits well with the nature of the crime problem as it manifests itself in the operational environments of their cities" (2002, p. 107).

This shortcoming can be avoided when conscientious analysts and intervention developers grasp the whole picture of a crime problem; one way of doing this is by gathering both qualitative and quantitative data (Scott et al., 2008). Place-based crime prevention policies are based upon the analysis of data related to a highly specific crime problem. To change a crime problem, a thorough process is required that will uncover the actual circumstances that cause an offender to recognize and exploit a crime opportunity. Geographic profiling is a holistic process in which multiple sources of information are consulted to understand a local crime problem. Many advocate for intelligence-led policies, but intelligence does not have to come in the form of numbers or official reports. These sources of data are important, but fail to provide the whole picture. In gathering information about a crime problem, analysts are wise to incorporate a variety of data types (e.g., calls for service, interviews, and officer reports) and sources (e.g., offenders, victims, neighborhood residents, and patrol officers) in their assessment. As such, geographic profiling, which synthesizes qualitative and quantitative data, is a best practice in the methods of crime science.

Yet, best practices are not always followed, and even superior crime science methods have shortcomings. As a result, a variety of applications result from the same theory; because there is diversity in the methods used, there is diversity in the speculated cause of crime, producing differences in crime interventions. One camp believes that broad social conditions (such as a lack of informal social control or neighborhood-wide legal cynicism) produce concentrations of crime in certain areas. Consequently, they advocate for programs that address the sociological features of a community that are conducive to crime. The other camp affirms that narrow environmental factors (such as poor street lighting) lead to crime hotspots. Accordingly, they institute solutions that are more tightly focused on the explicit and malleable cause that was identified.

As conveyed in Figure 2.1 (and discussed at the top of the chapter), the best approach to crime reduction involves attention to the characteristics of offenders that make them vulnerable to crime opportunities along with the immediate circumstances and community conditions in which offenders find themselves (Clarke & Eck, 2005). The methodological innovations of crime science, particularly through geographic profiling, help to provide a well-rounded picture of a crime problem. By gathering multiple sources of data, a truer understanding of crime opportunities is gained, leading to a more successful intervention (Wortley & Mazerolle, 2008).

INNOVATIONS IN PRACTICE

Changing the physical environment to prevent crime is nothing new. Place-based approaches to crime reduction have long tried to alter the benefits and costs (i.e., the targets and guardians) at a specific location. Prior to the introduction of crime science theories and methods, however, the prescriptions for crime problems were generic. Early environmental criminologists attempted to pinpoint the community characteristics that are associated with increases in social disorder. Yet the "place" side of the crime triangle (see Figure 2.2) can be misconstrued as either too vague or too definitive—or both at once. Community-oriented approaches to crime reduction widen the place-based idea to include the larger environment in which a crime problem takes place. Specifically, community-oriented policing aims to address how neighborhood structure impacts crime by focusing on the quality of life for residents therein (Reisig, 2010).

As an organizational strategy, community-oriented policing entirely redefines the function of law enforcement, suggesting new strategies altogether (Moore, 1992). There is no specific definition of community-oriented policing, with some scholars asserting that no such characterization can be made (Oliver & Bartgis, 1998). Yet while the practices under the umbrella of community-oriented policing are highly diverse, they differ because they share a common philosophy: context matters (Gentile, 1995). Crime reductions will be greatest when the analysis and response are highly individualized to a local crime problem.

As specified by Cordner (1999), four elements separate community orientations from other methods of law enforcement. First, the philosophical dimension provides new values for officers. Community policing seeks cooperation from local residents and organizations, and police must embody a personal service orientation while exploring the native culture. Next, the strategic dimension specifies that community policing should include much personal interaction between agents of formal social control and neighborhood residents. Not only does this foster positive relationships between police and the public, but it also allows officers to more fully understand local crime problems. Third, the tactical dimension conveys that officers must investigate, analyze, and address community-specific social disorder. This is achieved by establishing close relationships with neighborhood residents, which also cultivates a collaborative relationship in which community members actively work with law enforcement to reduce crime. Finally, the organizational dimension changes the structure of a police force, giving problem-solving authority to officers regardless of rank. This further implicates the need for officers to systematically seek and understand the local community conditions that may be responsible for a crime problem.

Unfortunately, research on the effectiveness of community-oriented policing is limited (Reisig, 2010). However, much is known regarding the neighborhood characteristics that mediate the relationship between structural disadvantage and crime. Drawing from social disorganization theory (Shaw & McKay, 1942), Kornhauser (1978) contends that disorder arises from a lack of effective social controls. A wealth of impressive studies indeed confirm that enhancing community relations (such as through social cohesion, mutual trust, collective efficacy, or willingness to intervene) can reduce community disorder, including offending (Browning, Feinberg, & Dietz, 2004; Carr, 2005; Lowenkamp, Cullen, & Pratt, 2003; Sampson & Groves, 1989; Sampson, Raudenbush, & Earls, 1997; Warner, 2007; Wilkinson, 2007). It logically follows, then, that if improved informal social control reduces crime, then law enforcement agencies should work to nurture resident relations (Kubrin & Weitzer, 2003). By encouraging neighborhood residents to take ownership of collective community spaces, social control can be more widely activated (Sampson, 2004).

Investigating the causes of a local crime problem, then designing an intervention to change those causes in order to prevent crime, seems a daunting task. It is of little surprise that the strategies used to reduce crime have differed depending on the crime problem. In response to this barrier, the SARA process was developed to streamline and synthesize these divergent methods (SARA = Scanning, Analysis, Response, Assessment; Clarke & Eck, 2005; Eck & Spelman, 1987a). In the first stage, scanning, multiple sources of information are consulted to develop a clear definition of the crime problem of concern. As more data become available, the description of the problem may change, though despite its characterization, the event must be something the police can reasonably be expected to control. Next, in the analysis stage, the specific problem is evaluated in order to develop an appropriate response. Information about police experiences in addressing a similar problem is gathered to inform the planned solution. In the third stage, the response, the findings from the analysis are used to design an explicit remedy of the crime problem. Notably, the police problem solver must explore a broad range of available strategies and choose the solution that best suits the results of the analysis. Finally, in the assessment stage, the impact of the response on the crime problem is measured. The findings from this evaluation should inform the current solution of the crime problem, and should contribute to the body of knowledge that future problem solvers consult.

A problem orientation to crime reduction refashions the theories, methods, and practices used to address offending. The SARA model tailors a response to a specific crime problem, measuring and adjusting the intervention as necessary. Traditionally, environmental criminology has focused on the "place" side of the crime triangle (see Figure 2.2). As the following section explores, the other components can be manipulated to prevent crime, as well. Rather than focusing exclusively on physical surroundings, the contributions of crime science can be used to address wider sources of opportunities for crime. Moreover, crime science can move beyond offending to look at individual offenders, altering their routine activities to limit the criminal opportunities they are exposed to.

Crime Science and Opportunity Reduction

To limit the opportunities for crime that an individual may encounter, a new way of thinking about offending and criminal justice solutions is required. Crime reduction practices must go beyond a blanket approach to physically changing high-crime environments. Problem solvers must understand the perspective of the offender (Wright & Bennett, 1990); specifically, they must uncover how certain surroundings create the perception that a crime opportunity is available and can be taken advantage of (Cromwell & Birzer, 2014; Wright & Decker, 1994). While police organizations have used problem solving to identify and change problem places, probation and parole agencies can use these same crime science methods to focus on crime problems as they relate to offenders. To prevent crime, practitioners must look beyond the physical elements of a place alone, and toward the circumstances that promote crime commission. By determining the stimuli that offenders interpret as conducive to crime, those characteristics can be removed, altered, or guarded, and the actual opportunity to commit that crime can be minimized.

Although some features of the physical environment may provide "cues for crime" to any ordinary person (e.g., unguarded cash), other factors require a better understanding of the individual offender. What emotions, actions, or possessions does the offender find rewarding? Where are these rewards located? What emotions or actions does the offender find punishing? Where do these punishments come from? What signals do offenders receive that make them think they will or won't be caught? By answering these questions, the situational precipitators of crime (see Figure 2.1) can be addressed in two ways. First, the daily activities of the offender can be designed to avoid contact with the crime opportunities they identify. Second, the offender's environment can be manipulated to reduce the rewards, increase the punishments, and improve detection/enforcement of the crime opportunities they will undoubtedly encounter.

These tasks go beyond the rational choice perspective that offenders will be deterred from committing crime if the benefits are few but the costs are great. Certainly this element of crime prevention cannot be ignored; however, beyond the manipulation of surface-level temptations and dissuasions, there must be a broader effort to minimize the chance to commit a crime in the first place. Using the lessons learned from crime science, the three sides of the outer crime triangle (see the crime controllers in Figure 2.2) can be exploited in order to reduce crime opportunities. By recruiting offender handlers, creating target guardians, and training place managers, the two aforementioned tasks can be addressed: Offenders will be exposed to fewer opportunities to commit crime, and the perceived crime opportunities that they do encounter will be less favorable for pursuit. We explore these issues in more detail in the following sections.

OFFENDER HANDLERS

Understanding why a person commits a crime is a noble goal, but discovering *how* that person comes to commit a crime is of greater importance in reducing offending opportunities (Clarke & Eck, 2005). One category of agents that discourage offenders from pursuing or engaging in crime is individuals who can influence the choices the offender makes. In thinking about all the possible people that could prevent someone from committing crime, it quickly becomes clear that the robustness of that list will vary from person to person. Offenders may report that the only people who prevent them from committing crime are the police (and their effectiveness at actually preventing the offender from committing crime is questionable). Non-offenders might acknowledge that in addition to a number of formal social controls such as criminal justice actors, they are prevented from committing crime by their family (e.g., parents, spouse, kids), friends (e.g., classmates, coworkers), and even more distant associates (e.g., boss, neighbors). It is reasonable, then, to assume that all the people non-offenders come in contact with contribute to their complying with the law. Thus, people who can prevent a particular offender from committing crime should be recruited to aid in encouraging desistance efforts and cooperate with formal control agents.

Some offender handlers, such as the police and probation and parole authorities, prevent crime by the definitions of their jobs. Yet agents of informal social control (such as a significant other, a family member, or a personal mentor such as a coach or a pastor) are a crucial element to crime reduction for two reasons. First, these potential offender handlers have a stake in the success of the solution; when that particular offender does not commit crime, they are directly benefited. Second, they may understand (or even be a contributor to) how that individual encounters and pursues crime opportunities; these prospective handlers are in a prime position to develop and institute solutions (National Research Council, 2008).

Community-oriented approaches to crime prevention are based on the context of a crime-specific population or place. By viewing and measuring crime as a native problem in need of a native solution, it becomes clear that the people local to the crime opportunity should be recruited to eliminate those opportunities (Community Policing Consortium, 1994). By contracting the support and involvement of the community in which the offender is embedded, the strength of formal social control agents such as the police is extended (Taxman, Young, & Byrne, 2004). As officers cannot persistently maintain a watchful and responsive eye on all prospective offenders, additional parties responsible for offender monitoring must be recruited. With these relationships comes less crime opportunity, whether from surveillance, distraction, or persuasion of the offender (Clarke & Eck, 2005).

Third-party policing is one such mechanism of this form of crime control, in which the cooperation of crime controllers is leveraged (Clarke & Eck, 2005; Mazerolle & Ransley, 2005). By recruiting a class of individuals who can influence offenders' primary environment, a number of barriers are created between the prospective offender and the offense (Buerger & Mazerolle, 1998; Ekblom, 2005). Even further, when these informal social control agents cooperate with police, compliance with the law is more likely to occur (Pew Center on the States, 2008b). The handlers are in a better position than the police to influence the activities of the offender, and may provide the police with useful information about available crime opportunities they should address (Murphy, 2005). By any process, research demonstrates that offenders with strong family and community ties are less likely to recidivate (National Research Council, 2008; Warr, 1998).

TARGET GUARDIANS

According to Cohen and Felson's (1979) routine activity theory, a crime will occur when a motivated offender meets an attractive target lacking a capable guardian. As previously discussed, motivation is not of concern for most opportunity theorists; this is because motivation is perhaps always present despite the available opportunities, or because motivation cannot readily be addressed. Other times, motivation may be created when a prospective offender takes note of an attractive target. Preventing crime, then, is a matter of guarding those targets that are likely to prompt criminal motivation. Yet, due to individual differences, what an offender defines as an "attractive" target will be unique to that one person (Smith, 2003). Although some targets can themselves be directly manipulated (e.g., a store keeping a limited amount of cash in the register or an individual not walking to his or her car alone at night), the personalized nature of target preferences among offenders makes their number virtually unlimited. Moreover, corrections agents trying to uncover what targets are attractive will likely have a very misrepresentative idea of an actual offender's perspective of the targets he or she is likely to notice or select. For these reasons, more general and flexible crime prevention efforts are needed to protect the array of potential victims or targets.

Indeed, guardianship can come in many forms, with the central mission of decreasing the vulnerability of a target to a possible crime. Routine activity theory (Cohen and Felson's 1979 formulation) indicates that guardians may be human actors or security devices (see also Hollis-Peel, Reynald, van Bavel, Elffers, & Welsh, 2011). With the development of the outer crime problem triangle that features various "controllers" (see Figure 2.2), "guardians" generally refers to individuals protecting their own and their acquaintances' persons and property (Clarke & Eck, 2005; Eck, 1994; Felson, 1995). Just as with offender handlers, informal guardians (such as neighbors, coworkers, or family members) augment the capabilities of formal guardians (such as law enforcement actors; National Research Council, 2008). Simply, the greater the guardianship, the less defenseless the potential target.

As listed by Ekblom (2005), there are a variety of methods to reduce the vulnerability of target property, persons, and enclosures. By removing access to a target (e.g., a security fence), concealing the target (e.g., placing shopping bags in the trunk of an empty car), or hardening the target (e.g., installing flood lighting), property is less susceptible to theft and vandalism. People can prevent victimization through target avoidance (e.g., avoiding places where offenders congregate) and reducing any potential offense provocation (e.g., turning the other cheek when insulted). Finally, enclosures can be safeguarded by controlling the perimeter of a space (e.g., clear space boundaries) or controlling access to that space (e.g., a security card reader at the entrance of a residential area).

Because the possible methods of guardianship are as numerable as the targets they are protecting, it is clear that not all can be accounted for and addressed. Without doubt, general crime prevention measures (such as typical target hardening provisions like surveillance cameras or security tags on merchandise) are effective. It is difficult to say how influential these target guardians are; what is known, however, is that the amount of crime a community experiences is noticeably related to the opportunities that the physical and social arrangements of that community make (un)available (Clarke & Eck, 2005). Nearly a century of social science research has demonstrated that, despite the motivation or propensity of the offender, fruitful crime opportunities *will be* exploited (Felson & Clarke, 1998).

Accordingly, crime prevention efforts must increase the guardianship of potential targets and victims. Or, preferably, those efforts should create the perception for any actor (with any motivation or propensity) that there are no attractive targets available or that they are being effectively guarded (Taylor & Nee, 1988). In any form, guardians must convey to potential offenders that the pursuit of a target comes with great risk; guards must cue for offenders that they will not successfully obtain the target or complete the victimization, or that they will be apprehended and punished for their attempt.

PLACE MANAGERS

The crime triangle (see Figure 2.2) indicates that an offense will occur when an offender and target converge in space and time, and there is an absence of effective controllers. Crime science theory and practices have vigorously pursued the circumstances of a place that promote offending. Even more importantly, many factors that prevent crime at a given place have also been discovered (Clarke & Eck, 2005). Typically, place-based crime reduction efforts have included measures that physically alter the environment. These efforts have included ways to increase the costs of crime, decrease the benefits of crime, maximize the effort needed to commit crime, reduce provocations that lead to crime, and remove excuses that are used to justify crime (Cornish & Clarke, 2003; Wortley, 2001). More recently, these programs have begun to solicit the aid of people related to these spaces. Specifically, individuals or groups can be trained as place managers, or people who can control the behavior that occurs within the space for which they are responsible (Eck & Weisburd, 1995).

From a purely pragmatic standpoint, recruiting place managers reduces the burden on police and other formal agents of crime control. Law enforcement agencies cannot address each physical space that is conducive to crime—they do not have the time, resources, or authority. Giving the surveillance and administration tasks of an environment to one of its natural owners (e.g., the residence's tenant, a store manager, or a front office worker) not only relieves police strain, but also extends the power to prevent and detect crimes. In addition, these managers know the place more intimately, allowing them to design and implement more appropriate crime prevention measures.

One prescription for crime-conducive places is to recruit, teach, and motivate the owners to better manage that space. This can be accomplished by training managers to make changes to the space in ways that will alter the uses of that space. For instance, crime could be prevented if a business owner would eliminate the loitering that takes place in the company's parking lot; by installing an entrance checkpoint (such as a card reader with a gate or a security kiosk) or making access to the place more difficult (such as speed bumps or fencing), the behavior of the space's inhabitants will immediately be changed.

Although typically the police are seen as the party most responsible for maintaining order, crime control can also be achieved when place managers are encouraged to structure and monitor their spaces so that offending is less likely. By removing the features of the environment that signal that crime is allowed, potential offenders perceive an increased risk of being observed, arrested, and sanctioned, thereby decreasing the likelihood that they will make the choice to engage in the crime. When place managers help to address the crime-conducive elements within their space, they send a message that crime will not be tolerated and that attempts will be intercepted. Even if the place is not actively monitored, the physical space is still maintained in ways that reduce opportunities for crime and give the impression that crime is not possible there. This also helps place managers to informally enforce social behavioral norms for that area (Walker, 1984), helping to negotiate the forms of behavior that are acceptable for the space they own (Sousa & Kelling, 2006).

One potentially difficult aspect for place managers is figuring out which characteristics of the place might lead to crime problems, and which environmental cues can be left unaddressed. Ensuring that place owners exercise effective management choices, as opposed to adopting a zero-tolerance or fortress-style mindset, is crucial to the success of place-based crime prevention (Sousa, 2010). As such, it is necessary that police and crime prevention scholars teach place managers how to gather intelligence about the causes of a crime problem, and how to prioritize possible responses to that problem (Ratcliffe, 2008). As data analysis has become a more common tool used by crime problem solvers, crime prevention and place management have become integral parts of everyday law enforcement work, shifting focus from its typical reactive role (Weisburd & Eck, 2004). Accordingly, sufficient place management is not a generic response to a generic crime "problem," but a means of minimizing the real opportunities for crime that offenders perceive and pursue.

Conclusion: Opportunity-Reduction Supervision

Traditionally, crime science approaches have been reactive problem-solving efforts, developing ways to reduce offending only after places have become crime hotspots. By contrast, probation and parole authorities can capitalize on the successes of these police interventions to create a proactive approach to limiting re-offending (Murphy, 2005). However, as opposed to focusing primarily on problem places, community corrections agencies can focus on problem offenders. As discussed above, recruiting offender handlers, creating target guardians, and training place managers are all effective crime prevention methods. Tailoring these three strategies to community-supervised offenders will effectively minimize recidivism (specific strategies will be discussed in the following chapter). Although crime science interventions are largely reactionary (such as the police enforcing law violations), a more preventative approach is required for active offending populations, in which behavioral change is substituted for behavioral control (Taxman et al., 2003). Although there is minimal existing research evidence that the theory of environmental corrections is an effective offender supervision strategy, the impressive success of crime science interventions suggests that the logic underlying the theory is reliable (Clarke, 2010; Farrell, Tilley, Tseloni, & Mailley, 2010; Sherman, 2011b; Travis & Waul, 2002).

One important aspect of this strategy is the combination of formal and informal control mechanisms. Inherent to this framework, then, are crime prevention efforts that operate through a number of different processes. Not only do additional crime controllers prevent crime through traditional means such as surveillance and enforcement, but the social capital that these controllers may provide for offenders will additionally encourage desistance (e.g., a steady job provides new routine activities with more handlers, guardians, and managers, but it also creates new pro-social associations; Farrall, 2004; Wright & Cullen, 2004). Further, by involving the community of origin in addressing crime, the problem is better understood, and the resources are better able to tackle the various roots of that problem (Community Policing Consortium, 1994; Travis & Waul, 2002). This framework advocates for the disruption of recidivism patterns through the development of strategic and collaborative solutions that influence all of the components that shape offender behavior (Ratcliffe, 2008).

As the discussion in this chapter has demonstrated, the best solution to recurring crime problems (such as relapsing community-supervised offenders) is the reduction of opportunity. Addressing the precipitators of crime is the most effective way to reduce the various forms of opportunity that probationers and parolees encounter (Taxman, 2011). The creation of a community supervision case plan should therefore focus on the three forms of opportunity reduction (see Figure 2.1). The plan must include interactions and programming that address cognitions—it must change the way that offenders interpret criminal opportunity. The plan must create stipulations that will attend to the crime-probable situations that offenders find themselves in—it must reduce offenders' exposure to environments where they are likely (based upon their past) to encounter criminal opportunity (Taxman, 2011). In combining these two strategies, supervision case plans must address the routines that have developed from that offender's cognitions and situations—they must restrict offenders' access to environments where criminal opportunity abounds.

Chapter 1 documented the reasons that probation and parole practices may be ineffective. Specifically, the balance of treatment and control does not work the way it is routinely practiced, in part because the constituent parts are exercised poorly, and in part because potential agents of change have become passive service brokers. Chapter 2 indicated that, as demonstrated by crime science, a revolution in probation and parole will require changes to the theory, methods, and practices of the problem of concern—in this case, how best to intervene with community-supervised offenders. Thus, changing the focus of offender community supervision to strategies that reduce criminal opportunity will require that the day-to-day operations of community-supervision officers and agencies also be changed. As outlined in Chapter 3, there are a number of specific tactics and techniques that will directly reduce the crime opportunities that probationers and parolees interpret, encounter, and pursue.

3

How to Supervise Offenders

Probation and parole often are largely ineffective in reducing recidivism because supervision is based on the failed strategy of generic deterrence (Glaze & Bonczar, 2011; Glaze, Bonczar, & Zhang, 2010; MacKenzie, 2006; Petersilia & Turner, 1993; Solomon et al., 2005; Taxman, 2002). As discussed previously, research has demonstrated that attempts to have offenders comply with strict rules or be "scared straight" through intensive supervision or by threats of revocation do not work. With this limited success, it is clear that a new approach to community supervision is past due. We argue that a promising alternative, rooted in the theory and research of environmental criminology, involves teaching probation and parole officers how to reduce their supervisees' exposure to criminal opportunities (Cullen, Eck, & Lowenkamp, 2002; Taxman et al., 2003; Travis & Waul, 2002).

This chapter seeks to extend this line of reasoning. Our discussion begins by examining current supervision practices, showing that much of what is done under the umbrella of probation and parole supervision is not well suited to affecting behavioral change in offenders. The limits of the standard model again suggest the need for an alternative perspective. Specifically, the goal of opportunity-reduction practices should be to promote desistance rather than simply controlling crime during the supervision term (McNeill, Farrall, Lightowler, & Maruna, 2012). Toward this end, the second section of the chapter will identify five key components that an opportunity-reduction model of supervision might include.

First, the chapter discusses strategies for identifying what crime opportunities the offender is routinely exposed to. Examples include antisocial associates, problematic times or days, high-crime places, and risky situations (such as substance use at social events). The following chapter develops some technologies that might be used to glean this information about crime opportunities for offenders; the current discussion, however, focuses on the process that probation and parole officers would engage in to collect and use these data.

Second, the chapter explores how the product of this data collection would be used; specifically, how probation and parole authorities can develop an offender's case plan according to the information gained about his or her actual crime opportunities. Rather than prescribing very general rules for all supervisees, the officer would create a personalized case plan with supervision stipulations tailored to manage the unique opportunities for crime that the client encounters in his or her day-to-day activities. The conditions of supervision must be centered on reducing opportunities to commit crime; included here is a discussion of how this can be accomplished.

Third, the chapter outlines reasons and processes for modifying an offender's case plan. Importantly, as offenders progress through their supervision term, their crime opportunities will change. The offender may encounter fewer chances to commit crime, he or she may encounter more chances to commit crime, or the nature of the offender's crime opportunities may change. In any of these events, the probation or parole officer should be responsive to these changes, and the case plan should be modified to reflect the current crime opportunities that the client is exposed to during his or her normal routine.

Fourth, this chapter discusses the graduated consequences that should be part of a probation or parole case plan. Community supervision typically includes a standard set of rules and punishments that apply to all offenders, often with no regard to circumstances. Conversely, the environmental corrections model advocates for rewards and punishments that are tailored to the behavior of each individual offender. Possible methods for individualizing consequences for probationer and parolee outcomes are explored.

Fifth, the chapter outlines recommendations for earned release and aftercare. Normal community supervision procedures include a mandatory window of supervision (e.g., 12 months of probation), followed by a blunt discharge with no period of transition or post-release services being offered. Opportunity-reduction supervision promotes a gradual return to an unsupervised life (such as decreasing the number of supervision meetings across time). Further, an offender's eventual discharge might be earned; if the probationer or parolee exhibits positive behavior and meets predefined goals, then his or her supervision term should be complete. This section discusses strategies for structuring earned release, and best practices for providing transition services during and after the supervision term has expired.

Current Offender Supervision Practices

Prior to outlining what environmental corrections may look like in practice, it is important to examine the ways in which current community supervision of offenders is flawed. In many ways, current probation and parole practices are suffering from an ideological crisis. The tug-of-war between treatment versus control orientations, combined with rising caseloads and diminishing resources, has led to an era of managerialism (Burrell, 2012). Rather than officers working to prevent recidivism or enhance public safety, many current probation and parole practices are aimed at processing cases. By focusing on the process of offender *management*, there is little room left for the more important focus of offender *change* (Feeley & Simon, 1992; Simon, 1993). This is not to say that efficiency should be disregarded, as it is a bureaucratic necessity. Yet offender supervision that is not built around preventing (as opposed to controlling) crime is fundamentally misguided. The vast majority of offenders will eventually be released from correctional control, so it is important to encourage lasting prosocial change before supervision terms expire.

Unfortunately, current community corrections strategies and corresponding practices, detailed in the discussion that follows, are in many ways inherently unsound. The limited effectiveness of probation and parole supervision can be attributed to two problems of conceptualization. First, many offender monitoring programs use atheoretical methods at multiple stages of supervision (including intake and assessment, case plan development, offender management, or review and discharge). This means that probation and parole agencies do not base their practices on a framework of how to reduce crime. Second, many community corrections frameworks are premised on faulty theories about the causes of crime (seen in misguided attempts to treat and control offenders). In both of these cases—having an invalid theory about how to prevent recidivism or having no theory at all—it is unreasonable to expect that offenders will desist from crime and lead prosocial lives.

Yet corrections agencies have a remarkable opportunity to help improve offenders' lives and enhance community safety. Traditionally, probation and parole are periods of community supervision ordered by a court following a plea, conviction, or sentence. Less commonly, a period of community corrections may be ordered following a term of incarceration as determined by parole authorities. In either case, offenders submit to a period of supervision, agreeing to exchange two freedoms: gaining the freedom to live in the community while sacrificing freedoms of lifestyle. This latter agreement involves requirements of the offender (participating in treatment or maintaining legitimate employment, for instance) as well as restrictions on the offender (such as abstaining from alcohol or abiding by a curfew). If offenders fail to abide by these requirements and restrictions, their freedom may be revoked and incarceration could result. Therefore, many offenders are highly vested in following the stipulations of their supervision plan, and officers can capitalize on this motivation to incite positive change (Clark et al., 2006). Given the impressive sway court and correctional authorities have over this active criminal population, probation and parole supervisions are ripe opportunities to alter offender behavior, and as a result improve public safety.

Unfortunately, however, the normal business of monitoring offenders in the community falls short of this goal; simply, we are not maximizing the chance to reduce recidivism. The interactions between corrections authorities and their clients are in most ways not reformative (Smith, Schweitzer, Labrecque, & Latessa, 2012). Routinely, offenders are being managed but not changed. This is not to say that there are not successful programs or even departments (MacKenzie, 2006), though considering the millions of hours spent meeting with offenders, we are not getting our tax dollars' worth. The status quo within probation and parole is a bureaucratic process focused on vague restrictions and nonspecific requirements. This results in momentary behavioral compliance (at best) rather than emphasizing lasting cognitive and lifestyle change. This downfall can be seen in four specifics that are characteristic of community supervision.

First, probation and parole officers are provided with minimal professional training and virtually no guidance in the performance of their job. At best, officers are provided training on how to manage their cases (e.g., completion of paperwork, particulars of the law, allocation of resources), yet they receive little instruction on how to change offender behavior (Bourgon, Gutierrez, & Ashton, 2011). Although in part a product of rising caseloads, the bureaucratic role embodied by most community corrections officers can largely be attributed to a lack of education: Probation and parole officers are not skilled in affecting behavioral change. If offender supervisors are expected to impact criminal behavior, then they must be provided with the knowledge and resources to do so.

Second, offender supervisors are not accountable for public safety. Rather than focusing on the prevention of recidivism through offender change, probation and parole officers are concerned with compliance. Indeed, contrary to the job title, hardly any time is spent by officers actually supervising or correcting their clients. Rarely does a probation or parole officer meet with an offender outside of the office or engage in prescriptively rehabilitative practices (Bonczar, 1997; Reinventing Probation Council, 2000). Supervisors must process cases by completing paperwork and communicating with the court, which shifts their attention away from the objective of preventing crime (Reinventing Probation Council, 2000; Smith & Dickey, 1998). Yet rather than judging officers' job performance on case-management objectives, probation and parole agents should be evaluated according to the outcomes of the offenders under their supervision. Although this improper focus is in part related to the lack of training officers receive in reorienting offender behavior, it also suggests a larger misunderstanding of the goal of community supervision (Pew Center on the States, 2008b). Largely, corrections agencies cannot anticipate reductions in re-offending until they explicitly define the goal of probation and parole as the enhancement of public safety through the prevention of recidivism (Smith & Dickey, 1998).

Third, the principles of community supervision are enforcement-based, as opposed to emphasizing risk reduction. Observational research demonstrates that the criminogenic needs of offenders are not discussed in meetings with their supervising officer (Bonta et al., 2008). The rules probationers and parolees are instructed to follow are as global and vague as to perhaps be meaningless. For example, offenders are often prohibited from possessing a firearm, though this misses the larger point of the daily routines and environments in which the offender is embedded and how these contribute to recidivism. Indeed, there is nothing inherent to gun possession that leads to crime, but the variables associated with gun possession (e.g., engagement in illicit markets, fellowship with antisocial associates, development of pro-crime values) may be more important targets for change. Many existing community corrections practices are atheoretical, while others are based on inaccurate theories that may actually increase re-offending. In order to evoke change, the conditions of supervision placed on offenders must be grounded in valid criminological theory.

Fourth, the guiding philosophy of probation and parole—a merger of punishment and treatment resulting in case management—is in many ways unsuccessful. In particular, the use of a vague deterrence orientation often guides offender supervision practices despite its limited effectiveness. Whether this is because the theory is unsound or the tenets of rational choice are untrue or we cannot practice true deterrence methods is beside the point. What matters here is that the model that guides community corrections is based on a theory that is demonstrably ineffective (Gendreau et al., 1994). Although deterrence and incapacitation are elements of a successful offender-management program, they must be used in constructive (as opposed to punitive) ways that adhere to valid criminological theory (Winstone & Pakes, 2005). Deterrence that is centered on surveillance and punishment (essentially watching offenders closely and threatening them with revocation for slight misbehaviors) is of little value. Yet *focused* deterrence interventions, often seen in problem-oriented policing interventions, can be a purposive crime reduction strategy. When designed properly, deterrence has an important influence in community corrections; however, supervising offenders based solely on the premises of monitoring, compliance, and control is ineffective (Pew Center on the States, 2008b).

These shortcomings are even further handicapped by the infrequency with which supervisors meet with their clients. Offenders may receive no more than 15 minutes of interaction with their supervising officer in each meeting (Clear, Cole, & Reisig, 2009; Teague, 2011). This is undesirable, as evaluation research shows that more in-depth interactions have crime prevention effects (Bonta et al., 2008). Importantly, short offender meetings (which may be a practical necessity given caseload sizes) can be effective if officers engage in proper cognitive-behavioral shaping (Robinson et al., 2012; Trotter, 1996). Again, however, this takes proper training and guidance of offender supervisors, and a theory of how meeting time ought to be spent (Burnett & McNeill, 2005; Smith et al., 2012). Overall, research consistently indicates that adherence to the risk, need, and responsivity principles (and the general application of the principles of effective correctional intervention) is most influential in minimizing recidivism (Bonta et al., 2011; Robinson, VanBenschoten, Alexander, & Lowenkamp, 2011; Taxman, 2008).

However, in order to reduce recidivism, the aforementioned limitations of existing probation and parole organization must be addressed: (1) Community corrections officers must be trained to affect behavioral change in their supervisees. (2) Community corrections officers must be held accountable for public safety through the reduction of recidivism of the clients under their supervision. (3) Principles of probation and parole must be specific to the individual offender and must be based on sound criminological theory. (4) The use of the philosophy of generic deterrence-oriented supervision must be replaced by an evidence-based model of probation and parole. The remaining sections of this chapter demonstrate how an opportunity-reduction model of offender supervision would reorient probation and parole to overcome these existing limitations.

Introduction to Environmental Corrections Supervision

Research in environmental criminology demonstrates the marked reductions in crime that are achieved when opportunities for offending are limited. Borrowing from these theories, the implications for probation and parole are now explicitly explored. By training probation and parole officers as problem solvers who are appreciative of the larger context that encourages or dissuades offending (and by providing them tools to do so), community corrections agencies reorient their goal toward one of crime prevention. As the conceptual model developed in this volume suggests, designing an offender's supervision conditions in ways that limit or restructure the person's exposure to crime opportunities may be a successful model to reduce re-offending. Rather than providing all community-supervised offenders with generic restrictions and prescriptions, the environmental corrections model of probation and parole would tailor supervision conditions to the unique and precise crime opportunities that each individual is vulnerable to.

The implications of this reorientation are promising. Probation and parole agencies are routinely in contact with active offenders, providing them with a bounty of opportunities to intervene. Moreover, supervising officers are potential super controllers, as they may be capable of managing the behaviors of other agents that influence the actions of offenders (Sampson, Eck, & Dunham, 2010). If given the proper tools, community corrections officers can become invaluable informal problem solvers, using various innovations to tailor a supervision plan to the offender or offending of concern (Cordner & Biebel, 2005). As Sherman (2011a) describes, "criminology as invention" requires an understanding of a crime problem in its original context, which then creates theories about the causes of that crime problem, in turn developing new ways of dealing with the crime problem. These solutions will include: (1) supervision stipulations that make it more difficult for offenders to access crime opportunities, (2) the inclusion of new agents of informal social control, and (3) restructuring offenders' daily routines with prosocial activities (Cullen, Eck, & Lowenkamp, 2002). While each probation or parole officer must rely on innovation for the unique circumstances of each offender and each community, the discussion that follows details methods that can be used to discover and restrict access to crime opportunities.

Identifying Exposure to Crime Opportunities

Following the theoretical contributions of environmental criminology, probation and parole can be refashioned to alter offenders' opportunities to commit crime. Opportunity-reduction supervision is guided by four tenets: (1) Offenders are constrained by their patterns of daily activity. (2) The environments encountered during these routines vary according to the real crime opportunities that they present. (3) Offenders will gauge each environment according to whether deviant behavior is socially acceptable and whether criminal behavior is feasible. (4) The clues offenders use in making their decisions are based on their perceptions of effort, ability, risk, and reward. The thrust of environmental corrections supervision is the reduction of offenders' exposure to situations that are conducive to crime. Thus, an important task in creating an individual's case plan and the conditions of his or her supervision is identifying the offender's exposure to crime opportunities. We hypothesize that there are four central questions that must be answered to discover a probationer or parolee's routine opportunities for offending. Each of these questions is discussed in the subsections that follow, accompanied by sample pictorial representations of data that can be used to detect environments where crime opportunities abound.

Thus, in order to prevent community-supervised offenders from accessing chances to commit crime, probation and parole officers must first identify those crime opportunities by asking and then compiling the data to answer these four questions for each supervisee: (1) With whom does the individual commit crime? (2) When does the individual commit crime? (3) Where does the individual commit crime? (4) Why does the individual commit crime? Addressing these "Four W's"—the who, when, where, and why of crime opportunities—will be a logistical challenge for any agency initially interested in implementing this sort of process, and procedures will obviously require adjustment to the local circumstances and available resources. While research is needed to evaluate the best methods for gathering and using offender-specific data about crime opportunities (see Chapter 7), it is probable that these processes will vary according to department size and offender population characteristics. As illustrative examples, four "infographics"—that is, graphical or visual presentations of data in a format intended to make the relevant information more easily understood—have been included in this chapter (see Figures 3.1 through 3.4). Readers should note that all the data used in the following infographics are fictional as are the names of people and places. The purpose of these infographics is to illustrate how various sources and forms of data can be organized and then used to create individualized and purposeful offender supervision case plans. While designing and using these tools will provide several initial challenges, we argue that they are worth serious pursuit. The upfront investment of assessing offenders and developing individualized case plans will be diminished by the benefits gained, particularly after these processes are streamlined and improved. Although each agency will develop different data tools and crime opportunity identification procedures, it is the novel approach used here that deserves special note.

To clarify, the four subsections that follow introduce infographics as illustrations of how to identify the crime opportunities of offenders. These data presentations are offered as examples of how offender supervisors can arrive at meaningful conclusions about offenders' routine activities from an abundance of peripheral information. Ideally, community corrections agents can recreate or approximate these figures in order to learn about opportunities for offending that are specific to each individual probationer and parolee. However, data about crime patterns (especially aggregated data from a specific jurisdiction) may still be helpful in creating specialized conditions of supervision relevant to local crime opportunities.

On that note, the next section, which discusses the creation of offenders' case plans, provides examples of how the information gleaned from these data syntheses can be used to develop supervision stipulations. Specific samples of conditions of offender supervision are presented to demonstrate the utility of the included infographics. Finally, the following chapter, which explores offender supervision technologies, addresses how the information displayed in these infographics can be gathered. In order to be useful for community corrections agencies, data must be collected in an organized and goal-oriented fashion, so as to serve as diagnostic tools for developing offender supervision conditions. Thus, the discussion of the figures in this chapter will speak to the following: (1) What kind of information can be used to determine an offender's crime opportunities? (2) How can this information be used to design the offender's supervision case plan? (3) Where does this information come from?

WITH WHOM DOES THE INDIVIDUAL COMMIT CRIME?

Antisocial associates are one of the strongest correlates of criminal behavior (Andrews, 1989; Andrews & Bonta, 2010; Cullen & Jonson, 2012; Gendreau, 1996; Van Voorhis et al., 2009). Knowing this, it is imperative that offender supervision case plans include stipulations that minimize this risk factor. However, traditional conditions of probation and parole include the blanket restriction that offenders do not *associate* with other *known* offenders. This creates two unfortunate problems.

First, the exact meaning of this phrase comes under frequent fire. Perhaps most obviously, is the interpretation of the word "known." Supervisees are quick to rebut that they did not know that an individual they were with had an arrest record. In addition, there is confusion over what the word *offender* is supposed to mean. It is unclear whether this term encompasses anyone with any criminal record, or people who are active criminals, or offenders who specialize in the same offense as the probationer or parolee, or even fellow gang members or previous co-offenders. Finally, there are disputes over what is implied by the word "associate." There is little understanding over whether this extends to whereabouts or social gatherings or solely criminal pursuits. This supervision rule creates problems of knowledge (who is known), interpretation (who is an offender), and breadth (what is meant by association). Taking the stipulation at face value, it seems a difficult task for anyone to achieve, as any person you encounter at any place may meet the definition of criminal association.

Second, even when offenders are known, the supervisee may have a difficult time eliminating all associations. It is not uncommon for a probationer or parolee to be intimately related to someone with a criminal record. In fact, an offender may live with other offenders (such as a parent, sibling, or spouse), without the option to terminate the relationship and relocate. Moreover, removing these social ties from supervisees may only worsen the problem, as family and friends are often part of the desistance process and can help to encourage prosocial behavior.

As a result of these limitations, community corrections officers often ignore violations of this rule. The infractions are too great in number to pursue, and too difficult to discover and sanction, and offenders can often excuse the misbehavior.

We acknowledge that an effective probation or parole plan will include some condition that recognizes the influence of deviant peers; however, a more pragmatic and impactful approach is necessary. According to environmental corrections supervision, the goal of probation and parole ought to be the reduction of opportunities to commit crime. The most important task in creating a useful case plan, then, is the identification of criminal opportunity that relates to an offender's associates. It is of little help to speak generally of all offenders. Rather, supervision officers must identify those individuals whom their client has committed crimes with before (co-offenders), those individuals whom their client may be at risk of committing crimes with (known offenders), and individuals who are associated with the offender but were not participants in his or her offenses (offender handlers). That is, this specific question should be asked: With whom does—or might—the offender commit crime?

Figure 3.1 provides an example of an infographic that depicts these data. This pictorial provides a social network analysis in which the associations of the offender of interest are plotted for analysis. These three kinds of relationships are graphed, and additionally indicate whether the information came from official reports (e.g., police reports, court records) or whether the offender divulged the information to the officer. Through this data synthesis, a great amount of data is reduced to a consumable and analyzable piece of information. Rather than having too much information and not knowing what to do with it (resulting in a generic restriction on who their clients can spend time with), probation or parole officers can now see an overview of the risky and protective people a client is associated with. In this way, officers can create a case plan (discussed in the next section) that is tailored to specific crime opportunities of their supervisee.

The central advantage of this infographic (Figure 3.1) is the ability to differentiate between various risks. Whereas traditional probation and parole supervision provides a blanket restriction (i.e., the client is not allowed to associate with any known offenders), this data presentation can distinguish between different types of crime opportunities. For example, in terms of causation (criminological theory), there is an important difference between associations that are adversarial (parties in conflict) and cooperative (parties working in concert). Officers can create a more realistic and impactful case plan when they can differentiate between co-offending that may occur at the same time and place but be adversarial (such as an assault in which both parties are arrested) and co-offending occurring together (such as two individuals breaking into buildings as a team). Community corrections supervisors can also tailor case plan restrictions by having information about the relationship between co-offenders and known offenders. Officers should be prepared for their supervisees to seek out new associations if they are restricted from spending time with their criminal peers, and recognize that offenders may steer away from specialization (e.g., branching out from drug dealing when they cannot associate with fellow dealers, and moving toward drug trafficking with friends of fellow dealers). Knowing ahead of time who may pose a risk in the future is an important crime prevention tool, so possessing and being able to assess information about prospective antisocial associates is beneficial to community corrections.

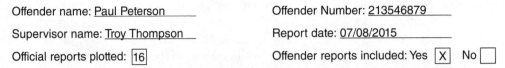

State Department of Parole

Offender name: <u>Paul Peterson</u>   Offender Number: <u>213546879</u>

Supervisor name: <u>Troy Thompson</u>   Report date: <u>07/08/2015</u>

Official reports plotted: [16]   Offender reports included: Yes [X]   No [ ]

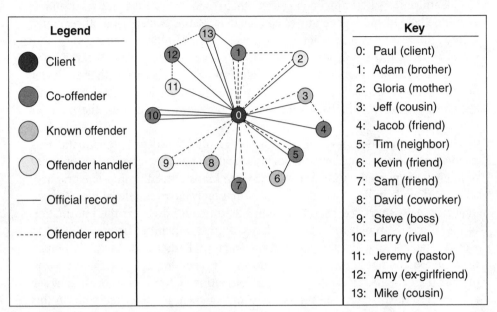

Legend	Key
● Client	0: Paul (client)
● Co-offender	1: Adam (brother)
● Known offender	2: Gloria (mother)
○ Offender handler	3: Jeff (cousin)
— Official record	4: Jacob (friend)
----- Offender report	5: Tim (neighbor)
	6: Kevin (friend)
	7: Sam (friend)
	8: David (coworker)
	9: Steve (boss)
	10: Larry (rival)
	11: Jeremy (pastor)
	12: Amy (ex-girlfriend)
	13: Mike (cousin)

Assessment: Paul has been arrested with six other offenders; of particular concern are Larry (a rival gang member) and Tim (his neighbor), though Paul reports using and dealing drugs with his brother (Adam) and friend (Sam). Paul's cousins (Jeff, Mike) are reported offenders, though they do not commit crime together. Potential handlers include Paul's mother, boss, and pastor, each of whom have influence over other offenders involved in Paul's network.

Figure 3.1   Social Network Analysis

WHEN DOES THE INDIVIDUAL COMMIT CRIME?

As Chapter 2 presented, criminological research demonstrates that offending is not distributed randomly in space (see the next subsection) or time. The commission of crimes is concentrated around a number of time points, such as time of the month, season of the year, or generational eras. Of concern for community corrections officers are the temporal crime patterns that emerge in shorter windows, such as across time of the day and day of the week. The graphical presentation of time geography gives a framework through which supervisors can recognize the patterns of behavior—both criminal and law-abiding—that their clients exhibit (Miller, 2005). Macro-level examples include offending hotspots at bars in the evening hours or in city centers during workdays (Ratcliffe, 2010). It is this pattern recognition that provides probation and parole officers with ideas for how to effectively prevent the convergence of their supervisees and crime opportunities at specific points in time (Ratcliffe, 2006).

For this reason, crime problem solvers would be remiss not to include temporal analyses in their address of offending. Unfortunately, the mapping of crime incidents across time is a woefully underdeveloped area in criminology and research methods (Ratcliffe, 2010). Even more difficult is that temporal geography is usually performed with aggregated data, providing evidence of patterns of offending across hundreds if not thousands of criminals and crime incidences. However, infographics of smaller scales are still valuable tools for identifying observable offending patterns. Depending on the individual offender, even a small handful of data points can prove useful in discerning when the probationer or parolee encounters and takes advantage of chances to commit crime. In any event, the strong association between time and crime commission demands the attention of offender supervisors. General correlations provide important supervision conditions; curfew, for example, is imposed based on the understanding that crime opportunities increase in the late evening and early morning hours. Offender-specific links between opportunities for offending and time are also valuable, giving community corrections officers information about the times of the day and days of the week when their clients are most likely to encounter situations that are conducive to crime. Thus, officers need to ask this question about each of their supervisees: When does the individual commit crime?

As seen in Figure 3.2, the times one offender converges with crime opportunities (in various circumstances, such as at a given place, with certain people, or in the presence of rewards) have been plotted. This pictorial provides two axes through which data points are graphed: time of the day and day of the week. Each of these levels of measurement provides offender supervisors with different types of information to use in identifying their client's pursuit of crime opportunities. For example, the figure demonstrates that the hypothetical offender accrues crime incidences most frequently in the afternoon and late night hours, with many of those events taking place on the weekends. As discussed in the following subsection, this information provides clear implications for how to structure the offender's time, in turn reducing his or her exposure to crime opportunities that have proved tempting in the past.

Of additional use for community corrections officers is the variation in the types of data points used in creating Figure 3.2. As not all encounters with the criminal justice system are equal, a quality data synthesis will be sensitive to the different forms of information included in the offender's record. Discussed in earlier chapters, the substantial difference between technical violations of supervision conditions and the commission of a new crime is important. Accordingly, this pictorial divides data points into three forms of criminal justice contacts: violations of case plan stipulations, contact with the police in which no further action was taken, and arrests. Again, by providing probation and parole officers with a diverse amount of information in a readily digestible format, recidivism can be more handily understood and prevented.

Of import is that this data presentation can be used to infer the causality of offending for the probationer or parolee. It is not helpful to merely note that the offender makes most of his or her contact with police during the afternoon hours. Rather, this observation should provide (1) an idea about why this is occurring, and (2) what case plan stipulations can be created to prevent it from continuing (examples of this are provided in the following section). The emphasis for

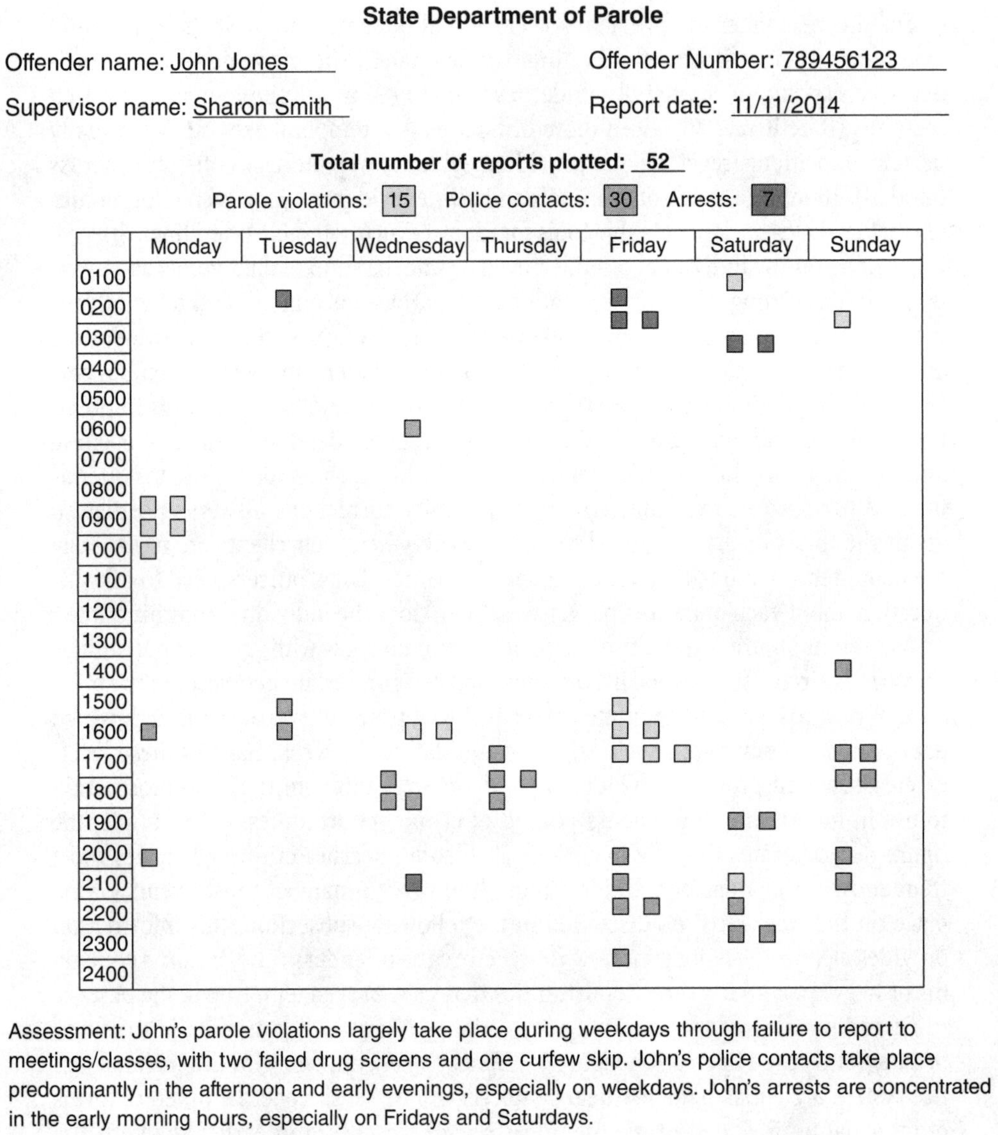

State Department of Parole

Offender name: John Jones   Offender Number: 789456123

Supervisor name: Sharon Smith   Report date: 11/11/2014

Total number of reports plotted: 52

Parole violations: 15   Police contacts: 30   Arrests: 7

	Monday	Tuesday	Wednesday	Thursday	Friday	Saturday	Sunday
0100						□	
0200		■			■		
0300					■ ■		□
0400						■ ■	
0500							
0600			■				
0700							
0800	□ □						
0900	□ □						
1000	□						
1100							
1200							
1300							
1400							■
1500		■			□		
1600	■	■	□ ■		□ ■		
1700				■	□ ■ ■		■ ■
1800			■ ■	■ ■			■ ■
1900			■			■ ■	
2000	■				■		■
2100			■		■	□	■
2200					■ ■	■	
2300						■ ■	
2400					■		

Assessment: John's parole violations largely take place during weekdays through failure to report to meetings/classes, with two failed drug screens and one curfew skip. John's police contacts take place predominantly in the afternoon and early evenings, especially on weekdays. John's arrests are concentrated in the early morning hours, especially on Fridays and Saturdays.

Figure 3.2   Time and Day Plot

community corrections officers must be on uncovering the crime opportunities that are associated with the observations made from the data.

WHERE DOES THE INDIVIDUAL COMMIT CRIME?

As the research presented in Chapter 2 demonstrates, there is a strong empirical and practical association between offending and place. The traditional concern for criminologists has been mapping the spatial dispersion of aggregate crime data, although lower levels of analyses have important uses, as well. First, knowing the places where an offender converges with crime opportunities is a necessary ingredient to general crime prevention. Place-based crime control measures are effective methods of avoiding potential problems for individual offenders in addition to large groups of readily motivated offenders. Second, when offender supervisors have information about where offenders commit crime, they can tailor a case plan to make access to criminogenic places less likely. Beyond general place management and situational crime prevention, probation and parole officers can create supervision conditions that restrict access to places where crime opportunities abound and cannot be easily controlled otherwise. Environmental criminology, in both theory and the practical application of place-based crime prevention policies, has unique applications for corrections that have yet to be explored.

Typically, community corrections agencies engage in "fortress supervision," in which probation and parole officers work in centrally located offices (Pew Center on the States, 2008b). This setup does little to help the officer understand the environment that promotes offending among their clients, and creates little deterrent effect for offenders who understand that their supervising officer is not present in their community. Opposing this model is "place-based supervision," in which offender supervisors have geographically based caseloads. This approach allows for a more efficient allocation of corrections resources, and places probation and parole officers directly in the communities where offenders meet with crime opportunities. By supervising offenders in their home communities, corrections agents can foster collaborations with the people who know and have some influence over the offender, and become familiar with the local resources and the high-risk areas for clients on their caseload (Pew Center on the States, 2008b; Reentry Policy Council, 2005; Solomon, 2006; Taxman, 2006).

To determine where the offender meets with crime opportunities (in order to then tailor a case plan and design interventions aimed at preventing offenders from meeting with those opportunities), community corrections officers would benefit from place-based crime data. Accordingly, they must ask this question about each of their supervisees: Where does the individual commit crime? Figure 3.3 demonstrates what a graphical presentation of offending hotspots for one individual might look like. This infographic provides a plot of arrest records and offender reports about where the individual participates in illegal activity. In addition to these data points are the locations associated with those crime opportunities, such as the offender's residence, his or her workplace, or places where social gatherings take place (e.g., friends' houses, bars, recreation centers). By having a visual presentation of where offenders spend their time and where they commit crime, the community corrections supervisor can strategically develop a case plan that restricts access to areas that offer high numbers of crime opportunities.

Importantly, the non-criminal activities of offenders and how their time is spent in a daily routine provide important information about the likely criminal activities of offenders (Brantingham & Brantingham, 2008). The crime opportunities that individuals encounter are intimately linked with their daily activity patterns, and it is therefore important that offender supervisors be knowledgeable about the activity and awareness spaces of their clients (Brantingham & Brantingham, 1993). Many times, offenders do not go out looking for places to commit crime. Rather, they may

State Department of Parole

Offender name: <u>Bob Brown</u>

Supervisor name: <u>Joe Johnson</u>

Official reports plotted: 17

Offender Number: <u>135792468</u>

Report date: <u>06/16/2015</u>

Offender reports included: Yes [X] No [ ]

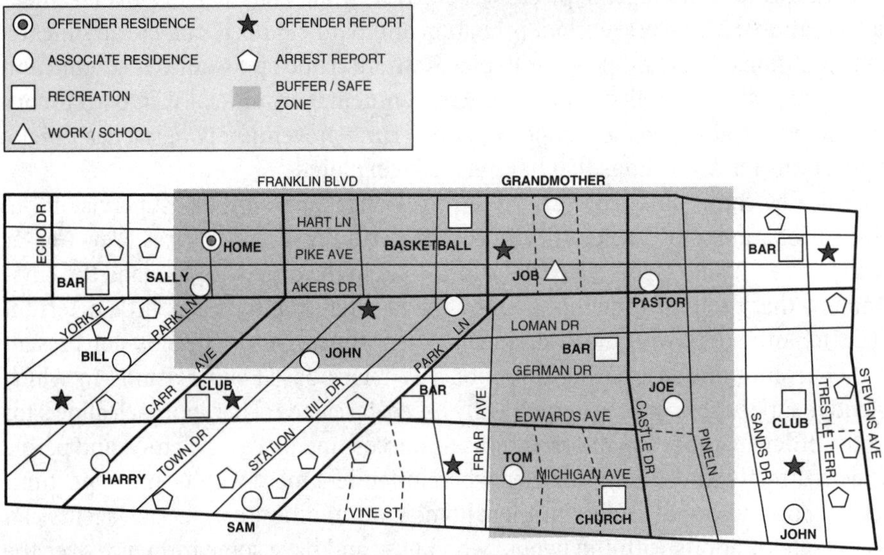

Assessment: Bob's arrest and self-report information reveal geographical areas of concern in the neighborhood of Oakley. This area contains a few bars and the homes of his friends Bill and Sam. The hotspot map shows a safe zone below Franklin Blvd. through the South Bank neighborhood, which includes Bob's residence, job, and church.

Figure 3.3 Offending Hotspots

encounter a crime-conducive place (filled with low risks, high rewards, and facilitating tools) that triggers criminal motivation, but only in the unfolding of non-criminal activities. There are different data that can be resourced in creating an infographic of hotspots for an individual; whether through qualitative interviews, hand-plotted by corrections officers, or by mapping geocached police reports, the goal is to analyze real data from the perspective of crime pattern theory (Brantingham & Brantingham, 2008). In order to create supervision stipulations that keep offenders away from risky places, probation and parole officers must first identify what circumstances are tempting for their clients and where those factors are located.

WHY DOES THE INDIVIDUAL COMMIT CRIME?

Figuring out what factors prompt an individual to take advantage of an existing crime opportunity is an important crime prevention tool. Yet many critics of criminology assert that after centuries of theorizing and studying offending and offenders, there is still no consensus regarding why people commit crime on the whole. True, the search for a general theory of crime is not complete, and no proposed explanation for an offense is perfect (i.e., there is unexplained variation remaining). Still, aside from these insurmountable faults, researchers have discovered a number of variables that are strongly associated with offending. After hundreds of studies (across decades, countries, and populations), we know that antisocial peers, antisocial attitudes and beliefs, and an antisocial personality pattern are highly predictive of criminality (Andrews & Bonta, 2010).

Yet some of these variables may be of little help to community corrections officers desiring to prevent crime there and then. As previously discussed, altering deep-seated propensities (such as someone with an antisocial personality pattern) is a difficult task requiring a great amount of time and effort. If probation and parole supervisors are to be held accountable for the relapses of their clients, then they require more usable information about the more immediate factors that prompt their supervisees to commit crime. Beyond internal inclinations, officers can more readily manipulate the environment and the situations that their clients are exposed to. To design an intervening case plan, then, the task for community corrections officers is to identify the situational motivators for offending.

Thus, officers must ask this question for each of their supervisees: Why does the individual commit crime? But in accumulating information to address this issue, they should take a specifc approach. Rather than focusing on the causes of crime that are difficult to determine and change, probation and parole officers should attempt to identify and manipulate those circumstances that encourage offenders to pursue crime opportunities—that is, those proximate factors that influence the individual to offend when an opportunity is available.

As described by Wortley (2001), one of the keys to reducing criminal opportunity is the control of crime precipitators, or, accounting for those factors that lead to a criminal event. Generally speaking, these precipitants include prompts, pressures, permissibility, and provocations. That is, environments can present cues that *prompt* the individual to offend, the situation may exert social *pressure* on people to offend, factors can reduce moral inhibitions and therefore *permit* someone to commit a crime, and the environment might create an emotional response from a person that would *provoke* a criminal response (Wortley, 1997, 1998, 2001). The trouble experienced by practitioners is translating these generic categories into clearly defined causes of crime within a given situation. If probation and parole officers must develop an actionable case plan centered around minimizing crime opportunities, then information about the specific variables that produce these prompts, pressures, permissions, and provocations must be available.

Examples of these crime precipitators are seen in Figure 3.4. Although the specific information used by community corrections officers will naturally vary by the data available, these provide an idea of the kind of considerations that may prove valuable. Five different kinds of categories are included in this illustration: motivation (what kind of reward the offender seeks when pursuing crime opportunities); mentality (what kind of mood the offender experiences when pursuing crime opportunities); company (what kind of setting is present when the offender pursues

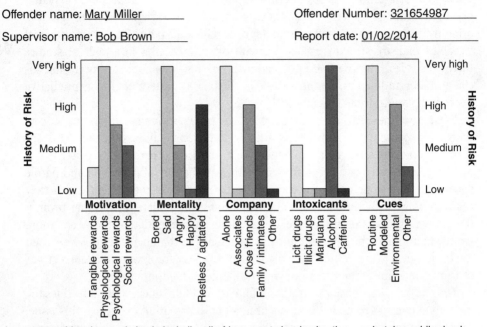

County Probation Department

Offender name: Mary Miller   Offender Number: 321654987

Supervisor name: Bob Brown   Report date: 01/02/2014

Assessment: Mary is an admitted alcoholic; all of her arrests involved actions undertaken while drunk, demonstrated in her risk history. Mary's primary impetus for offending is fueled by her addiction to alcohol, with crimes occurring when she is reportedly sad or agitated, and alone or in familiar social settings. Mary's cues for committing crime are largely a matter of routine (driving while intoxicated), though she is also spurred on when she becomes distressed at social gatherings (assault, public indecency).

Figure 3.4   Crime Precipitators

crime opportunities); intoxicants (what kind of substances influence the offender's behavior when pursuing crime opportunities); and cues (what chain of events leads the offender to pursue crime opportunities).

These distinctions are highly important, as they provide individualized information about the kinds of situations that are more or less likely to tempt an offender. There are too many crime precipitators to remove them all or to restrict a probationer or parolee's access to them. As a result, offender supervisors require a general understanding of the different triggers that their clients respond to. Specifically, officers need information about the reasons why an individual offender noticed, was attracted to, and decided to exploit an existing crime opportunity. Opportunities to commit crime are in every place at all times, but the appeal of and access to these chances to offend can be controlled. Consequently, the most effective combatant will be interventions (i.e., case plan stipulations) that address the specific situational antecedents that cause an offender to exploit the available crime opportunity (Wortley, 2001). Rather than assuming that offenders are readily motivated at all times, it is helpful to examine the situational circumstances that create, heighten, or facilitate offender motivation (Cornish & Clarke, 2003; Cromwell & Birzer, 2014).

IDENTIFYING SUPERVISEES' CRIME OPPORTUNITIES WITH THE FOUR W'S

The environmental corrections model of offender supervision reasons that in order to effectively reduce recidivism among probationers and parolees, vague and generic rules must be replaced by case plans that reduce the actual crime opportunities that offenders are vulnerable to. Taken together, we suggest that four categories of information about crime opportunities will be helpful for developing these targeted supervision conditions: who, when, where, and why. After gathering data about the particular circumstances surrounding individual supervisee's past offending, probation and parole departments are able to tailor case plans that help offenders to avoid coming into contact with these tempting situations altogether. Rather than using a broad deterrence model with blanket restrictions that are difficult to enforce (e.g., stay away from other offenders, be home by 10:00 p.m., steer clear of that suburb, and refrain from alcohol consumption), these "Four W's" of offenders' crime opportunities will help to produce unique case plans that are purposively corrective.

Considering Gender

At the core of environmental corrections is the assumption that supervision aimed at reducing exposure to crime opportunities should be as individualized as possible. That is why the Four W's emphasize asking questions about the *individual*. Still, any experienced probation or parole officer will enter an assessment session with some sense of the kinds of opportunities that the supervisee being interviewed is likely to have encountered and that are likely to be criminogenic. For example, similar to other sources of crime and desistance (Sampson & Laub, 1993), crime opportunities will be age-graded. Juveniles and adults may live in quite different social worlds and be exposed to quite different opportunities. Similarly, offenders from a structurally dense neighborhood marked by hot spots for crime encounter a vastly different illegitimate opportunity structure than those from a suburban community zoned primarily for residential use.

Although a range of these factors might well be pertinent, here we consider gender, where there is a long-standing debate over whether the causes of criminal conduct—including crime opportunity—are "general" (the same for everyone) or "gender specific" (different for males and females) (Daigle, Cullen, & Wright, 2007; Moffitt, Caspi, Rutter, & Silva, 2001). The general perspective extends to Freda Adler's (1975) *Sisters in Crime*. In this classic work, Adler argued that due to changing social roles, women had gained access to new crime opportunities that would both increase their lawbreaking and allow them to commit illegalities heretofore reserved for men. In the rehabilitation area, Andrews and Bonta (2010) are among those who argue that the criminogenic needs of offenders are general. At most, gender is a "responsivity" factor that affects the ways in which treatment might be delivered (see also Smith, Cullen, & Latessa, 2009; Smith & Manchak, 2015). By contrast, other scholars argue that gender intimately shapes the nature of crime opportunities, pathways into crime, and the criminogenic needs that should be targeted in treatment (for discussions of these issues, see Alarid & Wright, 2015; Miller & Mullins, 2006; Smith & Manchak, 2015; Steffensmeier & Allan, 1996).

Perhaps because its focus is mainly on the way opportunities are rooted in *situations*, environmental criminology has not paid considerable attention to how male and female *offenders* might differ in how they perceive, select, and respond to crime opportunities. Some insights can be gained from the work of Steffensmeier (1983), who has documented how sex-segregation and sexism restrict opportunities in the "underworld." With Allan, he also created a general paradigm for understanding female crime that has implications for understanding the gendered nature of criminal opportunity (Steffensmeier & Allan, 1996). For example, women will be unable to engage in some crimes due to a lack of physical strength but other illegalities are available because of their sexuality. They also may find the use of firearms and aggression to be inconsistent with their gender identity and may be less likely to see strangers as suitable targets for victimization. Other scholars have emphasized the role that sexual victimization and domestic violence play in pushing girls and women into homeless situations where criminal opportunities become available and are pursued out of necessity (Chesney-Lind, 2015). Trying to knife off crime opportunity might prove difficult if the reason why a female offender initially entered a risky situation is not addressed.

Again, at this stage, it is not clear how much the existing scholarship can assist probation and parole officers in developing a more effective case plan for helping offenders avoid criminal opportunities. Still, it is likely important that officers be sensitized to the potential role that gender might play in access to criminal opportunities. Over time, a knowledge base should be created by examining closely the case plans designed for male and female offenders to see if differential opportunity risks have been identified. Phrased differently, the role of gender and other factors (e.g., age, race) should be investigated systematically to see if they can sophisticate the ability of supervising officers to engage more effectively in opportunity reduction.

Creating the Offender's Case Plan

For probation and parole supervision to be effective, the conditions that offenders are subjected to must be based on their individual risk level, criminogenic needs, and responsivity considerations (Jalbert, Rhodes, Flygare, & Kane, 2010; Taxman, 2008). Moreover, the development of supervision conditions must be based on the actuarial assessment of these characteristics (the importance of proper offender assessment will be discussed in Chapter 4). The creation of an offender's case plan should therefore be based upon the crime opportunities unique to the offender that were uncovered during their assessment. As discussed in the previous section, the "Four W's"—with whom, when, where, and why offenders encounter and take advantage of chances to commit crime—provide individualized information that can be used to prevent recidivism. Although each agency will have access to different types of data and different resources for gathering and using those data, the general standard is that the case plan must reflect the real crime opportunities individual to each offender. Once data collection has taken place, however, general supervision conditions that reflect the crime opportunities relevant to a specific population or place might be gleaned. For example, probation and parole agencies may benefit from crime data about crime opportunity hotspots (see Chapter 6). In any event, the goal is to create supervision conditions that reflect the real chances for offending that each community corrections client is actually exposed to.

To begin, we note that a quality opportunity-reduction supervision case plan will require four reorientations from existing probation and parole practices, irrespective of the information that is used. First, real data should be used (as opposed to generic abstractions), even if the information is gained through qualitative interviews with the offender. Second, the information should be specific to the individual offender. Some general rules are fine (e.g., offending increases after sundown) and should be incorporated when original data are absent; however, the best predictor of future behavior is relevant past behavior (Andrews & Bonta, 2010), and looking at an offender's history provides detailed insight about what crime opportunities should be of greatest concern. Third, the data gathered or consulted as part of an offender's intake and assessment should imply a causal theory about his or her offending. Additional information may be useful as responsivity considerations, but the purpose of data analysis is the identification of those variables that increase the likelihood that the probationer or parolee will seek out or exploit an available crime opportunity. Fourth, the information that is gathered should provide usable recommendations for the offender's case plan. Moreover, these recommendations should be based on the theory of why that individual offender commits crime.

This process is fundamental to achieving the overarching argument made in this book: To improve probation and parole outcomes, the supervision of offenders must be based on their exposure and vulnerability to crime opportunities. Central to meeting this goal is a thoughtfully designed case plan that strategically accounts for the risks identified for each offender. Rather than a litany of generic prescriptions and restrictions, supervision conditions ought to be realistic, relevant, and research-based (Pew Center on the States, 2008b). That is, the stipulations of an offender's community supervision case plan must be attainable (and officers must be prepared to hold offenders consistently accountable to those conditions), tailored to each client, and based on evidence known to improve public safety and encourage offender desistance.

The development of supervision conditions must be customized to the risk level and criminogenic needs of the probationer or parolee (Crime and Justice Institute at Community Resources for Justice, 2009; Taxman, 2012; Taxman, Shepardson, & Byrne, 2004). Specifically, the tools used to manage criminal behavior must proactively reduce offenders' exposure and vulnerability to opportunities for crime (Solomon et al., 2008; Taxman et al., 2006). Importantly, supervision conditions are often more effective when they intrinsically enhance offender motivation to change (see Chapter 5 in this volume; see also Ginsburg, Mann, Rotgers, & Weekes, 2002). One method for encouraging offenders is to involve them in the development of the rules and requirements of community supervision (Pew Center on the States, 2008b). Not only do offenders provide invaluable information about their own crime opportunities, but they are also more likely to hold themselves accountable to the supervision conditions that they themselves help develop (Clark et al., 2006). Further, as a cooperative process, community corrections officers should communicate to offenders the rationale behind the restrictions and goals that are prescribed (Pew Center on the States, 2008b).

In any case, it is vital that the supervision plan of an offender reflect the assessment of his or her crime opportunities, prioritizing the criminogenic risks, needs, and responsivity factors that are most influential. In particular, the situational variables that trigger criminal behavior (that were identified during assessment) must be controlled through the stipulations of the offender's case plan (Taxman, Shepardson, & Byrne, 2004). Following the four categories of crime opportunities discussed in the previous section (i.e., with whom, when, where, and why offending takes place), the creation of case plan conditions must directly address these specific crime opportunities.

First, community corrections case plans must account for the offender's social network. Given what is known about the people the offender commits crime with (e.g., see Figure 3.1), how can this information be used to reduce his or her crime opportunities? Conditions of supervision should be reflective of the kind of relationship and the past and prospective influence of that relationship. Using the illustration presented in the previous section, supervision stipulations should be tailored to the offender's antisocial associates and prosocial handlers. For instance, the client should be prohibited from being around or communicating with co-offenders that the individual has a documented history of committing crime with (i.e., Paul is restricted from being in the same place as Larry, and must refrain from communications with Tim). Further, the offender should only be allowed to associate with potential co-offenders when identified prosocial influences are present (e.g., Paul is disallowed from spending time with his brother Adam except for in the presence of his mother Gloria, and is prohibited from associating with coworkers outside the supervision of his work manager). As opposed to providing vague and unreasonable restrictions about who the offender can associate with, the probation or parole officer should aim to provide stipulations, narrowly and explicitly, about (1) who the offender cannot associate with, and (2) under what conditions. Recall, the goal is to fashion the offender's case plan conditions to restrict exposure to crime opportunities, which in this regard includes the people that encourage or dissuade the pursuit of these opportunities.

Second, probation and parole case plans must reflect when the offender tends to get into trouble. Given what is known about when the offender commits crime (e.g., see Figure 3.2), how can this information be used to reduce his or her crime opportunities? Supervision conditions should structure the offender's time through the restriction of access to crime opportunities (such as curfew) and the replacement of access to crime opportunities with exposure to prosocial activities (such as employment). Using the previously introduced example, the client should be restricted from tempting activities at certain times of the day (e.g., John is prohibited from leaving his residence or having guests in his residence between the hours of 9:00 p.m. and 6:00 a.m.). Further, the offender experiences a number of police contacts and technical violations in the afternoon and evening hours; therefore, activities where crime is less likely to occur should be substituted in these time windows (e.g., John is required to attend work readiness training at Grove Recreation Center on Mondays to Thursdays from 3:00 p.m. to 7:00 p.m., and must participate in his assigned alcoholism support group on Saturday afternoons). Not only are these activities prosocial influences, but they are specifically designed and then employed to replace the unstructured use of leisure time that has previously been problematic for the offender.

Third, offender supervision case plans must address where the offender encounters situations that are conducive to crime. Given what is known about where the offender commits crime (e.g., see Figure 3.3), how can this information be used to reduce his or her crime opportunities? Case plan stipulations should restrict the offender's access to places where crime opportunities abound, but should also redirect the offender's activities to locations where crime opportunities are not as common. From the illustration that was introduced earlier, the parolee should be prohibited from being in or around crime hotspots (e.g., Bob is restricted from being in the neighborhood of Oakley during activities or from passing through it, or, Bob is restricted from being in or around AJ's Bar, Mike's Sports Club, Players Bar & Grill, Harry's apartment, and Sam's house). Further, the daily routines of offenders should be redirected to geographic "safe zones" where crime opportunities are minimal (e.g., Bob is encouraged to play basketball at the park on Hart Lane, or, Bob is allowed to attend church at Michigan Avenue and Castle Drive, though he is allowed to travel only through the South Bank neighborhood). It is of little influence or practicality to restrict offenders from all locations where alcohol is served or where criminals congregate. These prohibitions are vague, and are difficult to interpret and enforce. Moreover, such general restrictions are only distantly related (if at all) to the situations that entice offenders to commit crime. Contrarily, probation and parole officers can tailor supervision conditions to account for the places where crime opportunities are more or less likely to be present.

Fourth, community corrections case plans must account for why the offender takes advantage of opportunities to commit crime. Given what is known about why the offender commits crime (e.g., see Figure 3.4), how can this information be used to reduce his or her crime opportunities? Although there are a number of reasons why people commit crime, there are circumstances unique to each individual that make offending more or less probable, and supervision conditions should account for these factors. Following the illustration presented in the prior section, the probationer should be restricted from being in the presence of certain crime precipitators (e.g., Mary is required to refrain from any alcohol consumption and may not attend any social gathering where alcohol is provided, and, Mary is discouraged from driving or attending family gatherings when she feels depressed or agitated). In addition to these restrictions, the risk history for some of the triggers identified in Figure 3.4 imply treatment recommendations (e.g., Mary is obligated to attend family therapy on Wednesday evenings, or, Mary is required to participate in the Saturday problem-solving class held at First Baptist Church). As opposed to supervision case plan stipulations that are only loosely tied to criminological theory or are based on faulty theories about why people commit crime, the case plan should be created to account for the specific reasons why the individual offender finds himself or herself in situations that make crime more likely.

As these example case plans illustrate, probation and parole officers should create rules that disrupt the meeting of offenders and crime opportunities, which can be accomplished in two ways: (1) developing restrictions that eliminate an offender's access to situations that are known to be conducive to crime for that individual, and (2) creating new daily routines that contain prosocial activities. This approach is very different from the traditional model of community corrections that applies generic and global rules for all supervised offenders. Although these more targeted supervision stipulations may seem too specific to monitor, it is more effective (in resources and outcomes) to develop narrower guidelines for offender behavior (and as will be discussed in Chapter 6, the police are an invaluable partner in monitoring offender compliance with these supervision conditions). In addition to the conditions that will redirect offenders' activities away from crime opportunities and toward prosocial outlets, the case plan should also account for the individual's criminal propensity (specifically, how a probationer or parolee interprets environmental cues; see Chapter 5). Importantly, community corrections case plans must be established with no ambiguity about what is expected of offenders, in both restrictions and prescriptions. Central to environmental corrections, probation and parole officers must provide their clients with a clear message about the logic of their case plan: The rules that offenders are required to abide by are designed to reduce their opportunities for crime and increase their chances of desistance.

Modifying the Offender's Case Plan

Community corrections officers should see themselves as problem solvers (focused on offenders as opposed to places, as is often the case with policing interventions), and therefore must adjust their tactical solutions to offending problems as their clients' crime opportunities change (Clarke & Eck, 2005; Goldstein, 1990). Indeed, in accordance with the principles of effective correctional intervention, the conditions that offenders are subjected to should reflect their criminogenic risks and needs; because these variables change throughout the treatment window, so too should supervision stipulations be adjusted (Bernstein, Farrington, & Leschied, 2001; Bonta et al., 2008; Harland, 1996). An offender's exposure to crime opportunities and his or her susceptibility to engage in those opportunities for misbehavior will fluctuate across time, therefore supervision case plans require periodic modification (Healey, 1999; Reinventing Probation Council, 2000; Schlager & Pacheco, 2011).

In addition to the content of community corrections interventions changing across the supervision term, the quantity must be adjusted, as well. In accordance with the risk principle, a greater amount of resources should be targeted at offenders with a greater likelihood of recidivating (Andrews & Bonta, 2010; Lowenkamp & Latessa, 2004; Lowenkamp, Latessa, & Holsinger, 2006). Similarly, because the risk of recidivism is greatest in the first three months of supervision, resources should be frontloaded to account for these greater criminogenic needs (National Research Council, 2008; Pew Center on the States, 2008b). Then, as offenders progress through their community corrections sentence, the level of supervision they are subjected to should be altered in accordance with their decreased likelihood of relapsing (Reinventing Probation Council, 2000). This is not to say that all offenders should receive periodic adjustments to their supervision conditions, or that the adjustments across offenders should be the same. Some offenders will remain at moderate risk of recidivating throughout their supervision term, and thus their case plan should remain reflective of this level of risk the entire time. Yet for offenders whose risk level changes, supervision conditions and the level of intervention should change in reflection.

Importantly, the only way to know whether an offender's risk level is changing and whether the supervision conditions or intensity should be altered is through assessment. Because success in community corrections ought to be defined as recidivism reduction, offender progress toward this goal must be measured (Pew Center on the States, 2008b). Probation and parole officers invested in positive outcomes for their clients need to know whether supervision conditions are effectively changing offenders for the better, which requires intermittent reassessment (Lowenkamp & Bechtel, 2007). This appraisal should evaluate the offender's current exposure and vulnerability to existing crime opportunities, which includes positive changes the offender has made in addition to relapses in antisocial behavior (Clark, 2006; Maruna & LeBel, 2003). Then, just as with the initial creation of a case plan, the modification of supervision must reflect the real (and therefore contemporary) crime opportunities of each offender.

Graduated Consequences

Similar to supervision case plans requiring modification to reflect the offender's current criminogenic risks and needs, probation and parole officers must adjust the consequences they supply their clients to account for the offender's behavior. Misbehaviors require attention, but the consequence must be commensurate with the action. For example, it seems unreasonable to revoke a parole sentence because the offender missed a meeting with his or her supervising officer, yet it is also a mismatched result if an offender has multiple failed drug screenings with no changes to the nature of his or her supervision. As general principles of deterrence, punishment cannot be ambiguous, excessive, capricious, or arbitrary. Thus, undesirable actions must be met with consequences that reflect the severity of the misbehavior. And while the offender population is often characterized as persons who struggle with self-regulation and rebel against this sort of structure, carefully designed rules and consequences that are applied fairly and consistently do result in behavioral change (Dowden & Andrews, 2004; Gendreau, 1996; Gendreau & Andrews, 2001; Higgins & Silverman, 1999; Taxman, Soule, & Gelb, 1999).

The content of probation and parole meetings must be an address of the offender's risks and criminogenic needs, and the stipulations of the supervision term must be tailored to reflect and support that same goal (Bonta et al., 2011; Bonta et al., 2008). When properly assessed and classified (see Chapter 4), reduced supervision intensity for a large group of community corrections offenders does not result in higher rates of re-offending or threats to public safety (Barnes, Hyatt, Ahlman, & Kent, 2012). Evaluations on the practical application of graduated sanctions demonstrate effective crime prevention outcomes and reduced costs, especially with high-risk offenders (Whitworth, 2009).

In many ways, community corrections sanctions are already inherently graduated, reflecting the accountability of offenders and the proportionality of offenses in supervision sentences (Harris, Petersen, & Rapoza, 2001). Embedded within probation and parole programs, however, must be a continuum of consequences for supervision violations *and* consistent compliance; that is, there must be a range of consequences for the behaviors that offenders present, both positive and negative (Burke, 1997; Taxman et al., 1999). In this regard, analyses reveal that graduated interventions (as opposed to a one-size-fits-all or tough-on-crime approach to offender supervision) reduce recidivism (Lowenkamp & Latessa, 2004, 2005). For example, the success of drug courts is in part attributed to the graduated nature of rewards and punishments in response to offender behavior (Guastaferro & Daigle, 2012; Taxman et al., 1999). Relapses in criminal behavior and progress in prosocial outcomes are to be expected during the supervision term, so the case plan stipulations should be graded to reflect these changes (Lindquist, Krebs, & Lattimore, 2006).

When consequences for misbehavior are logically derived and swiftly imposed, offenders are dealt with in a way that approximates the treatment they will receive post-release. Community corrections officers aid in the behavioral change of their clients when they provide unambiguous rules about what is expected of them, and what will take place when those rules are violated (Reinventing Probation Council, 2000; Taxman et al., 1999). Readers should note the important distinction between punishment in criminal justice terms (such as supervision revocation and reincarceration) and punishment in the realm of behavior modification (any consequence that decreases the occurrence of an action). To change offender behavior, community corrections officers should not rely on the most severe (criminal justice) punishments at all times, but should use the least severe (behavior modification) punishments that the offender will respond to (Morris & Tonry, 1990; Petersilia, 1999; Reinventing Probation Council, 2000). That being said, probationers and parolees cannot be allowed to believe that their supervising officer will not swiftly and certainly punish misbehaviors with a noxious consequence, yet the strength of the punishment should match the severity of the infraction (Reinventing Probation Council, 2000).

Additionally, supervising officers should be mindful that reinforcement is a more effective behavior modification technique than punishment (Andrews & Bonta, 2010), and can be used to leverage prosocial behavior from probationers and parolees (Crime and Justice Institute at Community Resources for Justice, 2009; Robinson et al., 2012). The equation is simple: Offender behaviors that supervisors would like increased (i.e., prosocial actions) must be rewarded, and offender behaviors that supervisors would like decreased (i.e., antisocial actions) must be sanctioned (Taxman, Shepardson, & Byrne, 2004). The range of behaviors that receive reinforcement should be wide, from minor actions such as making polite conversation to major accomplishments such as gaining employment. When offenders are praised, whether with tangible prizes or verbal compliments, they are being trained to relocate the assessment, evaluation, and congratulation within themselves (Farrall, 2002). Enhancing intrinsic motivation, which includes helping offenders to value components of a prosocial lifestyle, is an important contribution to desistance and post-release success (Campbell, 2008; Clawson & Guevara, 2011; McNeill, 2006; Taxman, Shepardson, & Byrne , 2004).

An important distinction is that we do not advocate an approach that has graduated sanctions as the core framework for supervising offenders. For instance, Project HOPE (Honest Opportunity Probation with Enforcement) has its core feature the use of swift and certain punishments meant to invoke compliance. While there is some evidence that shows that this program has achieved some success, there are also limitations and downsides. Offender supervision philosophies that emphasize graduated sanctions above other tactics overstate the value of specific deterrence and downplay the value of other successful correctional practices (such as the risk-need-responsivity model; Duriez, Cullen, & Manchak, 2014). In some ways, probation and parole interventions focused on graduated sanctions may be too punishment-oriented, ignoring other contributors to criminality and effective prosocial mechanisms for achieving desistance. For these reasons, we envision graduated consequences as but one component of a larger opportunity-based offender supervision framework.

Earned Discharge and Aftercare

Just as immediate consequences for offender behavior should be graduated, so too must long-term outcomes reflect offender performance during probation and parole. Under the traditional model of offender supervision, probationers and parolees are discharged upon expiration of their term. This approach stands in contrast to the preferred method of releasing offenders from community corrections when they meet important goals *after* completing a minimum set sentence (such as completing a treatment program, committing no rule infractions for one year, or showing a marked reduction in the assessment of their criminogenic risks and needs; Petersilia, 2003; Solomon et al., 2008). One way to increase motivation and compliance, eventually leading to positive offender change, is to incorporate earned discharge or "accelerated release, whereby parolees have the ability to reduce the total length of their parole term by demonstrating arrest-free behavior and self-sufficiency" (Petersilia, 2007, p. 808). When low-risk offenders consistently meet strict supervision guidelines, they should be provided the opportunity to earn their release from probation or parole (Pew Center on the States, 2008b). Not only does this refocus resources on the offenders in greatest need of surveillance and treatment, but it also provides offenders with the incentive to change and meet prosocial goals.

Because the assessment of community corrections programs should be based on public safety, so too should offenders be held to comparable standards. Setting aside the justifications of certain philosophies of punishment (e.g., just deserts; Cullen & Jonson, 2012), offenders should no longer be supervised by the criminal justice system when their threat of recidivism subsides (Burrell, 1998; Reinventing Probation Council, 2000; Rhine & Paparozzi, 1999). To achieve this goal, community corrections meetings between supervisors and offenders must be reoriented toward behavioral change (Raynor & Vanstone, 2015; Smith et al., 2012). There must be an emphasis on risk reduction, reflected in a decrease of the offender's exposure to crime opportunities (Cullen, Eck, & Lowenkamp, 2002). This goal is achieved through a cooperative process between probation and parole officers and their supervisees (Schwalbe, 2012), in which daily routines are structured around practical (achievable) and desirable (prosocial) activities.

Criminogenic risks and needs typically decrease across the supervision term, which not only has implications for case management but also for their discharge and aftercare (Schlager & Pacheco, 2011). In order to prepare offenders for their eventual release, internal control (such as emotional self-regulation) must be cultivated, and should increase as external controls (such as drug testing) are reduced (Taxman, Shepardson, & Byrne, 2004). Because offenders will at some point no longer be under the sway of correctional authorities, supervision officers should ultimately be preparing their clients for a prosocial, independent life. If positive outcomes are observed when offenders are provided with structure during their supervision (composed of surveillance and treatment components), then naturally there should be a continuity of care after release (Smith, Gendreau, & Goggin, 2009). That is, whatever factors contribute to probationers and parolees demonstrating prosocial behavior during the supervision term, community corrections departments can help to encourage lasting desistance by working to make those same factors available after the sentence has ended (e.g., access to counseling). Aftercare should be in place to support the progress the offenders made during their probation or parole term, but should also be transitional to prepare offenders for life after correctional supervision (Dowden et al., 2000; Latessa & Holsinger, 1998; Taxman, 1999). Importantly, the services provided to offenders during their supervision sentence must be relocated in the offender's community (as opposed to those that are conditionally tied to the local department of corrections; Reinventing Probation Council, 2000; Solomon et al., 2008).

The development of coping skills is a necessary ingredient to post-release relapse prevention in community corrections (Dowden et al., 2000). Additionally, engaging the offender's social network aids in reintegration and helps to limit lingering crime opportunities (Burke & Tonry, 2006; Dickey & Smith, 1998; Solomon et al., 2008). These individuals, when prosocial themselves, offer lasting informal social control after community corrections control has expired (Laub & Sampson, 2003; Laub, Sampson, & Allen, 2001; Taxman, 2006). The goal for probation and parole officers is to prepare offenders for life independent of correctional supervision. This requires offender supervisors to understand their clients' environment and the crime opportunities it presents. To do so, community corrections officers require detailed information about the opportunities for offending their clients are exposed to, in what ways they are vulnerable to those crime opportunities, and what place managers, target guardians, and offender handlers they can recruit to minimize re-offending. Strategies for gathering these data are discussed in the following chapter.

Conclusion

As the opening chapter of this book demonstrated, current offender supervision practices are not as effective as they could be. The traditional model of balancing treatment and control results in a bureaucratic process of brokering services to probationers and parolees while holding them accountable to unrealistic regulations on their conduct, rather than intervening in the factors that are causing an individual's offending. However, as the second chapter explored, the advances in crime prevention achieved in environmental criminology have several helpful implications for community corrections. Crime science innovations can inform offender supervision practices, as the reduction of crime opportunities for probationers and parolees should lower re-offending. The present chapter more specifically discussed how offenders can be supervised in the community according to the tenets of environmental corrections (Cullen, Eck, & Lowenkamp, 2002).

In line with this model, the nature of offender-supervisor meetings must be restructured. These interactions must focus on the causes of the individual's offending, creating supervision conditions that restructure the offender's daily routines so as to avoid exposure to crime opportunities and enhance opportunities for a prosocial lifestyle. Although current probation and parole practices traditionally emphasize general behavioral restrictions that are only loosely tied to criminological theory, opportunity-reduction supervision creates case plan stipulations designed to reduce chances to offend that are specific to each offender. As this chapter has outlined, information unique to each individual must be consulted in the development of supervision case plans, changing as necessary to reflect the offender's current criminogenic risks and needs. To tailor supervision conditions to the crime opportunities of each offender, data about the individual's patterns of activity are required. Indeed, to create a new model of supervision, new information is required, and to gain this new information, new data collection techniques are required. In the next chapter, we present new offender supervision technologies, providing offender supervisors with a sample of tools to help gauge their clients' opportunities for crime.

4

Developing Offender Supervision Technology

Consistent with the crime-reduction effects observed in environmental criminology interventions, offender supervision within community corrections could likewise benefit from crime science principles. As discussed in the previous chapter, the foundational component of environmental corrections is limiting probationers' and parolees' exposure to crime opportunities. To restrict offenders' access to situations that contain these opportunities, however, the opportunities must first be properly identified. Chapter 3 presented resources that can aid in creating an opportunity-reduction supervision case plan; yet to obtain the data necessary to do so, new technologies are required. Accordingly, the current chapter presents examples of such technologies. Although each instrument would require tailoring for the context in which it is used (such as the data that are available, the population it is being used on, or the presence of proper staff training and computer software), the discussion that follows outlines sample assessment tools that correspond with the goal of crime opportunity identification among probationers and parolees.

In so doing, our discussion pursues three topics. First, an overview of offender assessment and classification is provided, demonstrating the importance of measuring offenders' risks, criminogenic needs, and responsivity considerations. We trace the evolution of offender assessments, documenting the validity of these tools and their impact on case management. Second, we present instruments that identify an individual offender's opportunities for committing crime. These tools produce output that provides community corrections supervisors with knowledge about their clients' risk of encountering and exploiting crime opportunities, and the criminogenic needs that contribute to finding and taking advantage of those crime opportunities. These technologies are designed to provide detailed information about the precipitators of offending specific to each individual, and the environments that contain these precipitators. Third, we introduce an assessment instrument that identifies possible crime opportunity-reduction partners. This inventory can assist probation and parole officers in locating potential crime control agents; specifically, by identifying offender handlers, target guardians, place managers, and prosocial activities, community corrections supervisors can more effectively limit the crime opportunities their clients are vulnerable to.

Following a discussion of these topics, a sample case plan is presented that illustrates how the information gathered from these assessments can be used to reduce the crime opportunities of probationers and parolees. Included in this discussion is a sample offender schedule that illustrates when and where crime opportunities are likely to emerge, allowing the supervising officer to develop conditions that address these situations. As such, the case plan provides requirements and restrictions that guide the offender's behavior. Importantly, these supervision conditions also address the activities and associates (and their correlates) that prevent the offender from encountering and taking advantage of crime opportunities. Notably, substituted for prior criminogenic routines, these new situations should serve not only to help the offender avoid antisocial behavior but also encounter environments that encourage prosocial behavior.

Offender Assessment and Classification

For a field concerned with the management of recidivism risk and responding to criminogenic needs, remarkably little is done in the way of proper offender assessment (Harland, 1996). As public and policy attention has turned toward crime control, the field has seen an increased interest in assessment and classification (Andrews, 1989). While the lure of empirically derived instruments should not be without a healthy dose of skepticism (Baird, 2009; Silver & Miller, 2002), proper assessment is one of the key components of effective corrections strategies. One meta-analysis reveals that high-quality community corrections programs reduce re-offending 20% to 60%, and that these interventions include evidence-based assessment practices (Gendreau, Goggin, Cullen, & Andrews, 2000). It is necessary for corrections programs to measure offender risks, needs, and responsivity in order to be effective (Latessa & Holsinger, 1998), so much so that a failure to use appropriate assessment procedures could be considered unethical and ignorant (Latessa et al., 2002).

The importance of offender assessment cannot be overstated. The principles of effective correctional intervention require that offenders be properly assessed and classified (Andrews, 1995; Andrews, Bonta, & Hoge, 1990). First, the risk principle states that intensive levels of supervision and service provisions should be reserved for high-risk offenders, while offenders with a lower risk of recidivating should not be subjected to extensive supervision and service. To classify offenders according to their level of re-offending risk, offenders must have their risk level accurately assessed. Second, the needs principle asserts that the targets of service should correspond with an offender's criminogenic needs. That is, those factors that are causing the individual to commit crime should be addressed in order to reduce criminality. To determine what these targets for change are, offenders must have their criminogenic needs assessed. Third, the responsivity principle posits that the style and mode of service should be matched to the learning style and abilities of each offender to maximize the effect of the intervention. To know what factors an offender is responsive to and what considerations might be barriers to treatment success, offenders must have their responsivity to treatment assessed.

Thus, for the principles underlying effective probation and parole programs, valid and reliable offender assessment is vital. Unfortunately, one of the major deficiencies in contemporary corrections programming is the lack of appropriate client assessment (Smith, Gendreau, & Goggin, 2009). Not only do program administrators and community corrections officers frequently rely on static predictors (i.e., things that cannot be changed) and clinical judgment (as opposed to actuarial measurement), but also, the results of offender assessments are often used inappropriately. Even when validated assessment instruments are in place, many agencies fail to incorporate the information gained into the creation of the offender's supervision case plan (Bourgon et al., 2011; Harris, Gingerich, & Whittaker, 2004).

For an assessment to contribute to effective correctional interventions, it must be evidence based, empirically validated, theory driven, multimodal, actuarial, predictive of dynamic factors, and usable. Probation and parole officers must use proper assessment tools, but then also must ensure that the products of these investigations are used to classify clients in order to match offenders to services and levels of supervision (Andrews & Bonta, 2010; Bonta, 2002; Bonta et al., 2000; Bonta et al., 2008; Latessa & Holsinger, 1998; Taxman, 1999). Fortunately, advances in offender assessment and classification technologies have put these goals within reach, and the adoption of quality offender assessment among community corrections departments is growing. The evolution through four generations of risk assessments demonstrates how far the measurement of offender risk, needs, and responsivity has come (Andrews & Bonta, 2010; Andrews, Bonta, & Wormith, 2006).

First-generation risk assessments relied on professional judgment. Clinicians and criminal justice personnel would make a judgment about an individual's risk of relapse according to their personal expertise. These assessments tend to be inaccurate and unreliable, because of the reliance on unobservable phenomena and offender characteristics that are unrelated to criminal behavior. The end result, an unstructured and subjective judgment that is often guided by intuition, is not an empirically derived calculation of risk. As a result, first-generation offender assessments tend to have low levels of predictive validity.

Second-generation risk assessments incorporate actuarial methods in the statistical determination of risk (i.e., clinical opinions are replaced with empirically derived evaluations); however, the items used to determine an offender's degree of risk are static considerations. While the incorporation of actuarial measurement is an important advancement, relying on factors that cannot be changed (such as the offender's arrest history or ethnicity) is limiting. The items included in second-generation assessments are evidence based, but are generally not theoretically derived or helpful in providing targets for change. So, although these tools provide information that is useful for classification purposes and release decisions, they do little in the way of accounting for the offender's criminogenic needs.

Third-generation risk assessments incorporate the assessment of dynamic risk and needs, using measurement items that are based on psychological and criminological theory. The Level of Service Inventory–Revised (LSI-R; Andrews & Bonta, 1995) is one prominent example; it gathers information across ten domains related to the variable causes of crime. An important contribution of this instrument is that the assessment of criminogenic needs may help to better indicate the level and drivers of an individual's re-offending risk, beyond what static measurements can predict. The LSI-R has been demonstrated as a valid prediction tool across correctional settings, with juveniles and adults, males and females, and various kinds of offenders (Andrews et al., 2006; Gendreau et al., 1996; Vose, Cullen, & Smith, 2008). Importantly, the LSI-R is based on knowledge accumulated through empirical research about the elements of social learning that contribute to criminal behavior; consequently, because the items measured are dynamic predictors, the assessment tool can be used to identify changes in offender risk and needs across time and interventions.

Fourth-generation risk assessments incorporate case planning into the instrument, by emphasizing offender strengths, responsivity, and the structured tailoring of the case plan throughout the supervision term. One example, the Level of Service/Case Management Inventory (LS/CMI; Andrews et al., 2006), measures specific offender risks and criminogenic needs in addition to responsivity considerations. The assessment also requires the operator to prioritize the needs that were documented, create targets for change, develop a means to meet those goals, and then monitor progress toward that end with each supervisory meeting. Accordingly, fourth-generation risk assessments provide offender supervisors with guidance on the development and modification of probation and parole case plans.

With the impressive strides made in offender assessment and prediction, it is unfortunate that more corrections agencies do not incorporate them into their practices (Latessa et al., 2002; Smith, Gendreau, & Goggin, 2009). For the model of offender supervision proposed in this book, assessment is integral to achieving successful outcomes. Upon intake, corrections authorities must gain personalized information about their clients in order to tailor the supervision case plan to each individual offender (Andrews, 1995). Given the current state of risk-assessment knowledge and technology, a four-step rational assessment model will prove useful (Harland, 1996). First, correctional agencies must specify their goals for environmental corrections supervision. Second, community corrections officers must define the options for case plan inclusions that are available to them. Third, agents must develop a set of information that will be used in making choices. Fourth, offender supervisors should select from the set of available options that which will be in greatest alignment with the agency's goals. If the goal is to reduce offenders' exposure to crime opportunities, then the information used to select stipulations of the supervision plan must identify the opportunities for offending that each probationer or parolee is susceptible to.

Identifying Opportunities for Crime

As discussed in Chapter 2, the crime science literature has identified a number of factors that precipitate offending. Some of these conditions are well known, creating crime opportunity maxims of sorts. For instance, when offenders, victims, and targets converge in a systematic or patterned way, crime opportunities can be identified in certain "routines." Probation and parole authorities can create overarching supervision conditions that minimize offenders' intimacy with such routines. Indeed, this is the approach generally taken in many agencies, as stipulations of community corrections sentences are often loosely tied to vague criminological theory (imposing curfews and drug testing, for example). Well-intentioned though these rules are, they discount the other two components that lead to an individual's likelihood of committing crime (i.e., cognitions and situations; refer back to Figure 2.1). To best prevent offending among probationers and parolees, community corrections officers must identify and address the cognitions and situations that are conducive to crime.

The remainder of this chapter discusses a process for discovering what situations present crime opportunities for an individual offender. While the following chapter explores the role of cognitions and how those are tied to an offender's environment, the current emphasis is on those environmental circumstances unique to a probationer or parolee that are related to his or her crime opportunities. Most assessments identify an offender's "risk level" (a categorization of re-offending probability that influences supervision intensity and resource assignment), but these technologies are not geared toward uncovering the environmental factors that inform that risk. Although these risk classifications serve valuable purposes, and their continued use is therefore highly encouraged, they provide virtually no insight into the specific *situations* that breed offending. As such, the instruments that are introduced here avoid these general labels and seek to uncover more detailed information about the situations that provide access and temptation to chances to offend, in addition to the conditions that serve as barriers to such access and temptations.

As a brief note, it is necessary to acknowledge the important role that process evaluations will have in implementing these new data collection procedures. Although some generic recommendations can be made (offender assessment should be a standardized and actuarial process, for example), other considerations will require research to inform best practices (see Chapter 7). Indeed, the data collection tools included in this chapter need to be trialed, validated, and appropriately altered prior to full-scale use. Additionally, it is unclear at this time how probation and parole offices might need to be reorganized to account for the data collection tools presented in the remainder of this chapter. Within smaller community corrections agencies, it is likely that officers can complete the offender assessments necessary for opportunity-reduction supervision. For larger departments, however, data collection procedures may need to be streamlined, and could benefit from a specialized unit that completes intake assessments for all incoming offenders. At any rate, in order to prevent probationers and parolees from encountering and taking advantage of existing crime opportunities, offender supervisors must gather information about the risk and protective factors that their clients are exposed to. We have created the assessment technologies that follow as initial examples of how this task might be accomplished.

RISK FACTORS FOR CRIME OPPORTUNITIES

In order to reduce an offender's exposure to crime opportunities, probation and parole officers must discover how the offender converges with those situations: specifically, with whom, when, where, and why an individual meets with the chance to commit crime. These situational inducements will vary by offender. This is because each offender interacts with different environments, and each offender is variably attracted to different kinds of crime opportunities. A useful assessment, then, must gather data about the specific conditions that have proven problematic for the individual offender. By inquiring about the details of past criminal behavior, offender supervisors can glean valuable information about the elements in an offender's environment that are likely to lead to further criminal behavior.

The Crime Opportunities Risk Reduction Action List (CORRAL; see Form A) provides an example of how an instrument can gather these data. Although the assessment would require pilot testing, revisions, and empirical validation prior to full use, this technology serves as a first step toward reorienting our methods of monitoring offenders in the community. The data collected through this instrument provide the assessor with basic information about situations the offender is routinely exposed to that contain crime opportunities. Additionally, the assessment provides details about the elements in that situation that led to the offender committing crime in the past, which give supervising officers information about the high-risk variables that should be addressed with case plan stipulations. This framework is a sharp departure from dominant approaches to offender assessment in which a recidivism risk classification is gauged according to a few generic variables. Yet, prior to discussing the content of the assessment, three points require explanation.

First, although the instrument that follows has not been empirically tested for its merits (and future research that explores the validity of this tool is encouraged), the included items are based on sound criminological theory. Appraising the research evidence accumulated through crime science interventions, we know a great deal about the variety of factors (and the environments containing them) that can trigger criminal behavior. As previously noted, however, the crime opportunities that an offender comes into contact with and is tempted by will vary for each individual. Accordingly, the assessment is loosely structured in order to guide data collection, but is also somewhat open-ended to encourage flexibility (because each offender is different). This format allows for the insights of environmental criminology to aid in the identification of individualized exposure and vulnerability to crime opportunities.

Second, the data sources that are referenced in the completion of this kind of assessment process will vary. This is preferable, as different resources will provide different perspectives on the offending problem. For instance, official data (such as court records and police reports) are valuable, as the information can largely be taken at face value; yet these records often provide little detail about the circumstances that surrounded the crime. Offender self-reports, on the other hand, provide deeper insights into the motivation for pursuing crime opportunities in the past; yet the information provided by offenders may not be reliable, as there may be incentives for dishonesty and the capacity for introspection and articulation may be limited (see Chapter 7 for an address of these limitations). Finally, third parties (such as a spouse, pastor, or counselor) may provide worthwhile angles, as well, giving information from someone who is both an outsider to and intimate with the offender. As a consequence, a variety of information should be assessed to provide the most accurate representation of the crime opportunities that the offender is likely to come into contact with and be tempted by.

Third, the processes for collecting these data should vary in method and intensity. While some information can be gleaned from quantifying the offender's records, other data can only be gained through qualitative exploration. Indeed, offender interviews provide the greatest prospect for gathering information about client-specific crime opportunities, although these data should be triangulated through other methods when possible. There are a number of steps that can be taken to ensure that quality information is gathered (as we discuss in the concluding chapter). Without a doubt, the depth of interview questions will vary. Throughout the semi-structured process, a more thorough exploration of specific crime opportunity details can be completed for situations flagged as being potentially high-risk. The instrument provides an outline of necessary information offender supervisors should collect about their clients' crime opportunities. When a question is particularly applicable to an individual, however, a more detailed understanding of the situation should be sought. This understanding can occur by asking the offender a variety of follow-up questions, or when possible, officers can seek out supplemental information (such as from official or third-party reports) to better appreciate why a certain situation induced an offense. Examples of this variation in methods for completing the assessment can be seen in the format of the instrument.

In reference to the content of this technology (see Form A), there are six data-collection sections, in addition to an end-of-assessment overview. The first five sections gather highly specific information about the offender's crime opportunities, which may be best obtained through a structured evaluation of official data sources, and then verified via offender reports. The sixth section, however, includes open-ended questions suitable for interviewing, allowing the assessor to follow up on the elements of an offender's surroundings that are conducive to crime. The data compiled in these six sections collectively inform the final component of the assessment, a risk reduction action list. This part of the instrument identifies a set of actionable supervision conditions. That is, based on the data gathered about the offender's exposure to crime opportunities that the individual is likely to be vulnerable to, a list of supervision requirements and restrictions is developed to avoid such exposure.

Form A: Crime Opportunities Risk Reduction Action List (CORRAL)

ASSESSMENT INFORMATION

Offender name: _____

Case #: _____

Supervisor name: _____

Assessor name: _____

Assessment location: _____

Assessment date: _____ Assessment time: _____

Assessment type: _____ Pre-sentence _____ Pre-release

  _____ Intake _____ Re-assessment

Additional information: _____

_____

_____

_____

_____

_____

_____

Completion instructions: Assessors should consult official records as appropriate in conjunction with offender interviews. To properly record the information received, see the corresponding manual. Where applicable, identify the primary crime opportunity categories of concern using the information collected.

These classifications provide corrections agents with information about the offender's situational crime inducements. These considerations should be used to create specific case plan restrictions and requirements.

SECTION A: <u>WHAT</u> KINDS OF CRIMES DOES THE OFFENDER COMMIT?

	Incident Identifier	Type of Report	Offense Severity	Offense Category
1.	_____	_____	_____	_____
2.	_____	_____	_____	_____
3.	_____	_____	_____	_____
4.	_____	_____	_____	_____
5.	_____	_____	_____	_____
6.	_____	_____	_____	_____
7.	_____	_____	_____	_____
8.	_____	_____	_____	_____
9.	_____	_____	_____	_____
10.	_____	_____	_____	_____

Documentation notes:

(a) Incident identifier: case number, report code

(b) Type of report: arrest, police contact, corrections, offender

(c) Offense severity: misdemeanor, felony

(d) Offense category: violent, property, vice

Modal offense severity: _____

Modal offense category: _____

Offense specialization classification: _____

Classification thresholds:

(i) Minor specialization: offenses are equally spread across categories

(ii) Moderate specialization: offenses are concentrated in two categories

(iii) Major specialization: offenses are concentrated in one category

SECTION B: <u>WHO</u> DOES THE INDIVIDUAL COMMIT CRIME WITH?

	Incident Identifier	Persons Present	Relationship	Criminal Association
1.	_____	_____	_____	_____
		_____	_____	_____
		_____	_____	_____
2.	_____	_____	_____	_____
		_____	_____	_____
		_____	_____	_____
3.	_____	_____	_____	_____
		_____	_____	_____
		_____	_____	_____
4.	_____	_____	_____	_____
		_____	_____	_____
		_____	_____	_____
5.	_____	_____	_____	_____
		_____	_____	_____
		_____	_____	_____

<u>Documentation notes</u>:

(a) Incident identifier: case number, report code

(b) Persons present: names of people included in the report

(c) Relationship: mother, husband, cousin, friend, co-worker, etc.

(d) Criminal association: co-offender, rival, antisocial peer, handler, etc.

Notable co-offenders: _____

Notable rivals: _____

Notable antisocial associates: _____

(Continued)

SECTION C: <u>WHEN</u> DOES THE OFFENDER COMMIT CRIME?

	Incident Identifier	*Date*	*Day*	*Time*
1.	_____	_____	_____	_____
2.	_____	_____	_____	_____
3.	_____	_____	_____	_____
4.	_____	_____	_____	_____
5.	_____	_____	_____	_____
6.	_____	_____	_____	_____
7.	_____	_____	_____	_____
8.	_____	_____	_____	_____
9.	_____	_____	_____	_____
10.	_____	_____	_____	_____

<u>Documentation notes</u>:

(a) Incident identifier: case number, report code

(b) Date: e.g., 10/25/2011

(c) Day: e.g., Monday

(d) Time: e.g., 2230

Modal days: _____

Modal time periods: _____

Activities corresponding with modal days and times: _____

_____

_____

_____

SECTION D: <u>WHERE</u> DOES THE OFFENDER COMMIT CRIME?

	Incident Identifier	Street Address	Neighborhood	Location Type
1.	_____	_____	_____	_____
2.	_____	_____	_____	_____
3.	_____	_____	_____	_____
4.	_____	_____	_____	_____
5.	_____	_____	_____	_____
6.	_____	_____	_____	_____
7.	_____	_____	_____	_____
8.	_____	_____	_____	_____
9.	_____	_____	_____	_____
10.	_____	_____	_____	_____

<u>Documentation notes</u>:

(a) Incident identifier: case number, report code

(b) Street address: e.g., 300 Main Street, Vine & 2nd

(c) Neighborhood: e.g., CBD, Lawndale

(d) Location type: e.g., residence, bar

Modal street segments / neighborhoods: _____

_____

_____

Problematic locations: _____

_____

_____

(Continued)

SECTION E: <u>WHY</u> DOES THE OFFENDER COMMIT CRIME?

Crime Precipitator	*History of Risk*			
1. *Motivation*				
(a) Tangible rewards	☐ Low	☐ Medium	☐ High	☐ Very High
(b) Physiological rewards	☐ Low	☐ Medium	☐ High	☐ Very High
(c) Psychological rewards	☐ Low	☐ Medium	☐ High	☐ Very High
(d) Social rewards	☐ Low	☐ Medium	☐ High	☐ Very High
2. *Mentality*				
(a) Bored	☐ Low	☐ Medium	☐ High	☐ Very High
(b) Sad	☐ Low	☐ Medium	☐ High	☐ Very High
(c) Angry	☐ Low	☐ Medium	☐ High	☐ Very High
(d) Happy	☐ Low	☐ Medium	☐ High	☐ Very High
(e) Restless / agitated	☐ Low	☐ Medium	☐ High	☐ Very High
3. *Company*				
(a) Alone	☐ Low	☐ Medium	☐ High	☐ Very High
(b) Associates	☐ Low	☐ Medium	☐ High	☐ Very High
(c) Close friends	☐ Low	☐ Medium	☐ High	☐ Very High
(d) Family / intimates	☐ Low	☐ Medium	☐ High	☐ Very High
(e) Other	☐ Low	☐ Medium	☐ High	☐ Very High
4. *Intoxicants*				
(a) Licit drugs	☐ Low	☐ Medium	☐ High	☐ Very High
(b) Illicit drugs	☐ Low	☐ Medium	☐ High	☐ Very High
(c) Marijuana	☐ Low	☐ Medium	☐ High	☐ Very High
(d) Alcohol	☐ Low	☐ Medium	☐ High	☐ Very High
(e) Caffeine	☐ Low	☐ Medium	☐ High	☐ Very High
5. *Cues*				
(a) Routine	☐ Low	☐ Medium	☐ High	☐ Very High
(b) Modeled	☐ Low	☐ Medium	☐ High	☐ Very High
(c) Environmental	☐ Low	☐ Medium	☐ High	☐ Very High
(d) Other	☐ Low	☐ Medium	☐ High	☐ Very High

Riskiest crime precipitators: _____

_____

Activities associated with these precipitators: _____

_____

_____

SECTION F: SPECIFIC RESPONSIVITY FACTORS

Responsivity Consideration	Applicability to Offender		
1. Poor verbal skills	☐ No	☐ Somewhat	☐ Yes
2. Poor reading / writing skills	☐ No	☐ Somewhat	☐ Yes
3. Poor social skills	☐ No	☐ Somewhat	☐ Yes
4. Mental illness	☐ No	☐ Somewhat	☐ Yes
5. History of abuse	☐ No	☐ Somewhat	☐ Yes
6. Low intelligence	☐ No	☐ Somewhat	☐ Yes
7. Physical disability	☐ No	☐ Somewhat	☐ Yes
8. Physical illness	☐ No	☐ Somewhat	☐ Yes
9. Primary caregiver of dependents	☐ No	☐ Somewhat	☐ Yes
10. No access to transportation	☐ No	☐ Somewhat	☐ Yes
11. Language barrier	☐ No	☐ Somewhat	☐ Yes
12. Cultural barrier	☐ No	☐ Somewhat	☐ Yes

Required accommodations: _____

_____

_____

_____

_____

_____

_____

_____

_____

_____

_____

_____

_____

CRIME OPPORTUNITIES RISK REDUCTION ACTION LIST (CORRAL)

| *Routine* | |
| *Criminogenic Risk* | *Restriction / Requirement* |

1. People

    (a) _____

    (b) _____

    (c) _____

    (d) _____

    (e) _____

2. Days / times

    (a) _____

    (b) _____

    (c) _____

    (d) _____

    (e) _____

3. Locations

    (a) _____

    (b) _____

    (c) _____

    (d) _____

    (e) _____

4. Precipitators

    (a) _____

    (b) _____

    (c) _____

    (d) _____

    (e) _____

5. Other

    (a) _____

    (b) _____

    (c) _____

    (d) _____

    (e) _____

To collect relevant information about a probationer's or parolee's environmental offending risks, past presentations of criminal behavior must first be analyzed. Section A of Form A examines the *kinds of crime* that the offender has committed. It is important to gain a general impression about the severity of the client's offending (i.e., a chronic misdemeanant vs. a technical felon), as well as the category of the client's offending (i.e., drug vs. violent offending). After detailing this information for each of the client's past offenses, the modal (most frequent) offense severity and offense category should be identified. These categorizations allow the assessor to classify the probationer or parolee's degree of offense specialization. An understanding of offender specialization helps to structure supervision conditions. For instance, an offender with very minor specialization (i.e., he or she commit lots of different kinds of crimes) requires broad behavioral regulations to inhibit a variety of antisocial activities. An offender with major specialization, on the other hand (such as an individual who only has a criminal history of driving under the influence), should be subjected to more narrow rules that reorient this specific behavior. Although this section of information does not reveal details about the offender's crime opportunities themselves, it gives offender supervisors an impression of a client's general environment where those opportunities are located. Different offenses imply different surroundings, such as the variation in the triggers for bar fights versus street corner drug sales, for example. The specific prompts for these larger categorizations are uncovered in the following assessment sections.

Section B gathers information about *who* the individual offender commits crime with. To produce a social network analysis (refer back to Figure 3.1), this portion of the assessment documents each person who was present during the probationer or parolee's criminal acts. Each listed person is then classified by his or her relationship to the offender and how he or she was associated with the offense. Using these details, notable offender associates are identified. In order to create an opportunity-reduction case plan, offender supervisors must know who their client gets into trouble with. Importantly, there are different categories included here to capture the range of interpersonal influences relevant to the offending behavior. These classifications include co-offenders (people the probationer or parolee commits crime with), rivals (people the offender commits crime against), and antisocial associates (people the individual identifies with who also commit crime separately) that are proximate to the client's offenses. These data help community corrections officers to create a daily routine for offenders that minimizes (or outright restricts) associations with the individuals identified as high risk for future crime opportunities. Notably, offender supervisors should be attentive to the different types of influences that are antisocial (e.g., an individual who helps the offender commit the crime by providing drugs vs. an individual who condones crime by providing justifications for the offender's behavior), customizing supervision stipulations to reflect these variations.

Section C documents *when* the offender commits crime. Listing the dates and times of past crimes allows the assessor to identify the modal days and time windows that have proven problematic for that offender (see Figure 3.3). Then, the instrument allows the user to link that information with the activities associated with those days and periods of time. This is important for probation and parole officers seeking to restructure the offender's daily routine. There is nothing inherently criminogenic about the time period of 3:00 to 6:00 p.m., for instance; however, the routine activities of an offender may bring him or her into contact with more opportunities (more attractive targets and fewer capable guardians) during that time period. As a result, offender supervisors can use this information not only to restrict those activities, but also to replace those high-risk days and times with prosocial activities (see the preceding chapter section). The expectation is that community corrections officers can arrange the offenders' daily schedules so that they avoid converging with the environments where crime opportunities prove tempting.

Section D outlines *where* the offender commits crime. The assessment gathers information about the geography of past crimes, associating different offenses with neighborhoods, addresses, and types of locations (see Figure 3.4). It is highly beneficial for probation and parole agencies to use geocoded data about the offender's activities, allowing the assessor to map the individual's movements. However, more general information is useful, as well, and may help community corrections authorities to make sense of a wealth of otherwise overwhelming data. For instance, having a list of 100 addresses where the offender has had contact with the police is meaningless without being properly categorized and presented. Offender supervisors can be greatly helped by knowing the sub-neighborhoods and categories of places (e.g., nightclubs, shopping districts, family members' houses) where their client encounters crime opportunities. By assessing problematic locations, both specifically and categorically, community corrections officers are in the best position to reorient the offender's activities in ways that avoid movement through these terrains.

Section E explores *why* the offender commits crime. This portion of the instrument assesses how risky common crime precipitators are for the individual supervisee. Such judgments are made based on the documented reasons for past offenses (e.g., the offender was heavily intoxicated), as well as the offender's self-reported guesses as to why he or she commits crime (e.g., to gain status among peers). Again, this section allows the assessor to associate high-risk precipitators with the offender's activities. In essence, this information provides insight into the elements of a crime-conducive environment that triggered the individual to take advantage of the available opportunity. By gaining an understanding about the factors that initiate the process of committing crime, offender supervisors can limit their clients' interactions with situations where those precipitators are present and influential over clients' choices.

Lastly, in order to gain a deeper appreciation for the nuances of the information gathered in the assessment, Section F generates an overview of the individual's *crime opportunities*. This component includes an open-ended qualitative exploration into the offender's environmental crime inducements. Without prompting or seeking specific pieces of information, the offender may voluntarily divulge revealing information pivotal to the development of an effective supervision case plan. The assessor is then able to follow up on potentially important statements the probationer or parolee makes about his or her offending. With proper training in interview skills, community corrections officers are in a supreme position to extract information about what triggers an individual's offending (McMurran, 2009).

Finally, the information gathered from Sections A through F can be referenced to construct the action list, which is a description of supervision conditions that reorient the offender away from the identified crime opportunities. This list is then used to create the offender's case plan (see the following chapter section). As an initial step, the assessor can develop requirements and restrictions that address the offender's vulnerability to the people, points in time, places, and precipitators that are associated with crime. Combined with treatment (see Chapter 5) and the substitution of prosocial activities, these changes to an offender's daily routine limit his or her chances to commit crime.

One limitation in this approach, although not at all an insurmountable challenge, is that probation and parole officers (or other corrections intake workers) would require appropriate training (see Chapter 7). Traditional processes of offender assessment and case plan creation would also need to be revised. Yet these changes provide the chance to improve community supervision. Founded in the logic of crime science theory, methods, and interventions, probation and parole can perhaps dramatically reduce re-offending by controlling crime opportunities. The technology presented above in Form A is one potential way of identifying these opportunities. The goal is for community corrections officers to prospectively limit their clients' encounters with high-crime environments, based on evidence of each offender's past of pursuing available crime opportunities.

It warrants repeating here that the current dominant approach to offender assessment (when evaluation takes place at all) still has merit, and it is in fact complementary to the approach advanced here. Traditional assessments aim to quantify the offender's risk of recidivating, using a propensity-scoring system to identify a category of "risk level." This classification scheme is important. Knowing the approximate probability of re-offense can be used to create caseloads (e.g., Officer A supervises 15 high-risk cases while Officer B supervises 40 low-risk cases), allocate resources (e.g., a low-risk offender does not require as much treatment), and suggest supervision intensity (e.g., high-risk offenders should be monitored more closely). However, these risk-level classifications do little in the way of indicating what factors are associated with the action of committing a crime for the individual supervisee. Thus, while third- and fourth-generation risk assessments are important contributions to effective correctional interventions, individualized information about crime opportunities provides precise and usable crime prevention aims.

Moreover, the transition from traditional forms of probation and parole supervision toward a model of opportunity-reduction supervision can perhaps be well served by these categorizations of risk. An intensive approach to community corrections for low-risk offenders can prove to be criminogenic, while high-risk offenders often exhibit criminogenic risks and needs that require specialized supervision tools. As such, early efforts to explore the effectiveness of the different components of opportunity-reduction supervision may find it helpful to first focus on moderate-risk offenders. However, the offender populations with which environmental corrections will be most effective (as well as the variable conditions that must be applied for different risk levels) is an empirical question that future research must address (see Chapter 7).

PROTECTIVE FACTORS AGAINST CRIME OPPORTUNITIES

In addition to circumstances that routinely bring offenders into contact with crime opportunities, there are a number of environmental elements that can protect individuals from those same opportunities. As we explore in the discussion that follows, community corrections officers can help their clients to engage in activities that avoid exposure to existing crime opportunities, and can also solicit the help of third parties to decrease available crime opportunities and offenders' access to them. There are also a number of strategies that can effectively reduce an offender's vulnerability or attraction to remaining chances to commit crime (see Chapter 5). Following the assessment of crime opportunities introduced above (Form A: CORRAL), the next step is to identify factors that can protect offenders from these opportunities.

The Crime Opportunities Regulators Rating Tool (CORRT; see Form B) was developed to accomplish this task. The assessment contains five sections. The first aims to identify the activities the offender engages in, rating them according to the type of influence each has on the client's behavior. The following three sections help to detect potential crime controllers, namely individuals who can handle offenders, guard targets, and manage places. The final section uses this information to create an action plan for how these identified activities and persons can be used to help control crime opportunities. The content of each of these sections and the rationale supporting their creation is discussed in turn below.

Section A in Form B has the assessor list the activities an offender engages in during his or her leisure time. There are categories of activities to help stimulate ideas for activities, though there is also an open-ended question to allow for a less structured exploration of what the individual enjoys doing in his or her spare time. The place and people involved in the activity are detailed, allowing the community corrections officer to make the determination about what type of influence the activity has on the offender's behavior. Importantly, the activities the offender is involved in can be used as points of leverage in shaping the supervisee's behavior. An activity the offender enjoys that is classified as being antisocial (because of the place it occurs or the other people associated with it) can potentially be redirected into a prosocial activity. For example, a probationer or parolee may enjoy playing basketball, although doing so has often led to trouble. Perhaps the games took place in a bad neighborhood or at a recreation center where aggressive behavior is encouraged, or maybe the offender played games with people who validate crime or also commit crime. However, basketball itself is not criminogenic, and can be a prosocial activity if the crime opportunities surrounding it are eliminated. Accordingly, the offender's supervising officer could restrict participation to a recreation center in a low-crime neighborhood, or help him or her to enroll in a league with anti-criminal associates. Participation in the activity, then, provides the offender with a tangible reward for positive behavior, and also helps to replace his or her typical routine with a pattern of prosocial behavior and influences.

Form B: Crime Opportunities Regulators Rating Tool (CORRT)

ASSESSMENT INFORMATION

Offender name: _____

Case #: _____

Supervisor name: _____

Assessor name: _____

Assessment location: _____

Assessment date: _____ Assessment time: _____

Assessment type: _____ Pre-sentence _____ Pre-release

_____ Intake _____ Re-assessment

Additional information: _____

_____

_____

_____

_____

_____

_____

_____

_____

Completion instructions: Assessors should conduct an informal offender interview to inquire about potential crime controllers, and should solicit information from third parties for elaboration as needed. To properly record the information received, see the associated technical guide.

This information offers offender supervisors options for crime opportunity reduction, allowing them to rate the potential efficacy of handlers, guardians, and managers. These considerations should be consulted when recruiting informal social control agents in the offender's community.

(Continued)

SECTION A: OFFENDER ACTIVITIES

Activity	Place	People	Type of Influence		
Sport					
	_____	_____	□ Antisocial	□ Mixed	□ Prosocial
	_____	_____	□ Antisocial	□ Mixed	□ Prosocial
Hobbies					
	_____	_____	□ Antisocial	□ Mixed	□ Prosocial
	_____	_____	□ Antisocial	□ Mixed	□ Prosocial
Religious / spiritual					
	_____	_____	□ Antisocial	□ Mixed	□ Prosocial
	_____	_____	□ Antisocial	□ Mixed	□ Prosocial
Community engagement					
	_____	_____	□ Antisocial	□ Mixed	□ Prosocial
	_____	_____	□ Antisocial	□ Mixed	□ Prosocial
Other					
	_____	_____	□ Antisocial	□ Mixed	□ Prosocial
	_____	_____	□ Antisocial	□ Mixed	□ Prosocial

What do you most like to do in your free time? Why? _____

_____

SECTION B: OFFENDER HANDLERS

Relationship	Name	Type of Influence			Strength of Influence	
		☐ Antisocial	☐ Mixed	☐ Prosocial	☐ Weak	☐ Strong
Family and intimates						
	_____	☐ Antisocial	☐ Mixed	☐ Prosocial	☐ Weak	☐ Strong
	_____	☐ Antisocial	☐ Mixed	☐ Prosocial	☐ Weak	☐ Strong
	_____	☐ Antisocial	☐ Mixed	☐ Prosocial	☐ Weak	☐ Strong
	_____	☐ Antisocial	☐ Mixed	☐ Prosocial	☐ Weak	☐ Strong
	_____	☐ Antisocial	☐ Mixed	☐ Prosocial	☐ Weak	☐ Strong
	_____	☐ Antisocial	☐ Mixed	☐ Prosocial	☐ Weak	☐ Strong
Friends						
	_____	☐ Antisocial	☐ Mixed	☐ Prosocial	☐ Weak	☐ Strong
	_____	☐ Antisocial	☐ Mixed	☐ Prosocial	☐ Weak	☐ Strong
	_____	☐ Antisocial	☐ Mixed	☐ Prosocial	☐ Weak	☐ Strong
	_____	☐ Antisocial	☐ Mixed	☐ Prosocial	☐ Weak	☐ Strong
Associates						
	_____	☐ Antisocial	☐ Mixed	☐ Prosocial	☐ Weak	☐ Strong
	_____	☐ Antisocial	☐ Mixed	☐ Prosocial	☐ Weak	☐ Strong
Others in the offender's community						
	_____	☐ Antisocial	☐ Mixed	☐ Prosocial	☐ Weak	☐ Strong
	_____	☐ Antisocial	☐ Mixed	☐ Prosocial	☐ Weak	☐ Strong

(Continued)

SECTION C: TARGET GUARDIANS

Previous victims / targets

Person / Place / Property Description	*Repeat Risk*			*Possible Guardian*
_____	□ Low	□ Medium	□ High	_____
Details: _____				_____
_____	□ Low	□ Medium	□ High	_____
Details: _____				_____
_____	□ Low	□ Medium	□ High	_____
Details: _____				_____
_____	□ Low	□ Medium	□ High	_____
Details: _____				_____

Potential victims / targets: _____

_____

_____

92

SECTION D: PLACE MANAGERS

Place Name	Place Type	Place Location	Place Manager
Familiar residences			
Neighbors (in the immediate vicinity of the offender's familiar residences)			
Work/school			
Leisure/recreation			

(Continued)

SECTION E: CRIME OPPORTUNITIES REGULATORS

Regulator	Action Plan

Prosocial activities

1. _____ _____

2. _____ _____

3. _____ _____

Offender handlers

1. _____ _____

2. _____ _____

3. _____ _____

Target guardians

1. _____ _____

2. _____ _____

3. _____ _____

Place managers

1. _____ _____

2. _____ _____

3. _____ _____

94

Section B in Form B evaluates prospective offender handlers. The assessment allows the user to identify different types of relationships (such as friends or community members), and then to determine the strength and variety of the influence of that relationship on offender behavior. By detailing this information, offender supervisors can not only discover the prosocial people in their clients' lives, but can also define which of these people will be most helpful in shaping a prosocial routine. A handler is someone who is in a position to exert control over an offender's actions. Although there are many individuals capable of influencing a probationer or parolee, community corrections officers would be wise to figure out who will be most effective in this role. One such consideration is the rapport between the potential handler and the offender (such as the level of trust, degree of respect, and the details of their history). By soliciting the help of people the offender is more apt to identify with (i.e., people the offender is more likely to listen to, to model their behavior, and to follow their recommendations), supervisors go beyond behavior control toward behavior modification. Ideally, community corrections officers can work cooperatively with an offender and his or her prosocial contacts to develop a network of people that positively influence the offender's behavior. A more thorough discussion of the role of offender handlers, including a discussion of how to recruit, train, and manage them, is included in Chapter 6.

Section C in Form B is designed to help indicate potential guardians of past and future victims or targets. First, this portion of the assessment documents the details of previous crime targets, classifying the risk of repeat victimization, and identifying a possible guardian to reduce the threat of such risk. Using information about these past targets and victims, there is also an open-ended component that allows the assessor to describe possible targets and victims of the client's future offenses. Because law enforcement and corrections officers cannot be every place at every time, additional parties are required to help prevent opportunities for crime to occur (see Chapter 6). When a threat of victimization is probable, probation and parole authorities can effectively limit future offenses by instituting effective guardianship. Examples include notifying a domestic assault victim of the perpetrator's community release (and providing information about enhancing personal safety), advising roommates to safeguard valuables, or informing the offender's neighbors of the threat of repeat property damage. In many ways, the role of offender supervisors in recruiting target guardianship is to provide encouragement to people to be the natural protectors of their persons and property, supplying them with information and tools to be effective in these tasks.

Section D in Form B explores potential place managers that can be useful in reducing opportunities to commit crime. This component encourages the assessor to identify places the offender frequents, within the categories of residences, neighbors, work/school, and leisure/recreation. For each place that is listed, the place type (e.g., a dance club) and the place location (e.g., the corner of 5th Street and Vine Drive) are documented so that the offender supervisor can note any emerging patterns in the offender's movements. Finally, the assessor is required to identify a possible manager for each place. Place managers are people (and their respective organizations) that control the behavior of the inhabitants there. Examples may include a homeowner, the shift supervisor at the offender's job, or the head clerk at a store. Community corrections officers can help to eliminate crime opportunities the offender is likely to come into contact with by recruiting and training the managers of the places the offender frequents. Later, we provide specific recommendations for soliciting these third parties in relationship to the role of police in reducing opportunities for probationers and parolees to offend (see Chapter 6).

The final component of this assessment, Section E in Form B, aids offender supervisors in rating the activities and persons that were identified as potential crime-opportunity regulators. A regulator here means any influence that controls the opportunities an offender is exposed to. Analyzing the information collected in the previous sections, probation and parole officers should list the prosocial activities, offender handlers, target guardians, and place managers that are most likely to reduce chances for their clients to offend. For each item listed, the offender supervisor must then develop an action plan for how the regulator is to be used. The assessor must be mindful of multiple considerations, such as the legality of the proposed solution, the likely cooperation of the third party, or the ability to provide the crime controller with the necessary tools. These ratings ought to provide probation and parole officers with actionable plans for reducing crime opportunities *beyond* traditional case plan stipulations (see the following chapter section). For example, an offender supervisor might enroll an offender in a music class that he or she has expressed interest in during a time that the offender might otherwise encounter chances to get into trouble. Supervisors can meet with the offender's family to inform them of the goals of the community corrections case plan, and to encourage them to contribute to its success and report any relapsing behaviors. Or an officer could notify the manager of a bar to contact the community corrections office if the offender attends the restricted premise. The overarching goal is to solicit the aid of the contributors to an offender's routine in minimizing his or her exposure to crime opportunities.

Opportunity-Reduction Case Plans

After completing these assessments, probation and parole officers should have a clearer understanding of their clients' crime opportunities and the potential controllers of these environmental risks. This information can then be used to create conditions of the community-supervision case plan that reduce these opportunities and the offender's vulnerability to them. An example outcome of this process can be seen in Figure 4.1, an infographic that details an offender's daily schedule for a typical week. Included in this schedule are the activities and locations that correspond with the offender's time use. By outlining the offender's schedule pictorially, community corrections officers have an overall impression of the routine activities of their client.

Included in this representation are three layers of data that complement this schedule. First, the locations of each activity are provided, including the name of

	Monday	Tuesday	Wednesday	Thursday	Friday	Saturday	Sunday
6:00 a.m.							
7:00 a.m.							
8:00 a.m.							CHURCH
9:00 a.m.			WORK	WORK			First Evangelical
10:00 a.m.	WORK	WORK	Miller Manufacturing	Miller Manufacturing			8800 E. Market Ln.
11:00 a.m.	Miller Manufacturing	Miller Manufacturing	4526 S. Smith St.	4526 S. Smith St.			East Sherwood
12:00 p.m.	4526 S. Smith St.	4526 S. Smith St.	South Sherwood	South Sherwood	WORK		
1:00 p.m.	South Sherwood	South Sherwood			Miller Manufacturing		
2:00 p.m.					4526 S. Smith St.	MPC GROUP	
3:00 p.m.					South Sherwood	Challenges, Inc.	
4:00 p.m.						444 Davis Dr.	
5:00 p.m.						Westside	
6:00 p.m.	COUNSELING	GED PREP COURSE	CHURCH		GED PREP COURSE		
7:00 p.m.	Amy Allen	Smith High School	First Evangelical		Smith High School		
8:00 p.m.	888 Monroe St.	123 Adams Ave.	8800 E. Market Ln.		123 Adams Ave.		
9:00 p.m.		West Pine Grove	East Sherwood		West Pine Grove		
10:00 p.m.							
11:00 p.m.							
12:00 a.m.	HOME	HOME	HOME	HOME	HOME	HOME	HOME
1:00 a.m.	Grandmother's house	Grandmother's house	Grandmother's house	Grandmother's house	Girlfriend's house	Girlfriend's house	Grandmother's house
2:00 a.m.	2552 W. Central	2552 W. Central	2552 W. Central	2552 W. Central	9876 Thompson Ct.	9876 Thompson Ct.	2552 W. Central
3:00 a.m.	East Sherwood	East Sherwood	East Sherwood	East Sherwood	Westside	Westside	East Sherwood
4:00 a.m.							
5:00 a.m.							

Figure 4.1 Offender Schedule With Dynamic Crime Opportunities

97

the place, the physical address, and the sub-neighborhood location. This information provides the supervising officer with important data at a glance without the need to reference other documents. Second, based on the problematic days and times identified in the offender's crime opportunities risk assessment (in particular, Section C of the CORRAL; see Form A), gradation in the likelihood of encountering crime opportunities is plotted on the schedule. Deeper grayscale in this figure indicates an increased risk of meeting with people, places, and situations when the individual has the chance to offend (e.g., white hue = low risk, dark gray hue = high risk for the offender converging with attractive targets and incapable guardians). Third, the type of crime opportunity is overlaid on the degree of risk. For example, a stick-figure icon represents the result from the assessment that at that time and in that place, the offender is likely to be surrounded by antisocial associates. The graphical icons reflect the type of temptation to commit crime the offender is likely to come into contact with, ranging from high-crime places to aggressive subcultures to substance use.

Taken together, these layers of information included in the schedule of an offender's weekly routine activities provide a snapshot of recidivism risk, and thus implicate points of intervention. For instance, in an examination of the hypothetical offender schedule in Figure 4.1, the probation or parole officer would immediately note that this client is in a high-risk place on Saturday evenings before staying the evening at his girlfriend's residence. After further investigation, the officer might determine that the offender's travel route should be redirected to avoid a particularly dangerous sub-neighborhood, thereby minimizing the risk of the offender converging with the crime opportunities that exist there.

These examples illustrate the larger point of the importance of creating supervision conditions that reflect the individual offender's opportunities to commit crime. As suggested, environmental criminology generally and crime science interventions specifically can be valuable resources in the development of community corrections interventions. Rather than attempting to balance treatment and control to the negation of one another, environmental corrections recommends tailoring probationers' and parolees' routine activities to avoid offender convergence with situations where crime is allowed to occur. Offender supervisors can use the leverage of conditional release to replace their clients' antisocial patterns of behavior with people, places, and situations where the chance to offend is minimized. As the present chapter has demonstrated, creating stipulations of community supervision that reflect the crime opportunities of each offender requires new data collection methods and assessment technologies.

Evaluating the information collected in the Crime Opportunities Risk Reduction Action List (CORRAL; see Form A) and the Crime Opportunities Regulators Rating Tool (CORRT; see Form B), a case plan can be designed that minimizes these identified crime opportunities. A sample case plan can be seen in Form C, an example Routine Activities Intervention Strategy for Opportunity Reduction (RAISOR). In addition to an introductory overview of compulsory information and a standard acknowledgment, the environmental corrections case plan includes five sections. These categories of content reflect the different crime opportunities that must be addressed. As has been theorized, there are different kinds of chances to offend, all of which must be controlled for with a supervision case plan if re-offending is to be reliably reduced. Thus, there are crime opportunities that most offenders are vulnerable to (general supervision conditions) as well as crime opportunities unique to each individual's history (special supervision conditions). There are also offender-specific temptations to crime opportunities (supervision requirements) and offender-specific exposure to those opportunities (supervision restrictions). These four categories of case plan stipulations are reflected in the intensity of supervision, detailed in the final section (supervision schedule).

Although this case plan is based on a fictional offender and hypothetical crime opportunities, the stipulations of the supervision term were created to reflect crime science innovations. The goal of each supervision condition is to minimize the probationer or parolee's exposure and vulnerability to crime opportunities. Additionally, it is important to note that this case plan would change to reflect alterations in the offender's risks and progress (see Chapter 3); however, this form provides a sample case plan that illustrates the utility of the offender supervision technologies created for this book. Each of the case plan's components is discussed in turn below.

Category I in Form C outlines the general supervision conditions to which the offender is subjected. These rules are often legislatively prescribed, including the standard court-imposed regulations that guide the offender's conditional release. Some of these conditions reflect guidelines that are meant to protect the offender's legal rights, and others outline the nature of the agreement between the offender and the court. Most of these general supervision conditions (which indeed apply across types of correctional interventions, across time, and across jurisdictions) are based on an unfocused deterrence theory, threatening the offender with a variety of sanctions for a number of detailed misbehaviors. Importantly, however, some of these generic rules the offender must abide by during his or her community supervision are based on understood associations between environmental features and crime. For example, typical supervision case plans forbid offenders to use or possess weapons or illegal substances, due to the idea that these things can trigger a re-offense. Thus, all offenders have certain freedoms restricted in an effort to minimize opportunities to commit further crimes.

Category II in Form C details special supervision conditions with which the offender is required to comply. These rules are unique to the individual offender, though commonalities across cases exist. For example, many offenders are required to pay restitution of community monitoring fees, although the costs will vary. Some conditions are a form of punishment in response to the specific offense (e.g., a revoked driver's license or mandatory participation in community service). Other specialized supervision stipulations are a clear effort to maximize public safety, such as restricting access to past and potential victims or targets, or to places where these victims and targets are located (e.g., an offender may be forbidden to live within 1,000 yards of a playground). Although typically court-ordered and not necessarily designed by the supervising officer, special conditions of community release are often aimed at preventing future offenses based upon the past crimes of the individual.

Form C: Routine Activities Intervention Strategy for Opportunity Reduction (RAISOR)

State Department of Corrections

ADULT PROBATION AND PAROLE AUTHORITY

Community Supervision Case Plan

Supervisee: <u>William Washington, #121343565</u>   Supervisor: <u>Thomas Taylor, PO</u>

Under the terms of your sentence, you have been granted supervised release. Your term of community correction is for a period of <u>12 to 24 months</u> commencing <u>04/01/2012</u>.

While under community correction supervision you are required to adhere to the stipulations outlined herein. A violation of any of these stipulations may result in the revocation of your conditional release. This supervision case plan can be reasonably modified with due notification.

While on supervised release you are compelled to abide by the conditions appended hereto. These stipulations are divided into the following categories:

    I. General Supervision Conditions
    II. Special Supervision Conditions
    III. Supervision Requirements
    IV. Supervision Restrictions
    V. Supervision Schedule

Acknowledgment

I have read, or have had read to me, the conditions included in this community supervision case plan. I understand the rules of my conditional release and accept that they may be modified during my supervision term. I understand that a finding of a breach of any stipulation may result in the revocation of my conditional release. I understand that I am subject to the appended conditions until notified by my supervising officer. I have been provided a copy of my community supervision case plan.

_____   _____
Supervisee signature   Date

_____   _____
Supervisor signature   Date

CATEGORY I. GENERAL SUPERVISION CONDITIONS

1. You shall obey federal, state, county, and municipal laws and ordinances, including those imposed by court order. You shall not commit any criminal offense. You shall notify your supervising officer of any questioning by a law enforcement officer within two business days.

2. You shall cooperate with your supervising officer at all times. You shall promptly and truthfully respond to any inquiry made by your supervising officer or agency.

3. You shall meet with your supervising officer as required. You shall permit your supervising officer to visit you at your residence, work site, or other community locations.

4. You shall be subject to warrantless searches of your person, vehicle, or premises by any authorized community correction officer if the officer has reasonable suspicion that you are not obeying the law or the conditions of your supervision.

5. You shall notify third parties of risks associated with your criminal record as directed by your supervising officer. You shall permit your supervising officer to monitor your compliance with the stipulations of your conditional release, including through contact with third parties.

6. You shall not leave the judicial district unless prior written authorization is granted by your supervising officer or agency.

7. You shall not change residence or employment without prior permission from your supervising officer or agency.

8. You shall not purchase, possess, own, use, or be in control of any firearm, ammunition, destructive devices, or weapons intended to cause physical harm.

9. You shall not purchase, possess, own, use, or be in control of any illegal intoxicants or related paraphernalia, including licit controlled substances (unless in pursuant to a medical prescription). You shall submit to a urinalysis drug screening as requested by your supervising officer.

10. You shall waive extradition and agree to return voluntarily if necessary to this judicial district upon arrest.

(Continued)

(Continued)

CATEGORY II. SPECIAL SUPERVISION CONDITIONS

1. You shall refrain from all contact with the victim __Rebecca Robertson__ in compliance with the restraining order issued by the Court. You shall not contact the victim directly, indirectly, or through third parties.

2. You shall refrain from unsupervised contact with your children __Wendy Washington__ and __Wendell Washington__ . You shall not contact your children directly, indirectly, or through third parties without the supervision of your case worker.

3. You shall complete four hours of community service per month as directed by your supervising officer.

4. You shall pay the following costs on or before the designated date each month to the Department of Corrections:

    —Supervision fee: __$20.00__   for a period of   __the duration of your sentence__

    —Court costs: __$12.50__   for a period of   __12 months__

    —Restitution: __$41.66__   for a period of   __6 months__

5. You shall not drive a motor vehicle until the suspension of your driver's license has expired. You shall meet the requirements of the Department of Motor Vehicles to have your driving rights reinstated.

CATEGORY III. SUPERVISION REQUIREMENTS

1. You shall participate in a psychiatric assessment as directed by your supervising officer. You shall comply with all recommendations arising from the results of the assessment.

2. You shall participate in the following treatments:

Treatment name: Individual counseling sessions

>Provider: Horizons Clinical Group; Amy Allen, LPC MSW
>Location: 888 Monroe Street
>Frequency: One hour each week
>Duration: Twelve sessions or until discharged by counselor
>Meeting time: Mondays, 6:30 p.m.

Treatment name: Making Positive Choices group

>Provider: Challenges, Inc.
>Location: Lewis Business Center, 444 Davis Drive
>Frequency: One session each week
>Duration: Four months
>Meeting time: Saturdays, 2:00 p.m.

3. You shall participate in the following service provisions:

Service name: GED Preparation Course

>Provider: ABC Education Services
>Location: Smith High School cafeteria, 123 Adams Avenue
>Frequency: Two sessions each week
>Duration: Until expiration of sentence or receipt of degree
>Meeting time: Tuesdays and Fridays, 6:00 p.m.

4. You shall maintain your part-time employment at _Miller Manufacturing_ . You shall notify your supervising officer within two business days if your employment status or working hours change.

5. You shall contact your case worker, _Matthew Martinson_ , for assistance with concrete needs (such as housing assistance, food security, transportation needs, employment training, or financial counseling) as necessary.

(Continued)

(Continued)

CATEGORY IV. SUPERVISION RESTRICTIONS

1. You shall have restricted communication with the following people:

Name	Relationship	Provision
Raymond Robinson	Co-offender	No contact
Peter Parker	Co-worker	No contact outside of work
Sally Simon	Ex-girlfriend	No contact
Mark Martin	Cousin	In company only at family gatherings
Kathy Klein	Neighbor	Cannot be inside her residence
Matthew Macdonald	Friend	No company between 8pm and 6am

2. You shall be limited in your activities during the following days and times:

Days	Times	Activity Restriction
All	10:00 pm– 6:00 am	Must be home
Fri. & Sat.	After 8:00 pm	Cannot be at Bill's Biker Bar

3. You shall not be permitted to be at the following locations at any time:

Location name	Address
Victim's neighborhood	Main St.–Parkway from Central Ave.–13th St.
Larry's Bowling Lanes	654 Strike St.
AJ's Bar and Grill	8852 S. Macarthur Ave.
Groves Park and Rec. Center	Berkley Dr.–Adams St. from 1st St.–3rd St.
Stratford Strip Mall businesses	300 – 550 Cunningham Ct.

CATEGORY V. SUPERVISION SCHEDULE

Your current schedule of supervision is outlined below. This supervision schedule may be modified by the Department of Corrections. The amount and nature of your supervision will be partly determined by your compliance with supervision conditions and your progress toward goals specified by your supervising officer. Information about your requirements, including meetings with your supervising officer and supervision stipulations, will be provided to you with adequate advance notice.

First three months of supervision (April through June)

    Meeting frequency: Once per week

    Meeting length: One hour

    Meeting format: Development of prosocial routine

    Meeting location: Alternating between your residence and DoC office

Next six months of supervision *(July through December)*

    Meeting frequency: Twice per month

    Meeting length: Thirty minutes

    Meeting format: Enhancement of cognitive-behavioral skills

    Meeting location: Alternating between community location and DoC office

Final months of supervision (January through December)

    Meeting frequency: Twice per month

    Meeting length: Fifteen minutes

    Meeting format: Promotion of life skills

    Meeting location: Alternating between community location and teleconferencing

In order to adjust your supervision case plan to reflect your current risks and needs, you are required to submit the following documents, completed with the assistance of your supervising officer, on a monthly basis:

    (a) Daily activity calendar (Form 964a)

    (b) Prospects and priorities goal checklist (Form 82.5)

Category III in Form C itemizes the supervision requirements the community-monitored offender must adhere to. These conditions address the offender's concrete needs (such as transportation assistance) and require the continuance of prosocial activities (maintaining current employment, for example). Additionally, this section details services that the offender is required to receive, including educational training, psychological assessments, individual counseling, or substance abuse treatment. Although in part these requirements reflect humanitarian concerns, the larger aim is to reduce an offender's likelihood of taking advantage of existing crime opportunities. By addressing a probationer's or parolee's situational propensity (see Chapter 5), his or her vulnerability to high-risk situations can be minimized. Interventions can adjust the offender's interpretation of opportunities to commit crime (Cromwell & Birzer, 2014; Wright & Decker, 1994) by helping to develop prosocial decision-making processes such as the proper evaluation of risks and rewards. Reducing recidivism is therefore achieved in part by requiring the offender to participate in programs and services that decrease the probability that he or she will notice and pursue available chances to break the law.

Category IV in Form C specifies the supervision restrictions that limit the offender's behavior during the community corrections term. Based on the information obtained during the evaluation of the individual's risk for encountering and pursuing crime opportunities, rules that guide the offender's activities away from the environments containing these opportunities are developed. Specifically, the probationer or parolee is restricted from communicating with certain people, attending certain places, or engaging in certain activities during particular days and times. These constraints are thoughtfully designed, steering the offender away from situations where crime opportunities are likely to emerge or where they would prove tempting to the individual. An important component of this aspect of the supervision case plan is the development of a routine of prosocial activities for the offender. So, when people, places, and activities are ruled off limits, offender supervisors should work to replace these high-risk situations with preferred patterns of behavior. In this way, offender actions are not merely controlled, but substitute routines are recommended. These restrictions reduce exposure to crime opportunities, but also reduce criminogenic needs through the replacement of values, skills, and influences.

Finally, Category V in Form C presents the schedule of supervision. As discussed in the previous chapter, the length, frequency, format, and content of offender-officer meetings will vary according to the offender's progress. When the offender's crime-opportunities risks change, the method of intervention must also change. Because the probability of relapse is greatest in the first several months of the supervision term, offender supervisors must be more intensively involved with their clients at this stage. It is also important that the location of these meetings is adjusted across time. Because offenders are expected to adopt new prosocial routine activities that they are reasonably unfamiliar with, probation and parole officers can contribute to the success of their supervisees by modeling these behavior patterns. For instance, supervising officers can rehearse and reinforce offender prosociality by shadowing their clients in the community as they adjust to new activities and associates. When offender supervisors walk through their client's routine with them, they set clear expectations and teach how to avoid and respond to crime opportunities. Officers are also able to observe an offender in the individual's "native setting," which provides additional information about what crime opportunities the person is exposed to and tempted by, as well as what skills and resources the individual has available to buffer these risks. The more familiar supervising officers become with the real-world situations that lead to and that prevent crime, the better able they are to create case plans that reduce recidivism and encourage desistance.

Conclusion

The current chapter has demonstrated the importance of offender assessment, detailing the strengths of new supervision technologies toward the goal of reducing crime opportunities. Indeed, the tools presented above provide processes that might reorient how we intervene with offenders under community corrections. Although having the potential to improve offender outcomes and public safety, the pursuit of a new direction would naturally involve several implementation hurdles (for a more detailed discussion of the limitations of opportunity-reduction supervision, see Chapter 7). There are three challenges that would require attention, though none are insurmountable. First, the data required to complete these assessments may not be available or easily accessed. Second, the resources necessary to gather the data (such as several hours of manpower, cooperation of third parties, and offender honesty) might be difficult to arrange. Third, offender supervisors would require training in how to complete the assessments and properly use their products. With thoughtful program development and enthusiastic agency participation, these challenges can be managed, although procedural revisions should be expected. Despite the initial "costs" of implementing these data collection strategies at the outset, as the processes become routinized and improved, the dividends will far outweigh the initial investments.

Further, collecting data through offender interviews poses several challenges. While some of these hurdles can be overcome through data triangulation methods and instrument validation procedures, the issues of offenders' awareness and honesty about their crime opportunity risks require a more considered approach. Importantly, several studies that have examined the reliability of offender narratives have concluded that the recollections offenders provide are actually chances in themselves to identify thinking errors, excuses, and insight into the social and psychological processes that led to crime (Auburn, 2005). Indeed, offenders may describe what seem to be "excuses" for crime, when in actuality this may be an effort to demonstrate how the offense seemed "rational" with that set of circumstances (Friestad, 2012). These narratives are valuable windows into the decision-making processes of offenders, and they may reveal the cognitive contents that require redress as well as the precipitators of crime that need to be "designed out" with the supervision case plan.

In this context, probation and parole officers should be provided sufficient training on the techniques of encouraging self-change (Miller & Rollnick, 2013; Robinson et al., 2012; Smith et al., 2012). Studies demonstrate that when community corrections officers combine influential relational skills with tools to promote offender change, desistance can be markedly increased and extended (Raynor, Ugwudike, & Vanstone, 2014; Raynor & Vanstone, 2015). With these skills in place, officers are in a prime position to first use their interviews with offenders to identify thinking patterns, crime opportunities, and routine activities, and then to redirect offenders toward building a prosocial identity (Burnett & McNeill, 2005; Maruna & Ramsden, 2004; Ward & Marshall, 2007). Although a host of best practices for offender interviewing and data collection are now available (Nee, 2004), we acknowledge that the processes required to use the types of instruments we have proposed here will encounter several barriers that will need to be addressed (see Chapter 7).

Yet despite these potential obstacles, the importance of offender evaluation cannot be neglected. To effectively reduce recidivism among community-supervised offenders, probation and parole agents must first have a clear understanding of the causes of crime. In this case, offender assessments serve the important task of determining what crime opportunities supervisees are exposed to, and what types of interventions will help to limit this exposure. Designing a new daily routine for offenders that limits their vulnerability to available chances to commit crime means first identifying what these temptations are for each individual. This shift in the goal of community corrections, from bureaucratic behavioral control to opportunity reduction, requires new offender supervision technologies. The instruments presented in the current chapter provide a first step toward this aim, offering a novel but promising solution to minimizing crime opportunities and relapse.

However, restricting offenders' access to available crime opportunities is but a partial remedy. Probation and parole authorities cannot be aware of every crime opportunity, and cannot fully insulate an offender from encountering those chances to recidivate. Crime opportunities remain, and community-supervised offenders will be exposed to them. Accordingly, two other components to opportunity-reduction supervision require development. First, the number of existing crime opportunities can be reduced, such as by recruiting offender handlers and training place managers (see Chapter 6). Second, an offender's interpretation of remaining crime opportunities requires address. As explored in the following chapter, altering the ways that probationers and parolees evaluate and appraise the elements of their environment is a necessary ingredient to limiting re-offending.

5

Getting Offenders to Think Right

The central argument advanced in this text is that reducing the availability of and access to crime opportunities will prevent re-offending among community-supervised offenders. Drawing on crime science innovations, the daily routines of probationers and parolees can be designed to limit offenders' exposure to situations where crime is more likely to occur. Community corrections conditions should be tailored to the individual supervisee's crime opportunities, fashioning his or her day-to-day activities to avoid chances to offend by replacing high-crime environments with prosocial surroundings. However, because it is not possible to provide supervision stipulations that would prevent an offender from encountering all crime opportunities, it is also necessary to address criminal propensity.

The traditional model of offender monitoring in the community orients treatment and control as adversarial ideologies. In the context of opportunities for offending, this divide may be artificial. As this chapter will argue, techniques of correctional rehabilitation can be expanded to incorporate elements of opportunity reduction. It is unreasonable to expect community corrections officers to identify and control all crime opportunities; consequently, effective approaches to offender supervision must address the offender's propensity to solicit and take advantage of existing opportunities to get into trouble. Many elements of criminal propensity are beyond manipulation, at least within the resource constraints of a typical supervision sentence. Rather than attempting to change deep-seated inclinations to offend (such as misconduct that results from a history of abuse or psychopathy), the principles of cognitive-behavioral interventions can be applied to recondition the way offenders interpret their environment. Probation and parole authorities can apply evidence-based best practices in correctional interventions to influence the way that supervisees view crime opportunities. Thus, in addition to offenders encountering crime opportunities less frequently, they will be more likely to view remaining crime opportunities as unattractive pursuits (i.e., the rewards are too low, the costs are too high, or the risks are too great) or as neutral stimuli (i.e., not seeing a chance to misbehave at all).

Contrary to the typical community supervision method of service brokerage, addressing criminal propensity encompasses more than enrollment in one program or making blanket program referrals. For example, simply encouraging or requiring offenders to participate in a substance abuse treatment group, irrespective of what actually causes each individual's offending, does little to identify and manage the conditions that lead to crime. As opposed to this broad approach, probation and parole supervision strategies must focus on dynamic criminogenic needs, altering the ways an offender interprets criminal opportunities and the environments that contain those opportunities. This chapter discusses effective mechanisms for creating prosocial cognitions and decision-making processes among community-supervised offenders. In this vein, the approaches explored in the discussion that follows demonstrate how correctional rehabilitation (in particular, the theoretical frameworks and techniques of intervention used in cognitive-behavioral therapies) can be aligned with the environmental corrections model of offender supervision. Specifically, we propose that effective forms of offender rehabilitation, such as thought replacement and situation processing, can be modeled in such a way as to enhance an opportunity-reduction approach to probation and parole.

As introduced in the beginning of this text, two ingredients contribute to crime: opportunity and propensity. Offenders must be motivated or able to commit crime, but there must also be a chance to act on it. The bulk of the environmental corrections model of offender supervision emphasizes the reduction of crime opportunities. Yet even when probation and parole authorities effectively limit their clients' exposure to environments containing these risks for relapse, some temptations will remain. For this reason, it is important that community corrections agents also address the way that offenders think about their surroundings and the potential crime opportunities therein.

Indeed, referring back to Figure 2.1 (see Chapter 2), one of the precipitators of crime events is offender cognition. How an offender thinks—what information is considered and how these data are processed—has direct consequences on recidivism. Offender supervisors can work with their clients and provide services that change the beliefs and values of probationers and parolees, as well as how offenders behave in response to these thoughts. In this way, offenders will be led to make prosocial decisions when they encounter environments that are accommodating to crime commission and to avoid environments that contain these triggers. Moreover, recall that the relationship between crime precipitators (cognitions and situations) is reciprocating. Thus, when offender supervisors address the thought processes of their clients, probationers and parolees are more likely to choose activities that are not conducive to crime. In the same way, by designing offender routines around law-abiding activities, probation and parole officers are working to supplant antisocial beliefs with prosocial ones. For these reasons, community corrections solutions must target the precipitators of a crime, both internal and external to the offender. Because corrections authorities cannot reasonably eliminate an offender's exposure to all crime opportunities, effective supervision programs must alter the way an offender thinks about the crime opportunities that he or she will inevitably still encounter.

To facilitate these goals, the present chapter discusses three central points. First, evidence from meta-analyses and program evaluations will be used to demonstrate the importance of addressing offender propensity. This section introduces evidence-based practices and the role of general responsivity, documenting the effectiveness of cognitive-behavioral techniques of correctional intervention. These processes have specific applications within an opportunity-reduction model of offender supervision, creating tools for offenders to resist and avoid chances to commit crime. Second, the chapter outlines specific techniques for building opportunity resistance skills among probationers and parolees—that is, ways to help offenders defy available chances to commit crime. Included in this section are discussions of how cognitive restructuring, emotional regulation, self-regulation, and problem-solving skills encourage offenders' ability to withstand available crime opportunities. Third, techniques for creating opportunity avoidance skills among community-supervised offenders are introduced; these are ways to help offenders steer clear of high-risk environments. This section provides information on the roles of personal schemas, behavioral activation and strengths theory, and situation appraisal and situation selection skills in helping offenders to circumvent situations where crime opportunities are likely to be present. The chapter concludes by presenting a model for the place of correctional rehabilitation in opportunity-reduction supervision, providing an overview of this reimagined role of cognitive-behavioral techniques in recidivism prevention among offenders monitored in the community.

Reducing Propensity

For a crime to occur, a motivated offender must converge in space and time with an opportunity to offend. Although the thrust of our analysis has been on the reduction of these crime opportunities, the other component of this calculus deserves attention, as well. Beyond the fact that motivation to offend is a necessary ingredient in a crime, propensity is important for two central reasons. First, reducing the inclination to commit crime is vital, provided that all crime opportunities cannot possibly be removed. Opportunity aside, fewer motivated offenders translates into less crime. Second, addressing offender propensity is complementary to opportunity reduction. Because all crime opportunities cannot be controlled, offender supervisors must concern themselves with how their clients interact with crime-conducive situations. Thus, an important component of reducing criminal opportunities is adjusting an offender's assessment of the efforts, risks, and rewards of the choices available in each environment (Clarke, 1992, 1995).

Termed herein *situational propensity*, the treatment aspect of community corrections should be geared toward changing the way that offenders interpret available crime opportunities. Propensity influences an offender's proximity to pro-crime environments, and also impacts that offender's likelihood of seeking, observing, and pursuing the available opportunity. Rather than assuming that there are two groups of people—offenders and non-offenders, differentiated by variations in criminal motivation—it may be more helpful to think about propensity as being fluid. People can be more or less inclined to break the law, and these inclinations are influenced by the situations in which they are embedded. Therefore, probation and parole authorities may find it helpful to consider the environmental features that trigger the transition from an unmotivated to a motivated potential offender, and then the jump from motivation to action. Although certain offenders may indeed be perpetually motivated (and there are interventions that should be resourced to address this criminal propensity), many community-supervised offenders may find themselves motivated to recidivate only in the presence of certain situational precipitators. Accordingly, community corrections officers can help to reduce re-offending among their clients by targeting for change the criminal propensity that corresponds with real crime opportunities in the environment.

Reducing propensity is a manageable task in light of the extensive knowledge base of effectiveness in correctional interventions. The scrutiny offender rehabilitation was subjected to in decades past motivated a search for evidence-based practices. The reign of rehabilitation as the guiding correctional philosophy was questioned after Martinson's (1974) assertion that "nothing works" to reduce recidivism (Cullen & Gilbert, 1982; Cullen & Jonson, 2012; Palmer, 1991). As part of a research team, Martinson had examined 231 studies that evaluated correctional interventions. In a classic essay published in *The Public Interest* reporting the results, he offered a stark and pessimistic conclusion: "With few and isolated exceptions, the rehabilitative efforts that have been reported so far have had no appreciable effect on recidivism" (1974, p. 25; for the full report, see Lipton, Martinson, & Wilks, 1975). Martinson's interpretation of the evaluation data was overly broad and ignored many positive findings in his own study (Palmer, 1975) and in research conducted elsewhere (Gendreau & Ross, 1979). But these more academic disputes were largely ignored because Martinson's "nothing works" inference affirmed what many people at this time already believed—that rehabilitation did not work (Cullen & Gendreau, 2001). Martinson's research and the credo that "nothing works" thus cemented the view that offender treatment was a failed enterprise. Still worse, it helped to open the way for a new punitive ideology that justified the creation of "commonsense" corrections programs meant to "get tough on crime." Without empiricism guiding program design, numerous community correctional interventions were instituted with no evidence to support their effectiveness (Aos, Phipps, Barnoski, & Lieb, 2001; Cullen et al., 2005; Cullen & Gendreau, 2001; Gendreau, Goggin, Cullen, & Andrews, 2000; Latessa et al., 2002; MacKenzie, 2006).

Yet despite the widespread impact of the "nothing works" movement, limited treatment efforts persisted. As Palmer (1975) notes, Martinson (1974) and his adherents paid little mind to the *degree* of effectiveness of the interventions that were evaluated, failing to note the numerous variables that provided substantial moderating effects on recidivism (see also Cullen & Gendreau, 2001). Following a healthy dose of what Gendreau and Ross (1979) called "bibliotherapy for cynics," progressive scholars began to note the features of correctional programs that were consistently associated with successful outcomes (see also Cullen & Jonson, 2012). The practice of meta-analysis, in particular, revealed a number of principles of effective correctional intervention that should be used to guide policy and practice (Andrews, 1995; Gendreau, 1996; Smith, Gendreau, & Swartz, 2009). These studies quantitatively synthesize the overall influence of varying treatment programs, and can identify the differential impact of the components of these programs. Accordingly, the past three decades have moved away from the mindless acceptance of the "nothing works" doctrine and toward an accumulation of knowledge regarding "what works" in offender interventions. This body of evidence is not a specific strategy, but provides a number of principles that produce marked impacts on positive offender outcomes (Andrews & Bonta, 2010; Andrews, 1995; Cullen & Jonson, 2012; Gendreau, 1996; Gendreau et al., 2006; Latessa & Lowenkamp, 2006; Smith, Gendreau, & Goggin, 2009). These principles are so influential, in fact, that numerous analyses have demonstrated that sanctioning offenders without rehabilitation, and treatment without regard to these guidelines for effective practice, cannot reasonably reduce re-offending (Andrews, Zinger, et al., 1990; Cullen & Gendreau, 2000, 2001; Lipsey & Wilson, 1998; McGuire, 2002).

Based on the systematic and empirical evaluation of correctional rehabilitation, the discipline has the evidence to demonstrate the best practices in reducing propensity. Research consistently establishes that adherence to the risk, need, and responsivity principles is most influential in minimizing recidivism (Bonta et al., 2011; Robinson et al., 2011; Taxman, 2008). Community corrections officials must be provided tools for changing criminogenic offender characteristics (Gleicher et al., 2013). In this case, offender supervisors must know *how* to target situational propensity. As this chapter details, cognitive-behavioral techniques can be used during offender-officer community supervision meetings and should also guide formal programming. Probation and parole officers can be trained to minimize offenders' motivation to seek out crime opportunities, and to reshape offenders' perceptions of their environments (Robinson et al., 2012; Smith et al., 2012). By applying the principle of general responsivity in efforts to reduce situational propensity, community-supervised offenders can be made to be less likely to take advantage of crime opportunities left unmanaged by probation/parole conditions.

Treatment within corrections "usually focuses on 'fixing' the 'trait' which causes the 'risk'" (Dickey & Klingele, 2004, p. 58), often attempted through mandatory enrollment in generic nonprescriptive programs. Although criminal propensity must be addressed in order to stifle offending, the deepest roots of criminality are typically beyond the scope of community correctional rehabilitation. Rather, the goal of probation and parole treatment must be to alter the personal dispositions that make individuals vulnerable to crime opportunities. As identified in numerous syntheses of evaluations of corrections programming, cognitive-behavioral techniques of intervention are the most effective means of altering pro-criminal proclivities (Andrews, Zinger, et al., 1990; Gendreau et al., 2006; Landenberger & Lipsey, 2005; Lipsey, Chapman, & Landenberger, 2001; MacKenzie, 2000, 2006; McGuire, 2002; Pearson, Lipton, Cleland, & Yee, 2002).

Cognitive-behavioral techniques are part of a larger approach known as functional contextualism. This pragmatic philosophy stipulates that the focus of therapies must be on observable variables; thus, to influence maladaptive *thoughts*, the practitioner should first aim to manipulate *behavior* (Biglan & Hayes, 1996; Gifford & Hayes, 1999; O'Donohue & Fisher, 2012). Reducing criminal propensity—the underlying *cause* of criminal behavior—is therefore achieved by addressing the manifested representations of that cause. An offender's thoughts and attitudes are malleable, and therapists can best change them by focusing on the behaviors that reflect those thoughts and attitudes. People choose behaviors that are reflective of their ideas and values, so it is important to associate the individual's actions with the thought processes that motivated the action.

Indeed, cognitive-behavioral interventions are effective because they link thoughts with actions, through skill building (via demonstration, role play, and rehearsal), reinforcements, and mental restructuring (Andrews & Bonta, 2010). If corrections agents want their clients to exhibit new behaviors, then offenders must be given the tools that are needed to address propensity and reduce recidivism. Techniques of cognitive-behavioral therapies vary, though they have in common the association of thoughts with actions. The role of the interventionist is to draw attention to the sequence of ideas that birth a given behavior (sometimes referred to in behaviorism as the three-term contingency: antecedent → behavior → consequence (new antecedent) → behavior → ...). When offenders gain the capacity to analyze their surroundings and their thought processes without the guidance of a corrections agent, they become empowered to change their behavior. Cognitive-behavioral techniques help offenders to recognize (and then alter) the features of a situation that produce given thoughts, and how those thoughts in turn produce given behaviors.

Reducing criminal propensity supplements the goal of opportunity-reduction supervision. Through cognitive-behavioral interventions, probation and parole officers can significantly impact the ways in which offenders choose and interact with their environments. In line with this goal, two strategies can be used to prevent re-offending. First, offender supervisors can train their clients in *opportunity resistance*, which involves developing the problem-solving skills necessary to withstand available chances to commit crime. Community-supervised offenders will invariably encounter crime opportunities, often through no purposeful action of their own; thus, correctional treatment must address how the individual perceives the situation and manages his or her response. Second, offender supervisors can train their clients in *opportunity avoidance*, which involves creating decision-making skills to help offenders steer clear of situations where chances to commit crime are present. When offenders are made aware of what their triggers for offending are, and can discover what situations contain those triggers, then they are able to design their activities and surroundings in ways that avoid exposure to those crime opportunities. As explored in the following discussion, there are several effective techniques of cognitive-behavioral intervention that can build the skills needed for probationers and parolees to resist and avoid opportunities to offend. Though the tools are diverse, community corrections officers can limit re-offending through skills training that identifies and changes the linkages between thoughts and actions.

Opportunity Resistance

It is inevitable that probationers and parolees will come into contact with crime opportunities. At several points during offenders' supervision terms the chance to commit crime will present itself. All people naturally encounter attractive targets, incapable guardians, proper crime tools, impressive rewards, minimal risks, and ample justifications for breaking the law. Chances to offend are in many places at many times, and while community corrections officers can control their clients' access to a great deal of these crime opportunities, not all criminogenic environments can be eliminated. To prevent the maximum number of re-offenses, then, probation and parole authorities must manage the decision-making processes that offenders experience when in the presence of remaining opportunities to commit crime.

By assessing offenders' crime opportunities, probation and parole officers should know a good deal about "what is going on" when their supervisees "get into trouble." The task is thus to diagnose the factors that lead particular offenders to fall prey to, rather than resist, the criminal opportunities they encounter (or perhaps help to create, such as an exchange of insults that escalates into an assault). Of course, anything that reduces overall criminal propensity will reduce the desire to offend across all of these opportunities. Still, officers might also be able to focus on what we might call "situational propensity" so as to help offenders understand the key challenges they face when a crime opportunity is "staring them in the face."

Based on the existing literature, it is useful to identify four situational challenges that an offender might encounter. Not all of these would apply to every offender, although some supervisees might face multiple challenges. The task for probation and parole officers is to talk with their supervisees about their participation in criminal events to try to uncover "what goes on" with offenders when deciding to take advantage of a criminal opportunity. What are these four challenges? One involves how offenders think about situations. Certain perceptions, interpretations, neutralizations, or definitions make the choice of crime "make sense." A second challenge is the emotions that offenders might feel that might arise and escalate to the point where opportunities are not resisted. A third challenge is the capacity of offenders to exercise self-control (or self-regulation) when a crime opportunity would provide them with immediate gratification and is easily within reach. And a fourth challenge is whether supervisees have the problem-solving skills to choose an alternative, noncriminal solution when the opportunity to offend is encountered.

For each of these four challenges—crime-conducive thinking, emotions, personal control, and problem solving—the discussion that follows includes two subsections.

First, an explanation of how each situational challenge is related to an offender's choice to pursue a crime opportunity is provided. The specific inducements for each offender will be different, but we believe that they can be categorized generally into these four groups. Second, specific cognitive-behavioral tools are presented that have applications for training probationers and parolees to resist the chances to commit crime that they will encounter. The cognitive-behavioral techniques used to reduce an offender's situational propensity will vary according to his or her specific criminogenic needs and capacity for change. Yet despite this individualization, the approaches that follow are widely applicable, flowing from the research of "what works" in changing problem behaviors. While implementing these strategies, either in formal programs or as a tool for officers to use when conversing with their clients, there are bound to be hurdles (see Chapter 7). However, we believe that the effectiveness of cognitive-behavioral therapies can augment opportunity-reduction supervision in many ways. Thus, the solutions we present below on how probation and parole officers can help offenders to resist taking advantage of crime opportunities are but initial ideas. These ideas would require experimental applications and evaluation, but are based on solid evidence of how best to reduce problematic behavior.

CRIMINOGENIC THINKING

The Challenge. One of the strongest and most reliable predictors of criminal behavior is antisocial cognition (Andrews, 1995; Andrews & Bonta, 2010; Gendreau, 1996; Glick, 2006; Van Voorhis et al., 2009). Cognitions refer to values (e.g., physical fighting demonstrates masculinity), beliefs (e.g., all police officers are corrupt), rationalizations (e.g., victims are deserving of the victimization), and emotional dispositions (e.g., a preference for defiance). The thought contents and thought patterns of offenders are important, because research shows that thinking bridges the gap between what people observe from the world and how they feel and act in response (Leahy & Rego, 2012). What this means is that when problem behaviors of any variety occur, they originate from dysfunctional thought processes (Spiegler & Guevremont, 2009). Biased ways of thinking can be based in biology or early upbringing, but the cause of the distorted cognitions is somewhat unimportant. Of greater concern for community corrections authorities is the cause of the undesirable behaviors (ranging from lying to drug use to violence), which are due, in large part, to maladaptive thinking.

There are multiple problems that can occur when an individual processes information (for a review, see Burns, 1989; also, Beck, 1976). Common thinking errors include exaggerating perceptions or making overgeneralizations (e.g., "Everybody hates me."), making irrational connections between causes and consequences, (e.g., "If I fail this exam I'm going to get thrown out of college and then I'll lose my job and then I'll be homeless."), and discounting important pieces of data that would contradict extreme outlooks (e.g., "I got second place out of fifty participants. I'm such a loser."). Interest in criminogenic thinking has surged in the past generation, with two recent constructs (among several others) being developed to pinpoint what kinds of thoughts are crime-conducive. One scale, called the Criminogenic Thinking Profile (CTP; Mitchell & Tafrate, 2012), contains eight dimensions; these include a disregard for others, demand for excitement, poor judgment, emotional disengagement, parasitic or exploitive worldview, justifying antisocial behavior, inability to cope, and grandiosity. Another measure, the Criminogenic Cognitions Scale (CCS; Tangney et al., 2012), consists of five categories; these include notions of entitlement, failure to accept responsibility, short-term orientation, insensitivity, and negative attitudes toward authority. Research evidence is accumulating that shows that these types of thinking patterns often lead to criminal behavior.

And although the adjustment of thinking errors is a relatively new addition to criminal rehabilitation, the link between thoughts and criminal behavior can be seen in earlier criminological theories. Perhaps most notably, Sykes's and Matza's "techniques of neutralization" (1957) include five personal justifications an individual might use to engage in deviant behavior. Indeed, removing excuses that condone criminal behavior is one of the components of situational crime prevention (Clarke, 1997; Cornish & Clarke, 2003; Felson & Clarke, 1998; Wortley, 2001; see also Yochelson & Samenow, 1976). Additionally, social learning theories of crime contain individual "definitions" (i.e., beliefs, attitudes, justifications, and orientations) that explain how wayward behavior develops (Akers, 1998; see also Cullen, Wright, Gendreau, & Andrews, 2003). Later research has even suggested that for many active offenders, criminal thinking is accepted and sometimes even expected, and prosocial thoughts and values require justification or new learning (Anderson, 1999; Brezina, Agnew, Cullen, & Wright, 2004; Stewart & Simons, 2010; Topalli, 2005).

There are dozens of thought patterns that the literature has identified as being criminogenic. To be consistent with the concepts of situational propensity and situational challenges, we propose that crime-causing thinking be organized around techniques of situational crime prevention (Cornish & Clarke, 2003). To teach offenders to resist crime opportunities, five categories of thinking errors must be controlled: an underemphasis of the effort involved in crime, inaccurate ideas about crime risks, grandiose perceptions of the rewards of offending, fallacies about what provokes crime, and excuses that facilitate offending. Space limitations prevent a thorough development of these categories (thereby prompting the need for further research; see Chapter 7), although they generate targets for change in training offenders to resist crime opportunities.

What Probation and Parole Officers Should Do. The underlying principle of cognitive-behavioral interventions is that if a person's thoughts are altered, his or her behavior will change (Glick, 2006). To reduce re-offending, then, the goal for probation and parole officers is to address situational thinking errors and replace them with prosocial attitudes and beliefs. One effective method of changing thinking errors is "cognitive restructuring." This process reduces distortions in thinking by (1) recognizing inaccuracies in how the client interprets and evaluates his or her surroundings (housed within the five aforementioned categories), (2) identifying proper alternatives to these cognitive faults, and (3) rehearsing prosocial thought patterns. Community corrections meetings provide a wonderful window in which officers can restructure criminogenic thinking in their clients in order to help offenders resist crime opportunities (Bonta et al., 2011; Raynor & Vanstone, 2015; Smith et al., 2012).

One cognitive restructuring tool that is useful for probation and parole officers is getting clients to talk about their thoughts. Many offenders have not learned to engage in "metacognition" (which is when a person thinks about thinking); intro-spection—examining your own thoughts and feelings—is a skill that requires training and practice. Through a specially designed dialogue (such as Socratic interviewing and vertical descent; Leahy & Rego, 2012; O'Donohue & Fisher, 2012), offender supervisors can guide their clients to understand how decision making occurs. Although it perhaps seems commonsensical on the surface, verbalizing a complex chain of thoughts and choices is a challenging task (i.e., Thought A → Thought B → Thought C → Decision Z). However, helping probationers and parolees to map these linkages is an important step toward producing rational choices (Beck & Clark, 1997; Hope, Burns, Hayes, Herbert, & Warner, 2010).

The three-prong cognitive restructuring process is an excellent teaching tool for opportunity resistance. For example, with help from his probation officer, John Smith identifies a common pattern of thoughts he has: That man looked at me rudely → I feel disrespected → I don't want my friends to think I'm not manly and tough → I have to defend myself → I punched that man in the face. The probation officer uses special interview techniques to help John realize what cognitive distortions were present in his decision-making process (e.g., maybe the glance was misconstrued as rude, perhaps rude glances are not an affront to masculinity, standing up for yourself is not the same thing as proactive aggression). John is then encouraged to evaluate the credibility of his original thought process. There are dozens of tools available for moderators to complete this activity, such as self-reflection, asking others, examin-ing logic, reverse role-playing, or behavior experiments (Leahy & Rego, 2012). The officer continues to help John outline his thinking errors by brainstorming about possible alternatives (e.g., The man looked at me rudely → I calmly asked him if I did something to upset him; or, I feel disrespected → I remind myself that not everyone has to like me). The final component of this process is purposeful practice. With the encouragement and guidance of his probation officer, John is given outlets to rehearse his new thought pattern. John and his supervisor might role-play several scenarios, or the probation officer could accompany John to an event where he might be required to use these skills. Through cognitive restructuring, John will eventually not require the help of his probation officer in thinking about how he makes deci-sions, what his thinking errors are, and how to develop prosocial alternatives. With practice, John will have the "self-talk" skills to complete this process independently. The expectation, then, is that the typical crime opportunity John is vulnerable to (signals of disrespect leading to physical violence) can be resisted because the proba-tion officer helped to restructure his criminogenic thinking.

As this example illustrates, addressing thinking errors is a pragmatic and effec-tive way to train offenders to think differently about available chances to commit crime. When officers are properly trained in cognitive-behavioral techniques, they can use these skills in client-officer meetings to shape the ways their supervisees think about offending (Bonta et al., 2011; Burnett & McNeill, 2005). Cognitive restructuring is an effective component of offender treatment, and should be incorporated into community corrections interventions (Petersilia, 2004; Wilson, Bouffard, & MacKenzie, 2005). Indeed, in a meta-analysis of cognitive-behavioral programs for offenders, Landenberger and Lipsey (2005) found that the treatment element of cognitive restructuring was significantly associated with the observed effect size, even after controlling for a number of methodological limitations (see also Lipsey, Landenberger, & Wilson, 2007). However, despite the strong empirical association between antisocial thoughts, values, and attitudes and criminal behavior, eliminating criminogenic thinking is not an all-inclusive solution to preventing recidivism. To equip community-supervised offenders to resist crime opportunities, corrections officers must also attend to the criminogenic emotions, personal controls, and problem-solving practices that probationers and parolees exhibit in their decision making.

CRIMINOGENIC EMOTIONS

The Challenge. When observing a criminal event, strong emotions are often readily apparent and salient in their effect (van Gelder, Elffers, Nagin, & Reynald, 2013). It is common to hear about offenders experiencing rage, jealousy, anxiety, boredom, or euphoria when committing crimes. Many times, criminal behavior is the consequence of these emotions (De Haan & Loader, 2002; Katz, 1988). Some theories speculate that the offense is a way to extend or terminate the feeling a person has (such as drug use to enhance sociability or assault to diffuse anger). When a crime opportunity exists, strong emotions may provide the motivation for a probationer or parolee to take advantage of the chance to offend. As such, an important component of individual crime prevention is ensuring that strong emotions are avoided or addressed through prosocial means; that is, that crime-conducive emotions are controlled and do not lead to crime.

Emotion regulation is the ability of a person to control his or her state of arousal in response to a particular stimulus. Emotions are discrete states of feeling that activate several other response systems, such as physiological, neural, or expressive reactions (Papa, Boland, & Sewell, 2012). Many of these emotional responses are biologically preprogrammed (like a hormonal reaction), while other emotional responses to stimuli are products of social learning (such as the association of excitement with risky behavior). People are taught to regulate their emotions based upon context; for example, the sensation of anger would be handled differently in the boardroom versus the football field versus the home. These socializations serve to modify existing knowledge and enhance an individual's adaptability to social situations (Levenson, 1999). Probationers and parolees may be more inclined to take advantage of a crime opportunity if they are not in control of their feelings. Community corrections authorities can work to reduce recidivism by minimizing the likelihood that emotions will trigger a criminal response. This is achieved by creating ways for offenders to independently regulate their emotions.

What Probation and Parole Officers Should Do. Several forms of emotion regulation aim to avoid activating the problematic feeling, such as staying away from bad environments, modifying the situation, or changing what the individual pays attention to (Gross, 1998); the following section of the current chapter discusses these strategies in greater depth. For existing emotions, however, alternative strategies are needed. That is, once an emotion arises, how can the intensity and duration of the arousal state be regulated? Once the offender already feels a certain way (i.e., restless, overexcited, enraged), how can the response be controlled? Probation and parole agents must address *how* their clients experience affective states in order to prevent them from pursuing crime opportunities (van Gelder et al., 2013). There are two categories of emotion regulation strategies that can help to train community-supervised offenders to resist the chance to commit crime even in the face of strong feelings.

First, probationers and parolees can be taught to engage in response modulation, whereby the experience of the emotion is altered. Emotional reactions themselves are often so deep-seated as to appear immutable; as such, changing the nature of this type of response may be an extremely difficult task. Indeed, some affective states are actually biologically based, either from birth, or the result of changes in the architecture of the brain following some environmental event. For example, a victim of childhood abuse may always feel fearful and defensive if she is yelled at, or a former alcoholic may always feel anxious and overstimulated when in the presence of alcohol. These reactions may always be present, and they generally cannot be addressed in the constraints of community corrections. Rather, the goal of offender treatment should be to influence the way that probationers and parolees experience feelings that may be criminogenic.

Common strategies for achieving this goal include thought suppression, relaxation and mindfulness, stifling the way the emotion is automatically expressed, and psychopharmacology (Papa et al., 2012). Popular corrections programs often incorporate these techniques, such as anger management training and instruction in coping skills (Andrews & Dowden, 2007; Sullivan, Helms, Kliewer, & Goodman, 2010). The aim of these interventions is not to extinguish the feeling, but to curb the reaction that the emotion typically invokes in the offender. For example, for an offender who reports that he is often angry, the goal of the supervising officer is not to eliminate all anger, but to redirect antisocial reactions (e.g., hitting someone) toward prosocial responses (e.g., going for a walk to "cool down").

Second, community-supervised offenders can be trained in cognitive reappraisal, whereby a person's evaluation of the situation that causes a problematic emotion is changed; this is done in order to prevent the emotional reaction that would generally be prompted. Thus, when taught to use alternative interpretations of situational triggers, offenders are less likely to experience negative affective states (Gross, 1998). For example, a domestic-violence perpetrator can learn through treatment how to reevaluate his or her home life, emphasizing the positive and downplaying the presence of conflict. Importantly, this technique has the additional benefit of highlighting the individual's activity patterns that create emotional distress, producing targets for change (Papa et al., 2012). A trained moderator can guide offenders through the identification of situations that lead to dysfunctional emotions. Then, in addition to avoiding those situations (see the following section), the counselor or offender supervisor helps the client to reinterpret those same triggers (e.g., appraising a disagreement of opinion as a normal exchange and not as a sign of disrespect).

When offenders can regulate their emotions, they are less likely to pursue an available crime opportunity. Whatever the source or the nature of the emotion, there is a consistent empirical association between an individual's inability to control personal feelings and aggressive or criminal behavior (Agnew, 1992, 2006; Davidson, Putnam, & Larson, 2000; Day, 2009; Karr-Morse & Wiley, 1997; Loeber & Hay, 1997; Sullivan et al., 2010). Adverse affective states like anger and fear are common human experiences, although perhaps especially when considering a criminal lifestyle; however, negative emotionality paired with poor constraint of these feelings is associated with offending (Agnew, Brezina, Wright, & Cullen, 2002; Caspi et al., 1994). Consequently, emotion control among community-supervised offenders should be enhanced; this gives supervisees the skills necessary to resist the temptation to commit crime when faced with an accommodating opportunity.

CRIMINOGENIC PERSONAL CONTROL

The Challenge. One of the most commonly hypothesized causes of crime is a lack of personal control. Self-regulation is the capacity of individuals to control their behavior in response to the thoughts and emotions that are produced in a given situation. Within criminology, Gottfredson and Hirschi (1990) labeled this ability "self-control" in their general theory of crime. Multiple studies have documented the fairly robust relationship between the capacity to regulate behavior and a variety of antisocial outcomes (Gottfredson, 2006; Pratt & Cullen, 2000). During terms of community supervision, offenders will at times have antisocial thoughts and antisocial feelings; even non-offenders experience these internal temptations to commit crime. What matters is whether probationers and parolees act on their criminogenic thinking and feelings, or whether they can regulate their behavior and resist the opportunity to relapse or re-offend.

As a result, community corrections agents can limit re-offending by addressing the way offenders control themselves in crime-conducive environments. Even when criminogenic thoughts are restructured and criminogenic emotions are constrained, some crime opportunities will still prove tempting. Perhaps the rewards are so abundant or the risks are so sparse that a criminal act may not be prevented by changing offenders' beliefs and feelings. Ultimately, when given the chance to break the law, probationers and parolees must have the skills necessary to resist acting upon the available opportunity. Offenders, a population of people not experienced in regularly exercising self-control, must be taught these techniques if they are expected to regulate their conduct.

What Probation and Parole Officers Should Do. When faced with a criminal opportunity, how can community-supervised offenders resist the urge to commit the crime? How can community corrections officers help to ensure that offenders will have the skills needed to resist these chances to break the law? There are dozens of techniques available to enhance self-control, although three may be of particular use for offender supervisors in teaching opportunity resistance.

First, and perhaps most central, is the executive modulation of attention. The ability to inhibit behavior depends upon the employment of voluntary attention (Karoly, 2012). In simpler terms, what people focus on and how they process information impacts how they behave. Although this capacity is usually developed in early adolescence, the skill can effectively be enhanced with coaching and deliberate practice for individuals deficient in this area (Rueda, Posner, & Rothbart, 2004). Training individuals to focus on top-down executive processes (i.e., increasing attention to the way decisions are produced) is one way behavioral regulation can be enhanced. To control their actions, people must become aware of the thought processes that lead to their behavioral choices.

Importantly, offenders often are not aware of what their thoughts are; metacognition (thinking about thinking) is a learned skill. The Effective Practices in Community Supervision model (EPICS) is an excellent example of this technique of attention in practice (see Smith et al., 2012; see also Bonta et al., 2011; Robinson et al., 2012). Probation and parole officers can help their clients to recognize the mental steps that take place in making choices. In EPICS, community corrections agents work with offenders to dissect their thought processes, verbalizing step by step what takes place in their mind when coming to a decision. When offenders learn to recognize how their thoughts lead to actions, they gain the insight needed to control their behavior.

Second, self-efficacy is an important ingredient of self-control. The definition of self-efficacy is the belief an individual has about his or her ability to organize and create action toward the accomplishment of a desired objective (Bandura, 1997). The way people appraise their ability to regulate their own behavior impacts the outcome. What this means is that people with greater valuations of their self-control are indeed better able to control themselves (Karoly, 2012). If offenders *believe* they can control their own behavior, they are more likely to *actually* control their own behavior. Creating motivation to change is increasingly being valued as an important contributor to treatment success (Clark et al., 2006; Ginsburg et al., 2002; Taxman, Shepardson, & Byrne, 2004; Walters, Clark, Gingerich, & Meltzer, 2007), but the ability of an offender to translate that desire into desistance is more complicated. By enhancing a person's capacity for forethought, confidence in personal control is increased (Bandura, 1986).

Officers can help develop this skill with their clients by having them consider a given scenario and then outline different decisions as to how they might act. For example, an officer might have a supervisee imagine and practice the variety of ways he or she could respond if a bar fight developed, and then have the offender verbalize the sequence of thoughts for each imagined course of events. Probationers and parolees are more likely to regulate their behavior when their competency for how this process develops is enhanced. When offenders learn that they are in control of how they respond in any situation, they are willful actors in opportunity resistance.

Third, the development of self-cueing and self-administered consequences influence a person's success in self-regulation. The ability of an individual to control his or her behavior is in part related to internal signals about anticipated consequences and the personal administration of incentives and punishments (Bandura, 1986; Watson & Tharp, 2002). People are more inclined to control their behavior when they can predict stimulus-response linkages (Karoly, 2012). When offenders feel more confident about what they can expect to happen in response to their choices, they can better regulate their actions. Offenders can be taught to engage in mental imagery (through successive guided rehearsals) that explores the cues and consequences associated with their behavioral choices. To help develop this skill, community corrections officers can role-play with their clients, having them identify what triggered a certain behavior and what happened as a result of that action. With practice, offenders can learn to better predict the outcomes of their choices, and are therefore more likely to regulate their choices.

These skills have important implications for offender supervisors hoping to initiate lasting behavioral change as opposed to momentary behavioral control (Taxman & Byrne, 2001; Taxman et al., 2003). We want probationers and parolees to stop committing crime for good—not just while under criminal justice supervision. The sway the criminal justice system has over offender behavior is diminished once community corrections sentences are complete; therefore, supervising officers interested in long-term desistance must provide their clients with the tools they need to regulate their own behavior. Behavioral inhibition is a vital part of opportunity resistance: When offenders are in control of their conduct, encountering a tempting and accommodating pro-crime environment is less likely to result in an offense.

CRIMINOGENIC PROBLEM SOLVING

The Challenge. In their daily routine, offenders will encounter a number of difficult scenarios. While under community supervision, one such challenge offenders may face is the desire to "go straight" and lead a prosocial life while still embedded in a criminogenic environment (e.g., the same criminal friends, the same neighborhood values that support crime, the same easy access to substance use). This is one reason why community corrections interventions try to change the situations offenders find themselves in. Yet sometimes circumstances are not easily changed; perhaps employment is hard to secure, housing is hard to locate, and addictions are hard to overcome. In these cases, resisting the temptation to take advantage of familiar crime opportunities can be a habit that is not easily broken, so offenders need tools to respond to pro-crime environments in a way that is different than what they are used to. As discussed above, probation and parole officers can help their supervisees to resist opportunities to commit crime by reducing crime-conducive thoughts and feelings and by maximizing personal control. Yet when these offenders are actually facing the chance to break the law, they must have the skills to assess and resolve the problematic scenario. How can probationers and parolees evaluate their environment and make prosocial choices? One strategy is to enhance the problem-solving skills of offenders. The way people approach situations helps determine how they will act (Nezu & Nezu, 2012). Problem-solving therapy gives clients the tools needed to behave thoughtfully when faced with a difficult situation (D'Zurilla & Nezu, 2007). As such, offenders can resist crime opportunities when they are taught to evaluate their environment and develop rational reactions.

What Probation and Parole Officers Should Do. In addition to modifying thoughts and emotions (discussed previously), probation and parole officers can teach their clients how to solve problems. This helps offenders to evaluate crime opportunities, understand what choices they have available, make rational links between their behavior and likely outcomes, and appreciate the benefits of resisting chances to offend. Developing problem-solving skills involves four steps (Chang, D'Zurilla, & Sanna, 2004). First, offenders must be trained to properly define the problem. Clients are taught to accurately identify the facts of the situation and separate them from assumptions, to develop a realistic goal, and to recognize the obstacles that prevent the solution from being implemented. Second, clients engage in the creation of alternative courses of action. Offender supervisors can help their clients to imagine all the ways that they could possibly behave to achieve the goal and overcome the obstacles (as identified in the first step). Third, individuals are taught to make the most rational choice. This process involves predicting possible consequences of each alternative identified, engaging in a cost-benefit analysis of each possible choice, and creating a plan to achieve the selected goal. Fourth, offenders implement the solution and verify whether the goal was achieved; if not, the four-step process starts again.

Although the process of thinking logically about problem situations and deciding how to act seems straightforward, community corrections populations may actually have considerable difficulty in completing these steps. To effectively limit offenders from pursuing available crime opportunities, probation and parole authorities must teach their clients how to rationally view and solve problems. Community corrections officers trained in EPICS, for example, discuss common crime-conducive situations with their clients, and talk through the proper way to think about their behavioral responses. With guidance, offenders can develop the skills to "solve the problem" of crime opportunities, learning to choose the prosocial outcome from the available choices. A promising strategy is to extend these discussions into the community, allowing the supervising officer to help the client practice rational problem solving in the real world (Pew Center on the States, 2008b; Reentry Policy Council, 2005; Solomon, 2006; Taxman, 2006). With rehearsal, offenders will internalize this process, leading to prosocial problem solving in the absence of their corrections supervisor. Indeed, empirical evaluations of correctional programs demonstrate that cognitive-behavioral interventions that include the component of problem-solving training achieve significant reductions in relapse behaviors (Antonowicz & Ross, 1994; Gendreau et al., 2006; Landenberger & Lipsey, 2005). Learning to rationally evaluate the environment and thoughtfully respond can be an important contribution to recidivism prevention, and should be considered as a valuable component to opportunity resistance training.

Summary

Offenders on probation and parole will invariably come into contact with crime opportunities. Whether the encounter is accidental or on purpose, and whether the individual wants to pursue the opportunity or not, the chance to commit crime will arise. Accordingly, it is important for community corrections supervisors to know about the things that make their clients vulnerable to these crime opportunities, and then implement solutions that will help their clients to resist these crime opportunities. As discussed in this section, there are four strategies that may be helpful in promoting opportunity resistance among offenders: restructuring criminogenic thoughts, managing emotional reactions, regulating behavioral responses, and enhancing problem solving. These skills can be developed within formal program placements (such as individual counseling, group therapy, or skills training courses), and traditional methods of offender rehabilitation are certainly encouraged. However, probation and parole officers can nurture these skills during their normal interactions with their clients (Bonta et al., 2011; Smith et al., 2012). Because the goal is to alter the way offenders respond to the crime opportunities they encounter (as opposed to "fixing" deeply rooted psychopathologies), corrections agents are in a prime position to help offenders recognize and resist these opportunities.

Opportunity Avoidance

The previous section introduced four ways probation and parole authorities can help offenders to resist engaging in available opportunities to commit crime. These strategies matter, because community corrections populations *will* encounter chances to offend. In line with the larger theme of this volume, however, a promising strategy is to identify crime opportunities that each offender is vulnerable to in order to design supervision conditions that avoid environments containing those opportunities. Offender supervisors can help their clients to avoid chances to offend when they have a good understanding about what kinds of opportunities each individual client has pursued in the past, and therefore what crime opportunities the offender is vulnerable to moving forward. Using the assessment approaches discussed in Chapters 3 and 4, probation and parole officers can create routine activities that circumvent situations where the offender is likely to be tempted to commit a crime.

In this way, offender supervisors contribute to crime opportunity avoidance by establishing community corrections conditions that limit exposure to crime-conducive environments. Yet what about crime opportunities that probation and parole officers do not know about? Perhaps the offender was not truthful during the assessment process, maybe the offender's recollection was not accurate, or maybe the crime opportunities the offender finds tempting could change during the term of community supervision. Moreover, officers cannot develop case plans that eliminate exposure to all crime opportunities, and offenders will have to make daily choices that affect such exposure. Probationers and parolees retain some freedoms, and those choices can present opportunities to offend. For this reason, offender supervisors should help their clients to recognize environments where crime opportunities might exist, and give their clients tools to personally avoid those opportunities.

Indeed, offenders know their environments, routines, and vulnerabilities better than anyone else. Probationers and parolees have intimate experiences with what kinds of situations are more or less likely to lead to them committing a crime. As a result, offenders are in an excellent position to determine the people, places, activities, and triggers that are associated with crime opportunities (see, for example, Mischel & Shoda, 1995). With this information, offenders can avoid the situations where these chances to relapse flourish. However, the process of assessing environments for possible crime opportunities (and then choosing prosocial surroundings) is another specialized skill that requires learning, practice, and coaching. Probation and parole officers are knowledgeable about their clients' crime opportunities, and can help nurture the skills their supervisees will need to recognize and avoid these opportunities. The offender's case plan will account for many probable crime opportunities, although the offender will be an active participant in choosing many of his or her daily movements (e.g., which route to take to work, whether to attend a social gathering, or how to spend leisure time). Consequently, it is vital that community-supervised offenders know how to make prosocial choices in order to avoid crime opportunities.

The current section contains two branches of discussion. First, specific skills for avoiding crime opportunities are introduced. Drawing on the knowledge of the effective components in cognitive-behavioral interventions, strategies are outlined for assessing and selecting environments free from crime opportunities. In addition to traditional forms of therapy, techniques are suggested that probation and parole officers can use in their meetings with offenders to help them avoid high-risk situations. Second, methods for encouraging desistance are explored. Research on the cessation of offending demonstrates several routes through which probationers and parolees could stop committing crime. Three theories are presented that associate prosocial routine activities (i.e., the avoidance of crime opportunities) with desistance. Strategies for community corrections officers are provided that suggest how to replace pro-crime environments with prosocial alternatives in an effort to prevent re-offending.

SITUATION APPRAISAL AND SELECTION SKILLS

Despite the structure that a community corrections case plan provides, and even with the guidance that supervising officers might deliver, probationers and parolees are responsible for making day-to-day decisions. Offenders must decide where to go, who to spend time with, what to do, and when to do it, and all of these choices can introduce (or circumvent) a host of crime opportunities (see Eck & Weisburd, 1995). No matter how many supervision restrictions are imposed on offenders, they still have to navigate their own way through their daily routines. Accordingly, offender supervisors can help their clients to avoid environments where crime opportunities are likely to exist by training them in two skills: situation appraisal and situation selection.

First, community-supervised offenders must learn to accurately evaluate their options. To avoid crime opportunities (i.e., to steer clear of environments where chances to offend are available), probationers and parolees have to be able to assess each possible choice. Community corrections officers can nurture situation appraisal skills among their clients by helping offenders to identify the thoughts, emotions, behaviors, and physical stimuli associated with different environments. Offenders can be taught to investigate their own personal schemas; these are pieces of information that are grouped together to help process decisions (Papa et al., 2012). How this information is grouped is very telling, and can reveal problematic situations offenders find themselves in (Gross, 1998). For example, a certain friend may be associated with aggressive conduct, a given street segment might be linked with temptations to commit a property crime, or participation in a leisure activity may lead to the desire to use drugs. Offender supervisors can guide their clients through the process of determining what factors trigger offending and when/where/with whom these factors occur. By understanding the association between environmental features and antisocial conduct, offenders are better equipped to conclude which situations are high-risk for crime opportunities.

Second, once offenders have assessed different situations, they must be able to choose their activities so as to avoid likely opportunities to offend. Having information about pro-crime environments will not be valuable unless probationers and parolees can use that information to design their daily routine. Offender supervisors can enhance the situation selection skills of their clients to encourage thoughtful day-to-day choices that will avoid exposure to crime opportunities. After assessing each possible choice, community corrections officers can guide offenders in thinking about how these situations are linked to one another, learning how the initial choice of environment triggers a chain of events that leads to other environments (Leahy & Rego, 2012). For example, choosing to walk one route to work will lead the offender to encounter antisocial associates, which may then lead to substance use, or, choosing to refrain from drinking alcohol while at a social event will lead to fewer feelings of anger, which will help to prevent a fight. While all of these environments will probably contain some crime opportunities, some choices are better than others; some situations have fewer chances to offend, and some situations will prove to be less tempting for the individual. As such, offenders must be aware of how situation selection can prompt an unfolding of events that leads them to trouble, even when the initial environment may seem innocuous (e.g., "I'm just going to a party. Where's the harm in that?"). Probation and parole officers can exercise and strengthen this skill by discussing how the initial selection of an activity naturally leads to other situations (e.g., the party may present chances to use drugs or get drunk, or previous co-offenders or victims may also be attending). Helping offenders to analyze a string of associated events that is more or less conducive to offending will aid in prosocial decision making.

ENCOURAGING DESISTANCE

In addition to helping community-supervised offenders make choices that avoid crime-conducive situations, opportunities to offend can likewise be discouraged by involving offenders in prosocial activities. Indeed, the principles of conditioning toward behavior modification indicate that patterns of activity are not eliminated, but replaced (Spiegler & Guevremont, 2009). Avoiding pro-crime environments is an important part of community supervision, but desistance is more likely if anti-crime substitutes are also provided (Farrall, 2002; Jannetta et al., 2009; Wilkinson, 2004). By engaging their clients in a prosocial lifestyle (and providing incentives for participation), probation and parole officers are helping offenders to develop the tools needed to desist from crime in the long term, beyond temporary compliance. Research on how people become involved and uninvolved in crime reveals that there are three dominant explanations for how an individual may cease offending after exposure to a prosocial routine.

First, research on life-course criminology (the study of how criminal behavior is initiated, maintained, and dies down) demonstrates that there are a number of "pathways" that lead people into and out of crime. These trajectories associate personal characteristics and experienced life events with social surroundings. For example, maturing past the teenage years usually corresponds with a new friendship network, and getting married often involves a change in how leisure time is spent. Crime theorists have speculated that these transitions are in part responsible for why offenders stop committing crime. Early studies of delinquency noted the powerful influence of "maturational reform," the idea that deviant youth often "grow out of" misbehavior (Matza, 1964). Similarly, in their landmark longitudinal studies of a single cohort across time, Glueck and Glueck (1950, 1968, 1974) demonstrated that criminal conduct peaks in late adolescence/early adulthood, and declines rapidly thereafter (see also Moffitt, 1993). The generation of life-course research that followed aimed to identify the life events that lead to these transitions in lifestyle. In particular, popular approaches to understanding desistance have sought to explain how these "turning points" produce an increase in informal social control through social ties (Laub & Sampson, 2001, 2003; Sampson & Laub, 1993, 2005).

Second, psychological studies of desistance indicate that when offenders become involved in prosocial activities, a cognitive transformation takes place. In-depth case studies of offenders show that the process of desistance (or of recidivism) is characterized by having internal and external influences match (Farrall, 2005). When offenders have a criminal mindset and are embedded in pro-crime surroundings, they are unlikely to stop committing crime. Yet when offenders are engaged in anti-crime routines and also have anti-crime attitudes, ceasing criminal behavior is more likely to occur. Qualitative research demonstrates that people's environments and mentality are symbiotic, or reciprocating (Giordano, Cernkovich, & Rudolph, 2002). This is important for community corrections populations: Involvement in prosocial activities leads to prosocial thinking, and anti-crime attitudes place offenders in anti-crime situations. These cognitive transformations can be instigated even if the prompting environment is initially forced (LeBel, Burnett, Maruna, & Bushway, 2008). Social events (such as a new job, a change in peer networks, or even a transition from prison to community) act as "hooks for change," allowing offenders to go through the motions of prosociality while their thinking changes to reflect the new lifestyle (Giordano et al., 2002). Whether through an apparent epiphany or a subtle alteration in attitudes, participation in prosocial activities helps to encourage desistance (Farrall, 2005).

Third, research that tracks offenders during the desistance process shows that the transition is gradual and often takes several years. This progression away from criminality involves offenders changing how they evaluate themselves and their opportunities—including chances to offend (Byrne & Trew, 2008; LeBel et al., 2008; Maruna, 2001). Offenders are enmeshed in a labeling process—derived from the "looking glass self" (Maruna, LeBel, Mitchell, & Naples, 2004)—in which their self-concepts for the future are largely derived from the definition the environment ascribes to them. For example, the activities associated with being on parole versus being a member of a church group imply different identities; in other words, what you do reflects who you are. In working toward a crime-free self, research suggests that offenders have a "working self," whereby desistance from crime develops only after opportunities consistent with a prosocial identity become available (Paternoster & Bushway, 2009). Accordingly, embedding active offenders in anti-crime environments helps to refashion how they conceptualize themselves (Kazemian, 2007). The expectation is that by exposing offenders to prosocial surroundings, they are encouraged to adopt an identity that is consistent with the behavioral expectations found there. Aside from providing their clients with anti-crime influences, community corrections officers can help offenders to understand that a past identity does not dictate future life choices (Maruna & Roy, 2007). Probationers and parolees must believe that they can redefine themselves outside of criminal justice labels. Indeed, the process of "knifing off" the old criminal identity (i.e., cutting bonds to a pro-crime lifestyle) is largely related to removing opportunities to maintain offending (Laub & Sampson, 2003; Maruna & Roy, 2007).

These three theories, though different in their proposed catalyst for change, offer a similar perspective: When offenders are embedded in prosocial environments, they observe and adopt prosocial behaviors. The context in which offenders are placed can help to encourage desistance by creating new life trajectories, producing changes in thinking, or transforming criminal identities (Bottoms, Shapland, Costello, Holmes, & Muir, 2004). For these reasons, community corrections officers can contribute to the success of their clients by enmeshing them in routine activities that are anti-crime. Probation and parole authorities can lead offenders through "behavioral activation," which is the guided practice of prosocial engagement to help increase positive reinforcement. For instance, officers can meet with their supervisees in the community, walking them through a daily prosocial schedule

(Pew Center on the States, 2008b; Reentry Policy Council, 2005; Reinventing Probation Council, 2000; Solomon, 2006; Taxman, 2006). Offender supervisors should try to arrange the situation so that probationers and parolees feel good about their new lifestyle and want to continue on this new path (e.g., being complimented for doing something nice for someone or receiving a tangible reward for success-fully filling out a job application). Furthermore, supplanting criminogenic routines with prosocial activities helps offenders to refine their skills in opportunity avoid-ance. When offenders are placed in anti-crime environments, they begin to develop new personal schemas; simply, situations that are high risk for crime opportunities are more easily recognized and avoided when compared to prosocial alternatives (Farrall, 2005; Giordano et al., 2002; Maruna et al., 2004; Paternoster & Bushway, 2009). Offender supervisors help their clients to stop committing crime when sub-stitutable and preferred activities are made available.

Conclusion

As we have proposed, offender supervision in the community can be refashioned according to the insights of environmental criminology and crime science. By determining what crime opportunities probationers and parolees are susceptible to, their surroundings can be redesigned (through case plan stipulations and other community interventions; see Chapter 6), effectively limiting their chances to offend. Unfortunately, however, community corrections authorities cannot elimi-nate all crime opportunities. Accordingly, offender supervisors are wise to also address their clients' susceptibility to these opportunities, termed here "situational propensity." Offenders will be more or less inclined to observe and pursue chances to break the law, and will variably respond to different forms of treatment. Probation and parole officers can capitalize on this reality by working to adjust the ways in which offenders think about their environments and make choices.

As discussed in this chapter, cognitive-behavioral interventions are particularly useful for altering crime opportunity-related propensities. Techniques of situational crime prevention (Clarke, 1997; Cornish & Clarke, 2003; Felson & Clarke, 1998; Wortley, 2001), organized around five categories, outline different ways of reducing opportunities to commit crime. We propose that reducing situational propensity can likewise be organized around these categories of intervention. The relationship between different targets of offender treatment and traditional situational crime prevention strategies is presented in Figure 5.1. An offender's relationship to crime opportunities can be addressed through three headings, using the five categories of situational interventions.

First, offenders may be inclined to break the law, despite what the environment looks like. Situational interventions that address this propensity should be aimed at decreasing the excuses offenders make. Ultimately, probationers and parolees are responsible for their actions, and this insistence (strengthened through self-control training and increasing problem-solving skills, for instance) will reduce their pro-pensity to take advantage of crime opportunities. Second, offenders must learn to

Situational Crime Prevention Interventions	Cognitive-Behavioral Interventions		
	Reducing Propensity	Crime Opportunity Resistance	Crime Opportunity Avoidance
Increasing Risk			✓
Increasing Effort			✓
Decreasing Rewards		✓	
Decreasing Provocations		✓	
Decreasing Excuses	✓		

Figure 5.1   Intersection of Cognitive-Behavioral and Situational Crime Prevention Interventions

resist available chances to break the law. Situational crime prevention interventions can contribute to this goal by minimizing the rewards and provocations associated with those opportunities. When the benefits of crime are reduced and the situational triggers for offending are decreased, supervisees will be better suited to resist the chance to offend. Third, offenders should be trained in the skills needed to avoid environments where crime opportunities are likely to be available. Based on the situational crime prevention literature, useful techniques for encouraging opportunity avoidance are increasing the risks associated with crime and increasing the efforts needed to commit the crime. If offenders see crime as more difficult to do, then they are in a better position to identify and avoid situations that are conducive to crime (e.g., stealing money from someone's desk that was in plain sight has fewer risks and effort than breaking into a bank vault; thus, the latter event is more recognizable as a crime opportunity, and can be understood as a situation to avoid).

This intersection of cognitive-behavioral techniques and situational crime prevention provides a novel approach to reducing offenders' exploitation of available crime opportunities. Although further theoretical refinements are necessary (achieved through empirical tests of the relationships proposed above), there is promising reason to believe that cognitive-behavioral and environmental criminology interventions can complement one another. With this new avenue in mind, it is important for readers to note that traditional offender treatments and program placements are still worthy pursuits. Probation and parole officers can be active participants in interrupting their clients' criminogenic opportunities and propensities. In particular, offender supervisors should not solely be bureaucrats or case managers, but should use meetings with their supervisees as chances to intervene (Raynor & Vanstone, 2015), substituting crime-conducive environments with prosocial routine activities.

E-technology might also be employed in these efforts. Notably, this technology is being used to provide "mobile persuasion" to assist individuals to meet performance goals, maintain diets, and manage chronic diseases (Fogg & Eckles, 2007). As Byrne and Pattavina (2013) note, it also opens the way for supervising officers to interact with offenders when the risk of recidivating is elevated. Much as a lifeline can be used by elderly who have fallen to summon immediate rescue, iPhone applications would allow offenders to request and receive help from officers when they feel vulnerable to breaking the law. Mobile persuasion also is a key tool for probation and parole officers to utilize strategically and situationally. Thus, Byrne and Pattavina observe that supervising officers "can send mobile reminders and support" to offenders "during risky times and places associated with relapse and use positive messages in real time for offenders as they make positive choices" (2013, p. 127; see also Cullen, Jonson, & Mears, 2015).

Still, there are certain aspects of crime opportunities and propensities that are beyond the job role and resources available to community corrections officers. For example, offender supervisors cannot give extensive attention to substance abuse treatment, psychotherapy, or employment training (especially if the focus of community supervision changes to opportunity reduction). For this reason, it is necessary for probation and parole agencies to become skilled in case plan coordination. This way, officers can focus on the immediate targets for change (i.e., crime opportunities), allowing for other service providers to meet these other criminogenic and concrete needs.

Indeed, there are a number of agencies outside of corrections authorities that can contribute to offender desistance and public safety. Crime problems are often community problems, therefore local community members and agents have specialized knowledge about what crime opportunities exist and how they can be combated (Community Policing Consortium, 1994). Probation and parole officers should foster collaborations with people familiar with offenders and their environments to extend the influence of correctional supervision (Pew Center on the States, 2008b; Reentry Policy Council, 2005; Solomon, 2006; Taxman, 2006). Because community corrections supervisors cannot watch and respond to all of their clients at all times, additional parties can be recruited to help reduce available crime opportunities and manage offender behavior (Taxman, Young, & Byrne, 2004).

One potentially fruitful partnership is between corrections authorities and the police (Schaefer, Eck, & Cullen, 2014). As the following chapter explores in great detail, police agencies and their representatives are in an excellent position to influence offender activities (Murphy, 2005). The discussion in Chapter 6 details how police officers can work with probation and parole agents to limit opportunities for offending. Moreover, the police are well positioned to solicit and train third parties in the community to provide aid that can likewise contribute to crime prevention and offender success (Mazerolle & Ransley, 2005). Collectively, the police and similar agents can assist corrections authorities in reducing crime opportunities for offenders under community supervision. This sort of police-corrections partnership has the obvious benefits of enhanced surveillance and enforcement for active offenders. Yet more subtly, by recruiting the assistance of police agencies to reduce and block access to crime opportunities, probation and parole authorities are able to pay more attention to minimizing their clients' situational propensity. Addressing both of these ingredients—opportunity and propensity—will reduce recidivism, but community corrections agencies would struggle to do it all alone. We recommend that probation and parole departments solicit the aid of police agencies in this new model of offender supervision. The following chapter outlines the important role that police might play.

6

How the Police Can Help

In the 1980s and beyond, increasing efforts were made to infuse community corrections with "get tough," deterrence-oriented practices (Cullen, 2002). Probation and parole officers were encouraged to carry guns, talk tough, and engage in "pee 'em and see 'em'" or "tail 'em, nail 'em, and jail 'em'" supervision (Cullen & Jonson, 2011; Skeem & Manchak, 2008; Stohr & Walsh, 2011). The rejection of rehabilitation in favor of control was typically done with much hubris and in the absence of empirical evidence that punitive practices are effective. As we have seen, this approach proved to be ineffective, failing to blunt offender recidivism and placing public safety at jeopardy.

Ironically, at around the same time, policing in the United States experienced a dramatic turn in the opposite direction. The crime-busters model—one that had the police arrive at a crime scene with sirens blaring and guns drawn—was seen for what it was: a failure. While probation and parole officers were encouraged to become more like police officers, police officers were encouraged to be what their corrections counterparts were once expected to be: problem solvers. In this model, crime can only be understood if it is studied and resources are allocated depending on the seriousness of the problem. Over the past thirty years, police officials thus have developed an array of methods for identifying problems (e.g., crime hotspots), analyzing the sources of the problem, and then developing responsive interventions. Many of these interventions are based on situational crime prevention aimed at opportunity reduction.

In this chapter, we propose that the police, who are far more advanced in techniques of crime-opportunity reduction than corrections organizations, have developed a wealth of insights and practices that can help probation and parole officers to supervise offenders more effectively. Specifically, following the advent of problem-oriented policing (Goldstein, 1990) and the development of tools related to this approach (Braga, 2002; Braga & Weisburd, 2010), many police departments have established expertise in the practice of analyzing and addressing crime problems. Thinking about community-supervised offenders and the risk of relapse as a specific type of crime problem, the police are well situated to assist probation and parole departments in creating tailored solutions. This assistance might come in the form of direct police-corrections agency partnerships or in the efforts of police officers supplementing the work of probation and parole officers. Both of these approaches pursue the model of "the new criminal justice," which reorients the components of the criminal justice system away from independent sequential work and toward meaningful collaborative partnerships in which resources are pooled to solve crime problems (Klofas, Hipple, & McGarrell, 2010).

Organized around the crime triangle, we identify three strategic categories of how the police can help community corrections officers wanting to reduce crime opportunities for their clients: (1) increasing the supervision of offenders, (2) increasing the surveillance of targets and places, and (3) increasing the surveillance of crime controllers. We discuss specific tactics within each of these three categories in turn below.

Increasing the Supervision of Offenders

Control theories of crime expect that people will break the law unless some other force stifles that inclination. According to Travis Hirschi (1969), an individual's "bonds" to society help to "control" criminal motivation. When people are attached to society, involved in conventional institutions, committed to conformity, and believe in the legitimacy of social rules, they are less likely to commit crime. A person who is connected to social order can therefore be controlled by that social order. Using Hirschi's (1969) control theory as a guide, Felson (1986) suggested that these social bonds are like "handles" attached to people. Anyone who can "grasp" this handle can influence the behavior of that person. As such, an offender handler is someone who supervises a likely offender and can moderate criminal motivation (Felson, 1995).

Offender handlers are often characterized as relying on informal social control. Importantly, however, the police can use their formal control to affect offender behavior. How can police officers use their authority to help supervise offenders on community corrections? As this section outlines, there are three ways in which the police help to "handle" offenders, reducing the likelihood that probationers and parolees will take advantage of available crime opportunities. Community corrections agents can partner with the police to (1) help ensure that offenders comply with supervision conditions so as to reduce access to crime opportunities, (2) encourage prosocial norms and develop/reinforce anti-crime routine activities among offenders to reduce the temptations of crime opportunities, and (3) monitor co-offender networks to minimize supervisees' exposure to crime opportunities. Using examples from existing partnerships between police and probation and parole officers, each of these tactics is presented in the discussion that follows, showcasing how police expertise in opportunity reduction can augment environmental corrections.

ENSURING COMPLIANCE

In a perfect world, community-supervised offenders would follow the stipulations of their conditional release. In fact, many scholars and practitioners alike have reasonably questioned why offenders are not *eager* to abide by their supervision conditions. When followed, these rules have two advantages that seem worthy of pursuit. First, community corrections case plans help to keep probationers and parolees out of trouble (thus avoiding a variety of punishments, including revocation of supervision and subsequent incarceration). Second, these restrictions and prescriptions for offenders' behavior provide a number of valuable prosocial pathways (such as social services) that promote desistance. Yet the motivation to "go straight" is not always predictive of positive corrections outcomes. Even when offenders feel inspired to follow the instruction of the courts and their supervising officers, they often still find themselves breaking rules.

As we have outlined in previous chapters, there are two reasons why this might be the case. First, some conditions are unreasonable (e.g., day-reporting requirements but also being required to work full time, or staying away from all other offenders). The argument we forwarded earlier is that these stipulations are only loosely (at best) tied to criminological theory, and that many of these generic conditions should be discarded or revised. Second, offenders wanting to do their best and "get back on the straight-and-narrow" can still be tempted by crime opportunities. For this reason, supervision conditions should be purposed around trying to reduce offenders' exposure to crime-conducive environments. Whether through restrictions (e.g., "do not go to that neighborhood because you are likely to get into trouble") or prescriptions (e.g., "do go to that church because it helps to keep you out of trouble"), the goal is to guide offenders away from crime opportunities. We believe that the ideas and tools proposed in this text will contribute toward that aim.

Probation and parole officers are the designated creators of opportunity-reduction initiatives for community-supervised offenders. The supervision conditions that these officers develop can present a strong line of defense against offender recidivism. Before detailing ways in which the police can (and do) help to enforce these opportunity-reducing stipulations, it is helpful to first briefly describe what compliance is, how it works, and why it is important.

The typology of offender compliance forwarded by Robinson and McNeill (2010) is a particularly useful heuristic. In their discussion of the differences in the length of compliant behavior, they note that short-term compliance can be either formal or substantive. Formal compliance (such as when offenders "go through the motions" and obey conditions on a surface level just to "get off paper") is a good start, but the desire of supervisors is for offenders to actively engage and cooperate with their orders. Explaining *why* offenders comply, Bottoms (2001) provides a four-pronged categorization: instrumental or prudential compliance (responding to incentives and punishments), constraint-based compliance (using physical barriers, reducing access to targets, or creating structural constraints to offending), habitual or routinized compliance (a lifestyle of activity that is engrained with prosociality), and normative compliance (accepting norms, social attachments, and beliefs about the legitimacy of prosocial behavior). Thinking about these two frameworks, it becomes clear that offenders on community supervision are going to comply at different rates, through different methods, and for different reasons. How can probation and parole officers flexibly respond to these differences?

Fortunately, the police are specialists at exercising their authority with variation. Under the problem-oriented approach to policing, line officers rely on multiple sources of information to understand the whole situation, use their discretion to solve the problem in the immediate context, and then apply resources to solve the underlying conditions that birth the problem (Peak & Glesnor, 2012). Police are intelligence experts when facing crime problems; their familiarity with their beat (and the community it is embedded in) and their understanding of the components of criminal opportunity are assets in preventing re-offending. Police officers often know many of the people in their jurisdiction who are on probation or parole (Leitenberger, Semenyna, & Spelman, 2003). The police have a wealth of information about situations (people, places, times, and crime attractors/buffers) that are criminogenic. This specialized knowledge alone makes the police qualified agents of opportunity reduction.

Beyond this routine crime prevention, probation and parole authorities can partner with the police to help maximize the reach and effectiveness of opportunity-reduction supervision. When offender supervisors provide police with information about their clients (e.g., who is on supervision, what environments are criminogenic triggers for different types of offenders, what the exact stipulations of the case plans are), police officers have another source of information. With this information, the police can solve crime problems even better, helping community-supervised offenders to avoid crime-conducive situations by complying with the conditions of their release. Existing corrections-policing partnerships show that there are two ways police officers can help to ensure that offenders comply with their supervision requirements.

First, the police are an ideal resource for formally enforcing known supervision conditions. These enhanced supervision partnerships involve police and probation/parole officers jointly checking up on key offenders and verifying that the rules of their case plan are being adhered to (and, if not, then collectively developing and implementing remediation measures). For decades, community corrections officers have worked with the police in fugitive apprehension units, serving warrants and performing roundups (Parent & Snyder, 1999). More recently, specialty programs have been developed to enforce specific supervision conditions (Reinventing Probation Council, 2000). One popular program, Operation Night Light, involves curfew checks for probationers and parolees as part of a larger focused deterrence strategy (reducing gang crime and gun violence; Jordan, 1998). Many comparable programs have been created with a similar purpose: By enforcing the rules already applied to offenders by the courts and corrections officials, the police were helping to stunt blossoming crime problems (Corbett, 2002; Parent & Snyder, 1999; Worrall & Gaines, 2006). Common tactics within these types of programs include joint patrols, home visits, employment and residency verifications, and consulting with the family and friends of supervisees. Through this collective and widespread presence, probationers and parolees have an increased certainty of detection and are therefore less likely to violate the stipulations of their conditional release (Hagenbucher, 2003).

Second, when the police know the opportunity-reducing supervision conditions of probationers and parolees in their beat, officers can regularly enforce those conditions while on patrol. The police represent the ultimate law enforcement authority to many offenders, and can therefore deter misbehaviors by relying on instrumental threats and constraints. Indeed, probationers and parolees may feel that they are safe to engage in criminal behaviors when beyond the reach of their supervising officer, so enlarging the pool of agents who are aware of supervision conditions (and can enforce them) is helpful. As place-based supervision becomes more common, "cop shops" are popularizing as locations (e.g., shared office space, coffee shops) where various arms of law enforcement work side by side. This results primarily in office personnel sharing information, but it also encourages joint problem-solving efforts. To enhance their presence, probation and parole officers are developing ways to provide the police with details about individual offender supervision conditions (Byrne & Hummer, 2004; Leitenberger et al., 2003). Examples include meeting to exchange notes, creating posters that police officers can take with them in their patrol cars, and giving briefings at the beginnings of policing shifts. Future solutions will likely include shared databases, where police officers will be able to view offenders' conditions of probation or parole on their patrol car computer (Griffin, Hepburn, & Webb, 2004). For the police to help ensure that community-supervised offenders comply with the stipulations of their release, police officers must first know what these rules are. As we discuss later, this task encounters many limitations (most surmountable, but still serious); therefore, probation and parole authorities should also seek to recruit police partners in developing other types of compliance.

ENCOURAGING PROSOCIAL NORMS

Ideally, community-supervised offenders would comply with the conditions of their case plan not only because they *have* to stay out of trouble, but also because they *want* to "go straight." Indeed, for long-term offender compliance once the community corrections sentence ends, offenders must comply with the law on their own, without the threat of correctional sanctions. How can this goal best be achieved? By being helped to make engagement in prosocial activities a habit, offenders should begin to invest in normative compliance; this occurs when offenders begin to participate in prosocial behavior because they believe in the legitimacy of prosocial values, as opposed to following the rules just to avoid being punished. Thus, in addition to removing offender access to crime opportunities, probationers and parolees should be immersed in routines that help to promote prosocial attitudes and beliefs (Farrall, 2002).

Community corrections officers encourage an anti-crime lifestyle in multiple ways, as discussed in previous chapters. Offenders are linked to treatments, social services, associates, and activities that discourage crime. Additionally, offender supervisors can reinforce positive demonstrations of prosociality, can use meeting time to develop prosocial skills, and can visit with their clients in the community to rehearse prosocial routines. Theories of desistance emphasize that conformity is in many ways due to social context and the "community" in which offenders are embedded (Bottoms et al., 2004). How can police officers help to supplement this groundwork for prosocial routines laid by corrections agents and their social service partners?

In this regard, there are two roles the police may be well suited to fill. First, the police are an outlet of service referral. Police officers' in-depth knowledge about the communities where they work gives them information about available services (La Vigne, 2008). It is a standard practice for line officers to divert juvenile offenders out of the criminal justice system and toward social services; this philosophy can and should be extended to community-supervised adult offenders. Where appropriate, police officers can encourage probationers and parolees to pursue the resources in their community, referring them to services that will contribute to reducing criminal opportunity and incentivizing desistance (Burke & Tonry, 2006; La Vigne, Solomon, Beckman, & Dedel, 2006). Second, the police are a source of offender praise. Police officers can encourage community-supervised offenders to be prosocial by reinforcing prosociality. Offenders can be coached to be anticriminal by rewarding positive behaviors as opposed to simply sanctioning negative actions (Robinson et al., 2012). Reinforcements can be negative (i.e., removing a noxious stimulus, such as reducing police questioning) or positive (i.e., adding a pleasant stimulus, such as giving compliments); either way, police officers are motivating offenders to keep engaging in prosocial activities and behaviors when the outcomes are enjoyable (Burke & Tonry, 2006; Taxman, Shepardson, & Byrne, 2004). As an important note, it is also likely that these actions may help to reduce police distrust and legal cynicism, which would produce a number of supplemental benefits (Goldsmith, 2005; Wells, 2007).

MONITORING CO-OFFENDERS

Criminological research has long acknowledged the potential criminogenic influences of peers. Indeed, one of the strongest correlations in criminological research is the positive association between the number of criminal peers an individual has and criminal involvement (Andrews & Bonta, 2010). There are many reasons why antisocial peers encourage antisocial behavior (see Felson & Boba, 2010; Warr, 2002). For community-supervised offenders, peers may bring crime opportunities to the offender, may bring the offender into environments that contain crime opportunities, may encourage the pursuit of crime opportunities, or may reinforce the offender when crime opportunities are acted upon. Thus, one component of crime reduction strategies is to disrupt the peer networks that stimulate and justify criminal behavior.

As discussed in previous chapters, probation and parole officers can help to prevent recidivism by guiding their clients away from certain peers and toward others.

Social network analyses can help supervisors determine the people who are high risk for offenders and their individualized crime opportunities. Beyond this formal approach to data collection and the development of related supervision conditions, the police are valuable assets in identifying and disrupting the peer networks that breed offending. With their familiarity of life in a particular community, police officers have expert knowledge of co-offending associations (La Vigne et al., 2006). The police are intimately aware of who knows who, and how these relationships present themselves—that is, where, when, how, and why the personal linkages emerge. Using this knowledge base, which individual patrol officers accumulate while on the job, police departments and their academic allies have been able to design interventions that disrupt the social networks that promote crime.

There are two crime prevention tactics in particular that can contribute to environmental corrections, each related to focused deterrence. Focused deterrence strategies seek to enhance the risk of apprehension would-be offenders are subjected to. Probation and parole authorities can partner with the police to apply focused deterrence methods in order to disrupt pro-crime peer groups. As opposed to generic threats of punishment, community corrections interventions can focus the intervention around certain points of leverage for each individual offender. We propose that the risk of offenders being detected and punished for committing crime can be enhanced in two ways: through highly specified threats/enforcements and through highly specific monitoring. In line with the SARA process within problem-oriented policing (see Chapter 2), these warnings and scrutiny are specific to a given crime problem. In this case, corrections-police partnerships can use two methods of increasing the risk that forbidden co-offender associations (through court order or through stipulations of the community supervision case plan) will be detected and reprimanded.

First, opportunity-reduction supervision can greatly benefit from the strategy of "pulling levers" (see Braga & Weisburd, 2012). Under this approach, a number of criminal justice and social service agencies combine their information about and approaches to a specific crime problem. By relying on these unique arrangements, the partnerships are able to "pull every lever" possible to apprehend and sanction offenders who contribute to that problem (Kennedy, 1998). In many of these arrangements, the focus is on eliminating the networks of co-offenders that contribute to crime problems (such as gang interventions). The police and their partners communicate to high-risk offenders (often probationers and parolees) a three-pronged message: (1) We know about your illegal activity and who is involved. (2) We are warning you that a failure to stop this activity by any member of your criminal network will result in swift and certain "hardball" punishments to all members of your criminal network. And (3) we can provide alternatives to those of you wishing to exit your criminal lifestyle. This message is delivered in a firm, repeated, and unwavering manner. Probation and parole agencies can cooperate with local police departments to tailor this strategy to the co-offender networks of community-supervised offenders. By focusing deterrence on the peers of probationers and parolees that get them into trouble (in addition to the probationers and parolees themselves), the number of available crime opportunities can be greatly reduced.

Second, knowledge about hotspots can be extended from places to social networks, in order to intensively monitor the activities of probationers and parolees and their co-offenders. Targeted enforcement of crime hotspots is generally effective at reducing the offending problem of concern (Braga, Papachristos, & Hureau, 2012), although these interventions are based around a particular physical place (such as a street intersection or nightclub). One important possibility is that these geographic concentrations of crime may involve groups of offenders and not just unrelated individual actors (Bowers & Johnson, 2004). As a result, hotspot policing may significantly help to disrupt co-offending networks. An alternative strategy is to broaden the definition of "hotspot." The policing tactics used to reduce crime concentrated in a certain place can likewise be used to reduce crime concentrated in a certain group. Probation and parole officers could provide police with information about the criminal associates of their clients, allowing police officers to monitor the peer networks in which community-supervised offenders are embedded. In this way, police officers would be able to ensure that offenders are complying with certain conditions of their supervision (i.e., activity/time/place restrictions based on known co-offenders), while also helping to discourage displacement from one pro-crime social network to another (Reiss, 1988; Sherman, 1992).

Increasing the Supervision of Targets and Places

As discussed in Chapter 2, environmental criminology creates theories that try to explain why crime is concentrated in certain places. Many police organizations no longer focus exclusively on offenders. Instead, their focus has shifted to include the criminogenic role of places, recognizing that features of a physical space might be attracting or creating offenders. As a result, crime science interventions have created new ways of analyzing and reducing crime problems in high-crime areas. Some of these approaches have been reactive (such as increasing the number of police in an area *after* an increase in crimes at a location), while other approaches are proactive (such as fixing signs of social disorder that might encourage offending in a place *before* it occurs).

Yet while the police have adapted a place-based orientation to how they view and address crime, corrections agencies have been slow to follow suit. Despite its conspicuous title, community corrections programs have not adopted theories and supervision practices that emphasize the role of place. The word *community* in community corrections merely indicates that the offender is subject to criminal justice control outside of an institutional setting. There are a number of benefits to community-based corrections programs aside from their being "less harmful than prison." Indeed, corrections sentences that are served in the community provide offenders with social supports and resources that encourage desistance. However, in addition to being potentially rehabilitative, an offender's community can also be criminogenic. If features of the community that caused a person to commit crime are not changed, then returning the person to that same community is not likely to prevent a return to criminal behavior.

For this reason, some experts have called for probation and parole supervision to be reoriented around offenders' communities, arguing that offender supervision should be a "corrections of place" (Clear, 1996; Clear & Corbett, 1999). Community characteristics are one of the major correlates of crime, so it makes sense that community corrections interventions should try to alter these crime-causing features in the community in order to eliminate some crime opportunities (Taylor & Harrell, 1996). The framework of place-based corrections seeks to understand an offender's community, making changes to the environment so that crime is less likely to occur there. This can be accomplished by recruiting the help of formal social controls (such as law enforcement officers, discussed in this section) and informal social controls (such as prosocial friends and institutions, discussed in the following section).

Realistically, what does it mean to supervise offenders in the community with a focus on "community"? While the previous section explored methods for enhancing the surveillance of offenders, the other two sides of the crime triangle must also be addressed: targets and places. Principally, probation and parole officers can create supervision conditions that restrict offender access to attractive targets and crime-conducive places. Case plans should (and generally do) contain stipulations that keep offenders away from risky situations where they are likely to relapse. As we have outlined in this book, it is important that offender supervisors create rules that are specific to the crime opportunities of each offender. For example, rather than telling clients that they cannot communicate with any other offenders, they might be given a list of five people that they are not allowed to speak to. Or, as opposed to telling offenders that they cannot go to any place that has certain triggers (e.g., drugs and alcohol, past victims, aggressive activities), the officer might list five specific places that they are not allowed to go to. These restrictions are based on the assessments of an individual offender's crime opportunities.

Yet even with these specialized supervision conditions, offenders are likely to encounter targets and places that may tempt them to commit crime. Many experts have argued that offender-officer meetings should occur in the community as opposed to a centrally located office (Pew Center on the States, 2008b; Taxman, 2006). In this way, officers can evaluate the daily routines of their clients, and revise supervision conditions to reflect current crime opportunities. Still, even with officers meeting with probationers and parolees in their home communities, offender supervisors cannot follow their clients around and patrol risky targets and places. The police, on the other hand, may be able to help fill this gap.

As the following discussion outlines, police partnerships with probation and parole agencies can contribute to a "corrections of place" in several ways. Community corrections can benefit from cooperation with the police through three related strategies: (1) specialized patrols of targets and places and enforcement of supervision conditions, (2) problem solving to identify and change places where crime opportunities are high, and (3) encouraging community crime control. Where they exist, examples of corrections-police partnerships are provided in the text that follows. Readers should note that there are practical hurdles and limitations to these partnerships (discussed in the concluding section of this chapter), although many can be overcome with careful foresight and organizational planning (see Chapter 7).

SPECIALIZED ENFORCEMENT

Police officers have skills that community corrections officers do not, especially related to patrol and surveillance (Parent & Snyder, 1999). Patrolling practices have become increasingly local, with the size of police beats shrinking; rather than patrolling an entire police district, officers are being assigned to small areas. As a result, police officers become intimately familiar with community life in their patrol. They become well acquainted with the dynamics in a given neighborhood, understanding how the people there interact with the physical space (e.g., patterns of movement around businesses at certain times of the day; La Vigne et al., 2006). These patrolling details are a key component of community-oriented policing, and increase the street presence of the law. In addition, the familiarity between police officers and community residents helps to develop trusting and timely exchanges about crime problems in the area (Jannetta & Lachman, 2011).

As a result of this familiarity, police officers are knowledgeable about the crime opportunities in the neighborhoods they patrol (Clear, 1996). Officers can identify the features in their beat that are conducive to criminal activity, whether it be a building, a street segment, a time of day, an activity, or the gathering of certain individuals. Through experience with crimes that have actually occurred, police have a knowledge base to also estimate what places and people and activities are likely to cause crime in the future. This intelligence can be a valuable reference for probation and parole officers when they are designing or revising conditions of supervision for their clients (La Vigne et al., 2006). Accordingly, police officers and community corrections officers should share information about offenders for which they are mutually concerned. Probation and parole officers want their clients to succeed in the community, and need information about the actual risks that their clients will face. Police officers want less crime in their patrolling area, and need information about the offenders who are embedded there. Likewise, community corrections officers are familiar with offenders and their risks for relapse, while police officers are aware of the crime opportunities in the community that reflect those risks (Jannetta & Lachman, 2011). By exchanging expertise, a partnership is created that more wholly addresses the risk factors that community-supervised offenders are vulnerable to, thereby reducing recidivism and enhancing public safety at once.

Moreover, when police officers are aware of specific case plan stipulations for individual probationers and parolees, they are well situated to help deter offenders from crime opportunities and enforce consequences for rule violations (Murphy & Lutze, 2009). This shared knowledge puts the police in the position to engage in specialized enforcements of existing supervision conditions. In the simplest form of this strategy, police officers can reprimand offenders for failing to comply with the rules of the their community supervision; these punishments can range from a warning, to reporting the violation to the supervising officer, all the way up to an arrest. In its more advanced form, specialized enforcements encourage police officers to help guide offenders away from environments where crime opportunities exist and are likely to prove tempting (Jannetta & Lachman, 2011). Probation and parole officers cannot account for all high-risk situations when they create supervision conditions for their clients. In addition, their knowledge of risks in the community does not update as frequently as it does for the police who work there. Consequently, police officers, as part of their normal patrol, can steer offenders away from antisocial influences (i.e., pro-crime places, people, and activities), and *toward* prosocial influences.

To focus these enforcements, probation and parole authorities might partner with police to develop task forces that are dedicated to policing high-crime targets and places. Some crime attractors may be off limits for all community-supervised offenders in a given neighborhood (e.g., all offenders released to Oak Ridge are forbidden to visit Al's Biker Bar or the Grove Street basketball court), so police officers can monitor these places for offenders who are not legally allowed to be there. More commonly, specialized police patrols might be revised to reflect *emerging* high-crime places, and could include ride-alongs with community corrections officers. Although such locations may not be mentioned in an offender's supervision conditions, officers can discourage probationers and parolees from placing themselves in risky situations. These joint efforts use "real-time" information to help guard targets and places that are welcoming of crime (Jannetta & Lachman, 2011).

In order to develop these partnerships, probation and parole and police agents must first share information. There are a number of methods for exchanging relevant data. Most commonly, officers meet periodically to discuss offenders of mutual concern. Within these partnerships, probation and parole officers will often reach out to police officers responsible for patrolling the area where their clients live, creating small-scale cooperation. In many instances, community corrections supervisors notify the police of at-risk probationers and parolees, and request that they be notified if any trouble emerges. At a larger level, interagency partnerships frequently develop a database that both parties contribute to and can access. These data sets include a wealth of offender information, such as photos and supervision conditions, that police officers can access in the field. Advances in police-corrections partnerships have led to the creation of specialized software programs that track offender interactions with officers, map offenders' locations (including areas that are off limits for particular individuals), pinpoint high-crime areas, and even link offenders to community resources and service referrals (Griffin et al., 2004; La Vigne, 2008; Lucht, La Vigne, Brazzell, & Denver, 2011; Rich, 1999).

Importantly, the framework of environmental corrections that we advocate in this book would make this type of data available. Through the assessments and outputs obtained by probation and parole officers, a great deal of information about offenders and crime opportunities is generated. Upon completion of the instruments presented in Chapter 4, offender supervisors shift their goal toward monitoring offenders' compliance with specific rules (as opposed to generic stipulations). This has important implications for police, as well. Rather than focusing their efforts on broad crime prevention, the police (through exchanges with community corrections agencies) can focus their attention on specific people and places. Databases could be built that would allow police officers to access information about offender-specific crime opportunities from their in-car computer. For example, a software program could be designed so that a patrol officer can specify a precise location, and have the computer generate photographs of people (and their corresponding information) who should not be there.

With these shared data, probation and parole officers can monitor police reports about their clients, and police officers can help to monitor community-supervised offenders while on their patrol. Specific techniques for creating and using these data resources are continually developing, as early data-sharing partnerships were hampered by a number of organizational issues (International Association of Chiefs of Police, 2007; Parent & Snyder, 1999). As previously stated, however, strong leadership, clear goals, and thoughtful planning can sidestep many limitations of information-sharing corrections-police partnerships (Murphy & Lutze, 2009; Murphy & Worrall, 2007).

OPPORTUNITY HOTSPOTS

Under the framework of environmental corrections, probation and parole authorities should seek to identify situations where crime opportunities are present. The crime opportunities that are "risks for relapse" are individualized for each community-supervised offender (see Chapters 3 and 4). Some offenders are tempted by certain targets and get into trouble at certain places, while other offenders are not very likely to commit crime with those targets and in those places. This specificity in offenders' criminogenic risks and needs is why supervisors must assess individual crime opportunities, and then develop a case plan that reflects these unique opportunity-related risks.

However, there is generally some overlap in the crime opportunities that probationers and parolees are vulnerable to. A large group of offenders may be tempted by similar targets, places, and activities. For this reason, it is helpful to consider "crime opportunity hotspots." Crime hotspot traditionally refers to concentrations of crimes in a certain area. The hotspot can vary by the type of crime (e.g., littering, burglary, gang violence), by the type of measure used (e.g., number of victimizations, calls for service, number of arrests), and by the area of interest (e.g., a specific street segment, a neighborhood, a region). Importantly: These hotspots are the product of crimes that have already been committed. Because community corrections officers want to prevent crimes from being committed, they should reframe their perspective to consider why crimes cluster in particular areas. Probation and parole authorities should question where crime *opportunities* are concentrated. That is, what targets and places attract and facilitate crime among offenders on community corrections supervision?

Answering this question requires different sources of information, and the varied perspectives of probation and parole officers and the police each contribute something unique. The police are aware of existing hotspots (where crimes *do* occur at high rates) and the detailed features of the communities they patrol. Community corrections agents know what crime opportunities are potentially risky for their clients and have a general idea about the kinds of environments that showcase these risks. By exchanging this information, it is possible to develop risk assessments for targets and places (Parent & Snyder, 1999). As stated by Eck, "Rather than concentrations of offenders or the absence of social controls, opportunity theories suggest that analysts should look for concentrations of crime targets" (2005, p. 9). As a result, corrections-police partnerships can identify situations that invite and allow crime.

In a way, probation and parole officers already do this when they tailor supervision conditions to a specific offender in a specific community. Yet these efforts can be augmented by police participation in two ways. First, the police can provide up-to-date information about crime opportunities that are emerging in offenders' neighborhoods. Second, some police organizations are highly skilled in situational crime prevention techniques that make targets less attractive and places less conducive to offending (Clarke, 1992). When hotspot policing emerged as a crime-fighting tool, many departments welcomed the strategy (Braga & Weisburd, 2010). The majority of police agencies now use hotspot policing (Police Executive Research Forum, 2008), so their knowledge of what works and why is a valuable resource for community corrections interventions. As problem-oriented policing has matured, research has better identified how crime hotspots develop and how to prevent crime in those places (Braga, Papachristos, & Hureau, 2014). Probation and parole agencies can maximize the success of their clients by incorporating this intelligence into their supervision strategies.

In order to respond to hotspots of crime opportunities, the crime problem first has to be measured and assessed (Clarke & Eck, 2005; Eck & Spelman, 1987a; Goldstein, 1990). Community corrections officers already know a great deal about the crime opportunities that are tempting for their clients, but they are less aware of how those opportunities relate to an offender's community (i.e., whether those crime triggers exist in the community and if so, where, when, and with whom). Probation and parole agents can better understand community-specific crime opportunities by meeting with their clients in the community (Pew Center on the States, 2008b; Reentry Policy Council, 2005; Solomon, 2006; Taxman, 2006). In addition to this "place-based supervision," community corrections organizations should confer with the authorities most familiar with the conditions in that community (Parent & Snyder, 1999). Police officers and neighborhood residents can help to detect the situations in their area that are likely to be attractors of crime.

Approaches to identifying hotspots of criminal opportunity will vary according to the size of the community, the resources available, and the needs of the probation or parole officer. Existing partnerships use individual contacts between officers (e.g., periodic phone calls to "catch each other up to speed"), scheduled brainstorming sessions (e.g., a weekly meeting between a community corrections officer and area police officers), and "town hall" meetings (where members of the community are invited to come and share ideas). Another helpful strategy might be for probation and parole officers to accompany police officers on their patrol on a regular basis (Jannetta & Lachman, 2011; Kim, Gerber, & Beto, 2010). These ride-alongs allow community corrections agents to see the actual crime opportunities in their clients' communities, and to learn from the police what targets and places are attractive to offenders (McKay & Paris, 1998; Moran & Guglielmi, 2001). Likewise, the police officers learn from the community corrections agents who is under community supervision, what stipulations offenders are subjected to, and how to use cognitive-behavioral techniques in interactions with offenders (Jannetta & Lachman, 2011).

Once identified, how can probation and parole officers partner with police agencies to eliminate these crime opportunity hotspots? While the solution must be specific to the individual crime problem, many techniques of situational crime prevention can be tailored to reduce vulnerable targets and crime-conducive places (Clarke & Eck, 2005). In addition to creating more crime controllers (e.g., training target guardians and soliciting place managers; discussed in the following section), community corrections authorities can recruit the help of police to blunt the hotspots where offenders might get into trouble. The police are experts at target hardening and can control access to places, reducing the factors that create crime opportunities (Weisburd, Groff, & Yang, 2013). For example, police officers can help to strengthen the crime defenses of previous crime victims and targets (such as victim notification of restraining orders and education about victim rights, or working with business owners to make their properties less vulnerable to victimization), and can patrol high-crime places for people who aren't supposed to be there.

When thoughtfully planned out with corrections authorities, police presence will increase the risks for offenders and the efforts they must make to commit crime (Durlauf & Nagin, 2011). Situational crime prevention can be highly effective, although information about specific crime problems (such as recidivism among community-supervised offenders) can help to reduce offending even more than broad interventions. Corrections-police partnerships can strategically deter offenders from taking advantage of crime opportunities, but only after such targets and places are identified as being tempting for probationers and parolees (Parent & Snyder, 1999). Joint patrols of "risky facilities" (see Eck, Clarke, & Guerette, 2007) can help to reduce the access of community-supervised offenders to crime opportunities. Community corrections officers can maximize the success of their clients by (1) working with police to figure out what crime opportunities exist in the community, (2) creating and revising supervision conditions that restrict access to those opportunities, and then (3) policing those targets/places for at-risk probationers and parolees.

COMMUNITY CRIME CONTROL

In addition to policing crime opportunities, community corrections supervisors may hope to eliminate those crime opportunities. In order to prevent probationers and parolees from recidivating, offender supervisors can work to change the conditions that encourage crime. Rather than generic crime prevention strategies aimed at the entire population of potential offenders, corrections-police partnerships can develop initiatives that reduce the environmental features that present specific chances to commit crime, and can encourage neighborhood residents to become active participants in crime control. One method for reducing crime opportunity hotspots (as well as enhancing the surveillance of those risky places that remain) is through the enhancement of community cohesion and collective efficacy (Kubrin & Weitzer, 2003; Sampson, 2004, 2011; Taylor, 1997). Through police partnerships with the community, (1) residents become active partners in crime control (contributing to preventative behaviors independently and through cooperation with the police), (2) fear of crime is reduced and the quality of community life is enhanced, and (3) potential offenders believe that the rewards of crime are fewer and the risks of getting caught are greater.

Within community-oriented corrections and policing strategies, enhancing pro-sociality in a neighborhood is believed to reduce crime opportunities and improve the overall quality of life for the entire community in which their clients reside. This is accomplished by soliciting the assistance of neighborhood residents and organizations (such as the police) to (1) address some forms of social disorder that can give the cue that crime is tolerated, and (2) enhance community relations so that area residents feel a sense of responsibility for controlling crime in the neighborhood (and are thereby more likely to reduce chances for crime to occur, and will supervise and intervene in crime events when necessary). Advocates of this method propose that by educating community members on how to eliminate crime opportunities, the entire neighborhood is helping to facilitate effective community supervision (Reinventing Probation Council, 2000). Examples of existing strategies include street clean-ups, community outings and meetings, and frequent personal and informal contact between probation and parole officers and their clients' friends and family members. By creating a community-wide sense of trust, cohesion, and the shared goal of public safety, offender supervisors gain the assistance of many other people and agencies in reducing crime opportunities (Browning et al., 2004; Karp & Clear, 2000; Sampson et al., 1997). These improved social relationships between community corrections agencies and neighborhood residents can be facilitated through police partnerships (Schaefer et al., 2014). Enhancing informal social control and guardianship may motivate residents to take ownership of community spaces, thereby activating several sources of crime control (Kubrin & Weitzer, 2003; Sampson, 2004; Taylor, 1997).

Arguably, these strategies can be improperly implemented and sometimes abused. Under the heading of "broken windows" (see Chapter 2), some policing and corrections initiatives that emphasize order maintenance or zero tolerance can backfire, leading to increases in rates of minor offenses, police mistrust, and legal cynicism. Although some of these community corrections frameworks emphasize opportunity reduction and community cohesion (Rhine, 2002), unfortunately they also focus on swift consequences (which we know are often ineffective). Accordingly, broken windows supervision and order maintenance may place too great an emphasis on surveillance and control; these frameworks tout the benefits of "community policing" but become infatuated with the "policing" parts and neglect the "community" aspect (Taxman & Byrne, 2001). Indeed, research is lacking, but existing empirical evidence has found little support for broken windows styles of corrections and policing, with some interventions doing more harm than good (Harcourt, 2001; Lilly, Cullen, & Ball, 2015; Reisig, 2010; Thacher, 2004).

That said, there are ways to solicit the cooperation of communities in controlling crime, short of micro-policing problematic behaviors and areas (Clear, 2000). Through partnerships with police, probation and parole authorities can better foster community conditions that minimize offenders' chances of re-offending, and encourage neighborhood relationships that inhibit crime. The goal here is to create community features that send a message to offenders (i.e., that crime is unwelcome and will be noticed and punished) and to develop community cohesion that sends a message to neighborhood residents (i.e., that they should be responsible for their area and to help prevent and report crime). This approach removes chances for offenders to commit crime, but also lets probationers and parolees know that informal and formal controls are in place to react to crime should it occur. Developing community cohesion and collective efficacy in crime prevention is part of a larger call to return community supervision to the community (Clear, 1996). As such, the police officers in those communities are natural partners in opportunity-reduction supervision.

If probation and parole agencies want to address the community disorder that their clients are exposed to, how can the police contribute to that goal? Partnerships should place probation or parole officers with police officers in the community, through ride-alongs, home visits with offenders, or meetings with neighborhood residents. Collectively, these officers "negotiate the rules of the street" that members of the community (including offenders) are subject to (Wagers, Sousa, & Kelling, 2008). It is important that offender supervisors and the police interact one on one with offenders and other community residents so as to informally communicate what kinds of behaviors are expected (Braga & Bond, 2008; Clear & Corbett, 1999; Sampson, 2011). This tactic is very different from monitoring and reprimanding minor disorders and incivilities, but rather aims to improve conditions of community life so that crime opportunities are reduced and the number of cooperative crime controllers is increased.

Offender supervisors should help probationers and parolees to develop and maintain prosocial daily activities to create stable routines, which will invariably include contact with other community members and organizations. Most commonly, corrections-police partnerships work with community organizations (e.g., neighborhood watch, citizen action groups, victim empowerment boards, community restoration groups) to develop initiatives that reduce crime opportunities and encourage offender reintegration and desistance (Reinventing Probation Council, 2000). These partnerships are community oriented, based on the premise that the community that causes the problem (an available crime opportunity) should be part of the solution to that problem. There are already strong associations between many citizen groups and police organizations with the collective goal of crime prevention (Greene, 2000); community corrections agencies would be wise to seek their help in creating community conditions that facilitate the success of probationers and parolees located there.

Increasing the Surveillance by Crime Controllers

Environmental criminology research reveals the importance of context in explaining crime. The situations in which people are embedded influence their behavior. Regardless of how or why this process unfolds, it is indisputable that offending is in part caused by features of the social and physical environment.

People can only commit crime when there is an opportunity to do so, and these opportunities vary according to environmental characteristics. As demonstrated previously, studies show that the crime opportunities of probationers and parolees are related to the communities in which they reside. Accordingly, to prevent the recidivism of their clients, community corrections authorities must change the features of an offender's community that present crime opportunities or allow them to be taken advantage of.

The previous section discussed the importance of reducing crime-conducive targets and places. Unfortunately, not all attractive targets and suitable places for crime can be eliminated, policed, prevented from developing, or controlled through probation or parole conditions. As a result of this reality, offender supervisors must find ways to extend their authority. That is, what can community corrections officers do to help control the availability and use of crime opportunities? How can partnerships with the police help? Through the use of community-oriented policing strategies, it is possible to recruit the help of other people and organizations (and their resources and tools) to control crime (Reisig, 2010). At a general level, studies demonstrate that improving certain community conditions reduces offending (Browning et al., 2004; Carr, 2005; Warner, 2007). More specifically, research shows that fostering a number of informal and formal social controls can diffuse many crime opportunities. As such, corrections agents can help to prevent recidivism among their clients by nurturing relationships with crime controllers in the community (Kubrin & Weitzer, 2003). Given the experiences of police in carrying out this task, combined with the legal authority they represent, corrections-police partnerships are an effective strategy for creating, recruiting, and training crime controllers (i.e., the people who control the availability and use of crime opportunities).

This section presents two categories of tactics that can enhance opportunity-reduction supervision. First, we present the strategy of using "super controllers," and discuss how these highly influential persons can increase the number of lower-level crime controllers that monitor offenders and situations. When super controllers solicit the help of additional offender handlers, target guardians, and place managers, community-supervised offenders will encounter fewer chances to commit crime (or will at least be subject to increased surveillance). Second, we outline the strategy of third-party policing. Through civic regulations, the police (along with their community corrections partners) can leverage target guardianship and place management actions to reduce the number of crime opportunities that are available. Notably, both of these strategies—the use of super controllers and third-party policing—are consistent with the principles of problem- and community-oriented policing (for a review of these interventions, see Chapter 2).

SUPER CONTROLLERS

An accumulation of research evidence has revealed how best to prevent crime. For example, we know a great deal about the features of the environment that send signals to prospective offenders and how these signals influence their decision making. A large collection of studies has identified what some of these signals are, and how they inform prospective offenders about what might happen if they commit the crime (e.g., what effort or tools are needed, what the rewards might be, what the possible risks are). Importantly, then, these signals can be removed or altered to change the decisions made by prospective offenders. Crime prevention interventions rely precisely on this information to structure the environment in ways that reduce crime opportunities for offenders (i.e., increasing the effort, reducing the rewards, and increasing the risks). After decades of research and a generation of experiments in crime prevention, academics and their police partners understand what interventions can help to make situations less conducive to crime. Less well known, however, is why people and organizations fail to take these actions. Why do offender handlers, target guardians, and place managers fail to get involved? In what ways do these controllers fail to effectively prevent crime? And perhaps more important, how can potential crime controllers be motivated to exert their influence and help to stymie crime opportunities?

To answer these questions, Sampson, Eck, and Dunham (2010) introduced the concept of "super controllers." Super controllers are "the people, organizations and institutions that create the incentives for controllers to prevent or facilitate crime" (p. 40). They do not directly influence crime opportunities. Rather, super controllers influence the actions of handlers, guardians, and managers, who then in turn help to control crime. As previously discussed, probation and parole officers are primary offender handlers, as they are able to influence the behaviors of their clients. Likewise, police officers are formal target guardians and place managers, as they help protect against victimization and influence the social processes in their areas of surveillance and law enforcement. Yet beyond these principal roles as crime controllers, community corrections and police officers are also super controllers; that is, they can lobby other handlers, guardians, and managers, and can influence the actions those controllers take, thereby decreasing crime opportunities.

First, community corrections agents should recruit offender handlers. Corrections and police officers cannot always monitor offenders, so other parties can be solicited for offender surveillance. Moreover, research consistently shows that offenders with strong family relationships and community ties are more likely to desist from crime (National Research Council, 2008; Warr, 1998). Probation and parole officers can use the information from their assessments (see Chapter 4) to work with people in their clients' lives who are prosocial and can help to keep offenders out of trouble. For instance, family members should be consulted in creating supervision conditions, and can encourage offenders to "go straight" (Taxman, Young, & Byrne, 2004). Informal social controls and role models can be actively woven into offenders' daily activities to ensure that they are surrounded by positive influences (Pew Center on the States, 2008b). Moreover, probation and parole officers can work with the police to notify community members about offenders and their supervision conditions (Reentry Policy Council, 2005; Taxman, 2006). As illustrations, a probationer is less likely to violate curfew if her neighbors know that she has to be home by 9:00 p.m., and a parolee is less likely to attend a bar he is not supposed to be at if the owner is aware of that restriction. These additional handlers are not eliminating crime opportunities so much as they are encouraging offenders to comply with their supervision conditions.

Second, probation and parole officers should train target guardians. There are a number of guardianship behaviors that can be used to reduce crime opportunities (Clarke, 1992; Ekblom, 2005; Wortley, 2001), and corrections-police partnerships are especially useful in putting those practices in place. Community corrections officers know which targets their clients find attractive. Police officers know how to make targets less attractive. Through collaboration, officers can work to create more and better target guardians. General examples include victim or neighborhood notifications about returning offenders and community safety initiatives (such as police-citizen workshops on target hardening and "block watch" programs). Specific strategies for extending guardianship are highly variable, depending on the unique circumstances of a given crime problem (Clarke & Eck, 2005).

Third, community corrections authorities should educate place managers. Probation and parole officers have detailed information about high-crime places, including knowledge of the features of these places that promote criminal activity. By working with the owners (and representatives) of these places, a number of these crime opportunities can be effectively eliminated (Cherney, 2008). Corrections agents may have little influence over place managers, and may therefore find it helpful to partner with police authorities. Probation and parole officers might invite police officers to accompany them on visits to high-crime places in a given neighborhood, to speak with place managers about how to prevent crime by making changes to the space itself. The police can also work with place managers to improve surveillance, thereafter communicating back to probation and parole officers about emerging crime opportunities for offenders on supervision. Getting place managers to reduce the features of their space that promote crime may require additional legal leverage (see the proceeding subsection), although the task is necessary to maximize crime prevention.

As stipulated by the crime triangle (and verified by a large body of theoretical and empirical research evidence), we know that three elements are necessary for a crime event to occur: motivated offenders, attractive targets, and facilitating places. Equally important, studies demonstrate that a variety of controllers can reduce or disincentivize opportunities for crime to occur. Yet sometimes offender handlers, target guardians, and place managers fail to effectively control crime. The reasons for this are many, although the action of front-line crime controllers in addressing crime-conducive situations is important for preventing recidivism among probationers and parolees. Accordingly, community corrections agents and their police partners should leverage their authority as super controllers, influencing the people in offenders' lives to act in ways that limit chances to commit crime.

THIRD-PARTY POLICING

Probation and parole officers, especially in collaboration with the police, are excellent super controllers. After identifying their clients' crime opportunities, community corrections officers can create and influence the actions of offender handlers, target guardians, and place managers. Because corrections and police officers cannot eliminate all chances for offending, they are eager to solicit the help of others who can reduce crime opportunities. Further, the knowledge base of "what works" in place-based crime prevention is impressive. Thus, we know how offenders get into trouble, and how to prevent them from doing so. Unfortunately, not all prospective crime controllers will cooperate with the requests of probation or parole authorities. Even with many incentives to do so (e.g., offender successes, less victimization, safer places), people and organizations may refuse to help in controlling crime opportunities. Offender supervisors know about specific actions that individual crime controllers could take to prevent recidivism among their clients; but when those controllers won't cooperate, are there any ways to compel them to take those actions?

Third-party policing is one way to recruit crime controllers to remove crime opportunities (Buerger & Mazerolle, 1998). Police departments often use third-party policing during crackdowns on specific crime problems (Mazerolle & Ransley, 2005). Officers facilitate or coerce the owners of crime opportunities (usually place managers) to control the relationship between offenders and the problematic target or place. Using a number of civic regulations (such as a noise or traffic ordinance), the police can compel place managers to take appropriate actions that will reduce crime. In some cases, the police work directly with legal rulers (e.g., city councils, liquor licensing boards, health inspectors) to pressure people and organizations to remedy the situation that facilitates offending.

Probation and parole officers can benefit from this model. Importantly, community corrections authorities can and should try to approach the owners of crime-conducive targets and places independently and supportively (i.e., without the police and without the threat of legal recourse for failure to comply with the proposed remediation). It is possible that some target guardians and place managers will be willing to cooperate with simple crime prevention requests. When a probation or parole officer explains how the removal of a crime opportunity is beneficial to guardians or managers themselves, people may gladly participate. However, when the owners of crime problems refuse to cooperate, the police can help to enforce (already legal) conditions that solve those crime problems (Mazerolle & Ransley, 2005). In this way, police officers help community corrections agencies to "pull levers" that coerce place managers into actions that make crime less likely to occur there.

Within problem-oriented policing, many police departments already rely on civil remedies as a means to leverage crime prevention efforts. It is also important to note that regulatory threats are supposed to be a last resort, and that the police can first try to help place managers to solve the problem (Cherney, 2008). Probation and parole officers understand the crime opportunities of their supervisees, and may have detailed information about why these opportunities exist. In partnering with the police, community corrections agencies can help to eliminate these opportunities at their source by compelling third parties to take crime-preventive measures in their spaces.

Conclusion

The police have a wealth of information about crime opportunities and know the places, people, and activities that are most likely to get at-risk offenders into trouble. In addition, they have experience with specialized crime prevention strategies and have learned how to structure situations to reduce those chances to offend. Given their expertise in environmental criminology, the police are valuable sources to look to in environmental corrections. As we have discussed in this chapter, community corrections authorities should solicit the aid of police officers in order to (1) learn about community-specific crime opportunities, (2) extend their ability to get probationers and parolees to comply with the conditions of their supervision, and (3) reduce remaining crime opportunities. These goals can be accomplished through partnerships that increase the surveillance of offenders, increase the surveillance of targets and places, and increase the supervision of additional crime controllers (Schaefer et al., 2014).

Although there are numerous benefits to corrections-police partnerships, there are several important limitations that must be accounted for if the collaboration is to be successful. Many of these hurdles can be overcome by tailoring the partnership to the unique crime problem that a community is experiencing. Different probation and parole officers will have different kinds of offenders with different types of crime opportunities in different sorts of neighborhoods with a variety of resources. As such, there is no one-size-fits-all approach that community corrections agents can rely on in working with the police. However, there are common problems encountered by most probation/parole-police partnerships (for a review, see Murphy, 2005), so efforts to resolve these issues and to learn from past mistakes are under way. Fortunately, as these collaborations have become more common, the research on these programs has expanded. As a consequence, there is a small but growing foundation of best practices for community corrections agencies working with the police (Jannetta & Lachman, 2011; Parent & Snyder, 1999). This desire to produce research on "what works" in correctional interventions is important, and will be needed to validate and improve the propositions set forth in this volume. It is to this topic that the concluding chapter now turns.

7

Making Offender Supervision Work

There are nearly 5 million people on probation and parole: 1 in 48 adults in the United States is under some form of community correctional supervision (Glaze & Bonczar, 2011). Although underfunded in many ways, we still devote an enormous amount of resources to the task of supervising these offenders. For instance, America has more than 100,000 probation officers (and expects to add 25,000 more officers in the coming decade; Allen, Latessa, & Ponder, 2013), and each year the nation spends $12.9 billion on non-institutional corrections (Kyckelhahn, 2012). These expenditures are justified by promising that community supervision will protect public safety. We restrict the freedoms of millions of people because we believe that it helps to prevent crime and improves the lives of those under correctional control.

At the core of this promise is the assumption of utility—that probation and parole supervision "works," such that supervision reduces re-offending and makes positive changes in offenders' lives. Too often, however, what community corrections officers do with their clients (in the standard delivery of community supervision) has proven to be ineffective (Solomon et al., 2005). In part, the fault lies with probation and parole authorities because a true profession would have been more vociferous in calling for effective strategies to handle offenders. But criminologists are also to blame for not providing officers with evidence-based tools to help them do their jobs better (Gleicher et al., 2013; Latessa et al., 2002).

Recently, there have been attempts to use criminological knowledge to equip probation and parole officers with the ability to reduce the criminal propensity of persons under their supervision, including training in the risk-need-responsivity model and the principles of effective intervention (Andrews & Bonta, 2010). These efforts have included programs such as the Strategic Training Initiative in Community Supervision (STICS; Bonta et al., 2011), Effective Practices in Community Supervision (EPICS; Smith et al., 2012), and Staff Trained at Reducing Re-Arrest

(STARR; Robinson et al., 2012). Much less attention has been given to how criminology can help probation and parole authorities to reduce the criminal opportunities of supervised offenders (Cullen, Eck, & Lowenkamp, 2002). The goal of this book is to advance this effort, to make use of validated crime theories in order to make community supervision "work."

In particular, insights from environmental criminology—or crime science as it is now increasingly called—have been used to articulate a new paradigm of probation and parole supervision: environmental corrections. Research in environmental criminology (including situational crime prevention and problem-oriented policing) demonstrates the causal importance of crime opportunities. Offenders cannot commit a crime if there is no chance to do so. As such, community corrections officers should be equipped with the knowledge and technologies to reduce opportunities for their clients to offend. In this book we have outlined the principal components of a model of opportunity-reduction supervision. In exploring how probation and parole supervision might be reoriented as "environmental corrections," much has been learned. Although not an exhaustive list, eight lessons stand out in considering how to make offender supervision work.

Lesson #1: Punishment Does Not Work Well

Probation and parole supervision are traditionally seen as embodying two functions: treatment and control. In this latter role, offender supervisors police their clients. Offenders on community corrections are provided a number of rules they have to follow, and the job of the officer is to monitor offenders' compliance with these rules. This model of supervision is based on a generic use of deterrence theory, assuming that the threat of punishment (such as the revocation of conditional release and a return to prison) will "scare" offenders into behaving. Despite the popularity of this form of "corrections" (that is to say, nothing about what causes the offender to commit crime is actually being corrected), deterrence-oriented supervision is largely ineffective (Gendreau et al., 1994; MacKenzie, 2006; Petersilia & Turner, 1993; Solomon et al., 2005; Taxman & Byrne, 2001). Although some deterrence interventions can work to prevent re-offending (such as focused deterrence and lever-pulling within problem-oriented policing strategies; Braga & Weisburd, 2012), current probation and parole practices that use intensive surveillance and generic threats of punishment are not designed in a way that would make them effective.

It is important to understand that no one is advocating for the abandonment of all control. People with a history of criminal behavior are at greater risk for future criminal behavior, and as such, it would be irresponsible for the criminal justice system to *not* impose restraints. Moreover, punishment is (in a limited sense) appropriate and beneficial. When someone breaks the law, we expect that "the scales of justice be rebalanced." It is also likely that there is some general deterrent effect, whereby criminal justice punishments prevent some people from becoming involved in crime in the first place. Thus, retribution and surveillance are necessary responses to criminal behavior, although these alone are insufficient.

Yet proponents of punishment-oriented offender supervision argue that the threat of punishment will prevent probationers and parolees from recidivating. Unfortunately, this line of thinking is handicapped by two notable problems.

First, the logic underlying punishment as an offender-supervision strategy is, at its core, flawed. If a person commits a crime because of some stimulus, then it follows that this same stimulus must be changed to prevent crime from reoccurring. The stimulus could be a mental illness, delinquent peers, substance abuse, poverty, opportunity, or any other of dozens of plausible explanations for criminality. Irrespective of the criminogenic need, the same equation applies: A failure to change the cause of crime will lead to the same effect (Andrews & Bonta, 2010). Thus, watching offenders more closely or threatening and applying more severe consequences to misbehaviors does nothing to change the impetus for their criminal behavior. As concluded by Cullen and Jonson, "For offenders who are already in the correctional system, there is just not much evidence that trying to punish them makes them less criminogenic" (2012, p. 89).

Second, deterrence has its limits. Certainly, the healthy majority of people can be discouraged from engaging in a behavior if the punishment is certain, swift, and severe. But due to practical and ethical considerations, punishments will never be certain, swift, and severe enough to dissuade all re-offending. Community-supervised offenders often believe that detection of misbehavior is unlikely, that consequences are slow to come, and that punishments are mild enough to be worth the offense. And in many cases, they are right. Probation and parole officers cannot watch offenders closely enough to detect all crimes or violations of supervision conditions, they cannot ignore due process, and they cannot impose unjust or excessive punishments. As a consequence, the threat of punishment in community supervision often remains just a threat. In order to be effective, deterrence must be focused, and must be tailored around the actual crime opportunities (i.e., the risks and rewards of offending) for each probationer and parolee.

When followed through, attempts to control (as opposed to change) offender behavior create more problems than they solve (Taxman, 1999). By subjecting offenders to scrupulous surveillance and meticulous rules, they are bound to fail (MacKenzie, 2000; Pearson & Lipton, 1999). Additional monitoring and threats may indeed lead to more punishments, but that does not therefore lead to less crime. As it stands, the generic application of deterrence theory is one of the weakest predictors of crime (Pratt & Cullen, 2005). A control orientation to community corrections *can be* effective, but only when partnered with effective treatment and when conformity is incentivized (as opposed to wayward behaviors being punished; Cullen & Jonson, 2012). As they are largely practiced, however, efforts to deter offenders from recidivating through threats of punishments do not work well.

Lesson #2: Reducing Crime Opportunities Reduces Crime

If threats of punishment do not discourage probationers and parolees from re-offending, then what does? There are a great number of criminological theories and related interventions that address offender propensity. Many identified causes of crime can be corrected, although this is typically a time-intensive task (e.g., a year of behavior modification therapy to reverse criminogenic attitudes). In many instances, a quicker resolution to active crime problems is required, so minimizing criminal propensity cannot be the only approach to reducing crime. Rather than solely addressing what makes a person a criminal, it is helpful to also consider what makes a crime occur (Clarke, 2010). By reducing the precipitators of a crime, the crime itself is less likely to take place. The task then becomes a matter of figuring out what leads to a criminal event, and disrupting those conditions.

Fortunately, many scholars and practitioners have taken up this task, and new criminological theories and interventions have been successful in reducing crime. Using the innovations of environmental criminology, "crime science" aims to discover and change the characteristics in the immediate situation that provide occasions for an offense to occur. Dozens of crime-reduction initiatives, driven by the scientific method and environmental crime prevention theories, have demonstrated that a focus on crime opportunities (as opposed to the criminals themselves) is a successful approach. A number of explanations have been forwarded and validated that show what crime opportunities are, where/when/why/how they arise and are pursued by prospective offenders, and how to eliminate them. Perhaps most notably, routine activity theory (Cohen & Felson, 1979) and the crime problem triangle (Eck, 1994, 2003) provide excellent insights into these queries. According to these frameworks, a crime occurs only if there is an opportunity to do so. These opportunities arise when a motivated offender finds a suitable target in a crime-conducive place. These opportunities can be thwarted when there are appropriate and effective crime controllers in place (i.e., offender handlers, target guardians, and place managers).

Problem-oriented policing in particular has shown that, rather than simply enforcing punishments when people violate the law, criminal justice agents can create conditions that prevent the crime from occurring in the first place (Eck & Spelman, 1987b). Moreover, as opposed to generic, broad-based crime prevention efforts, problem-oriented policing and situational crime prevention have demonstrated that the *chance* to commit crime can be minimized (Scott et al., 2008). The logic underlying these interventions is that by reducing the opportunity for crime to occur, there will be less crime (Clarke, 2008). Even if no changes are made to the motivations of offenders, a reduction in criminogenic places—that is, addressing the features of the environment that make that place an area where crime can occur—automatically reduces the opportunities for those inclined persons to commit crime. The next order of business, then, is to develop ways to extend environmental criminology and crime science to community corrections supervision.

Lesson #3: Environmental Corrections Can Reduce Crime Opportunities

Using these insights from environmental criminology, Cullen, Eck, and Lowenkamp (2002) created a new model of probation and parole, which they call "environmental corrections." Although there is little existing research evidence that this is an effective framework for supervising offenders in the community (see, e.g., Miller, 2012), the reliable logic and impressive results within crime science interventions suggest that environmental corrections is promising. Our goal in this book is to flesh out these ideas, outlining how an emphasis on opportunity reduction can reorient offender supervision. Although pilot studies and research evaluations will be necessary moving forward, probation and parole outcomes might be improved by a new focus.

Current community corrections practices are not centered on crime prevention, but around case processing; offenders are managed rather than changed (Burrell, 2012; Simon, 1993). Misguided criminological theories, diminished resources as well as rising caseloads, and the lack of a guiding framework for supervising offenders all contribute to poor outcomes. Probationers and parolees are subject to vague behavioral restrictions that are loosely associated with the causes of crime. As a consequence, the criminal justice system is not capitalizing on the chance to encourage desistance among these active offenders. By shifting community supervision away from rule enforcement and toward risk reduction, public safety is better served. Rather than making threats for noncompliance and then punishing offenders for misbehaviors, how can offender supervisors prevent their clients from relapsing in the first place?

To reduce re-offending, probation and parole officers must limit the crime opportunities to which offenders are exposed. Instead of using generic supervision conditions, the stipulations of community corrections can be tailored to match the specific risks of each offender. In this way, offender supervisors become problem solvers, inventing individualized case plans that create a new routine activity for each offender. This model of opportunity-reduction supervision would structure offenders' lives in such a way as to minimize exposure to crime-conducive people, places, and events, to include new agents of informal social control, and to fill offenders' time with prosocial activities. Ideally, these supervision conditions should be developed following a quality offender assessment (see Lesson #4), although general ideas from environmental criminology are also useful.

In any event, it is important to note that a reorientation of offender supervision around crime opportunities is a reflexive process. That is, each offender's criminogenic risks are different, and each offender's vulnerabilities to crime opportunities will change throughout the person's supervision term. Accordingly, probation and parole officers must respond to the situational vulnerabilities for recidivism that each offender faces during each period of his or her correctional sentence. This requires an understanding of where, when, with whom, and why the individual gets into trouble, which can only be gathered through novel methods of offender assessment. New tools to assist in meeting this goal might include social network analyses, geospatial activity mapping, or officer-offender meetings in the client's home community to rehearse prosociality. Although the "package" of environmental corrections is new, the focus on reducing probationers' and parolees' opportunities to commit crime is in line with core correctional practices, which provide evidence-based principles regarding how to best prevent recidivism (Clawson & Guevara, 2011; Dowden & Andrews, 2004; Gendreau, 1996; Gendreau et al., 2006).

Lesson #4: Crime Opportunities Must Be Assessed

Crime science interventions are effective because they are based on valid criminological theories, focusing on the situational precipitators of crime. These crime-reduction efforts also benefit from their reliance on the scientific method. To create a solution to a crime problem, the problem itself must first be understood. In the instance of offender supervision, the solution proposed by environmental corrections is opportunity reduction; therefore, the problem of crime opportunities has to be properly evaluated. As mentioned before, all offenders are different; they are each exposed to various triggers in their daily routines, and are tempted by different rewards and deterred by different efforts and risks. Developing an individualized opportunity-reduction case plan thus requires the identification of each offender's specific contact with and vulnerability to available crime opportunities.

Chapter 4 outlined examples of data-collection instruments that identify these crime opportunities. One important consideration is that, in addition to discovering what environmental factors (e.g., friends, places, emotions) lead to the probationer or parolee committing a crime, these assessments also identify protective factors that prevent offenders from getting into trouble. Most offenders are not engaged in crime (or the "lead-up to crime") all the time, and spend much of their day-to-day existence as "non-offenders." This reality can be used to encourage desistance by creating supervision conditions that bring correctional clients into more frequent contact with these prosocial influences. Offender supervisors also can assess the "controllers" of crime opportunities, or the people and institutions that prevent the development (or regulate the pursuit) of criminogenic situations. Taken together, the information collected from these different assessments results in a case plan that not only restricts offenders from crime opportunities, but also places offenders in contact with chances to help them "go straight."

Designing new routine activities for probationers and parolees requires information about the crime opportunities of this population. Although this information may be a challenge to obtain (see Lesson #7), data about the crime opportunities of community-supervised offenders can transform our approach to corrections, moving away from crime control and toward crime prevention. Ideally, information about crime opportunities should be gathered first-hand from a variety of sources (such as offender reports, police/court records, and interviews with the offender's social network), and should emphasize the situational risks of each individual offender. The processes necessary for this type of data collection will surely vary according to the resources available to each community corrections agency and the characteristics of the offenders being supervised. Yet when individual-level data collection is not possible, it is still conceivable that opportunity-reduction supervision can prevent recidivism even if not based on data from the offender. As problem solvers, probation and parole officers can evaluate the crime opportunities that exist in the communities of their clients (and should consult other crime controllers to learn about this information, as well). In fact, community corrections authorities can rely on existing data about crime hotspots or offending patterns to account for relapse opportunities of probationers and parolees. In this way, no matter the source of the data, an offender's case plan will reflect the chances to commit crime that he or she will actually face.

Lesson #5: Cognitive-Behavioral Techniques Can Help

Although reducing offenders' exposure to crime opportunities can help to prevent re-offending, probationers and parolees will undoubtedly come into contact with remaining chances to commit crime. Offender supervisors cannot know about all of the crime opportunities of their clients, and cannot control all of those opportunities of which they are aware. At some point, community-supervised offenders will be confronted with situations that tempt them to break the law. Fortunately, there are effective methods to reduce criminal propensity. Some of these techniques, such as those used in cognitive-behavioral correctional interventions, have unique applications for opportunity-reduction supervision. Rather than addressing the deep-seated psychological causes of crime, community corrections officers can work to change the ways offenders are at risk of perceiving and pursuing crime opportunities. Specifically, two strategies can help to address this "situational propensity" of probationers and parolees.

First, community-supervised offenders can be taught skills to help them *resist* existing crime opportunities. Because correctional clients will invariably have the chance to commit crime, they must have the tools to withstand those temptations. During meetings with their clients, probation and parole officers can work to overcome four challenges that offenders face in deciding whether or not to take advantage of a crime opportunity. Offenders must reduce their crime-conducive thinking, control their criminogenic emotions, enhance their self-control, and learn to properly engage in problem solving. Although traditional correctional rehabilitation programs can assist in meeting these goals, community corrections officers can also help to nurture these skills during their regular interactions with their clients (Raynor & Vanstone, 2015; Smith et al., 2012). Through intentional focus and structured practice, offenders can learn to identify and resolve their susceptibility to crime opportunities.

Second, probationers and parolees can be educated on how to *avoid* available crime opportunities. By training offenders to better evaluate the situations in which they place themselves, they can learn to circumvent environments where they are likely to be tempted to commit crime. Community corrections clients may not be skilled at assessing environments and selecting the most prosocial of those options, but it is an ability that can be developed by teaching and rehearsal. In addition, probation and parole officers can help to encourage desistance by embedding their clients in prosocial routine activities that bypass crime-conducive scenarios. As it is not possible to eliminate all offender risks, environments that contain triggers for those risks must be sidestepped when possible. And because officers cannot be solely responsible for this task, offenders must be taught to evaluate their own routine activities to avoid pro-crime environments and surround themselves with prosocial influences.

Both of these strategies fundamentally transform the way that probation and parole officers interact with their supervisees. Rather than simply prescribing rules and mandating participation in typical treatment programs, offender supervisors should actively work with each client as change agents. Provided the proper training, community corrections officers are in an ideal position to change the ways that offenders think about crime opportunities and make decisions about whether to pursue those opportunities (Bourgon et al., 2011).

Lesson #6: The Police Make Excellent Community Corrections Partners

As noted, the police are experienced at reducing crime opportunities. Police departments have expertise in evaluating crime problems and creating suitable interventions to prevent those crimes. Community corrections agencies have been slower to consider crime prevention frameworks based on opportunity reduction. Probation and parole authorities can learn from the successes of past problem-oriented policing practices, but can also augment the benefits of environmental corrections by forming strategic partnerships with the police. By creating a shared vision for how to prevent recidivism among probationers and parolees, corrections-police initiatives reduce crime opportunities in ways that are beneficial to both parties without overextending existing responsibilities and capabilities (Murphy & Lutze, 2009; Murphy & Worrall, 2007; Parent & Snyder, 1999). That is, community corrections partnerships with police agencies enhance opportunity-reduction offender supervision by pairing the current expertise of each.

Perhaps most notably, the police are well situated to be offender handlers. Not only can police officers monitor probationers and parolees for compliance with their supervision conditions, but they can also help to steer offenders away from existing crime opportunities. Necessary to this task is information sharing between corrections and law enforcement officers; agents should exchange information about supervisees and emerging crime-conducive situations in the community. As these partnerships develop, it is likely that corrections and police officers alike will learn about attractive crime targets and places. Accordingly, the police can work to guard and manage those targets and places, and probation and parole officers can revise supervision case plans to reflect those targets and places. Through a joint problem-solving approach, community corrections authorities can solicit the police to embody the role of formal crime controllers. Success is maximized when probation and parole authorities instruct the police about at-risk offenders and the police provide information about risky environments in return (Jannetta & Lachman, 2011).

In addition to the roles of offender handlers, target guardians, and place managers, probation and parole agents can also encourage the police to serve as super controllers. Given the assistance of community corrections authorities, police officers can solicit additional sources of informal social control. There are a number of persons and community organizations in offenders' lives that are responsible for crime opportunities, and the police can engage these prospective crime controllers in two ways. First, probation and parole agents can partner with the police to educate and incentivize other handlers, guardians, and managers to (1) eliminate existing crime opportunities, (2) prevent new crime opportunities from developing, (3) encourage offenders to comply with the conditions of their opportunity-reduction case plans, and (4) report issues of noncompliance. Second, third-party policing tactics can be used to address lingering problematic crime opportunities. By relying on legal levers, the police can coerce crime controllers to address the environmental characteristics that allow crime to occur.

In the absence of formal corrections-police partnerships (that include features such as shared databases and joint patrols), probation and parole officers should consider gathering information from police officers about crime opportunities as a necessary component of case plan development. The police are intimately familiar with the features of their patrolling areas that cause crime and help to prevent offenses. As such, community corrections officers should solicit and use that information to tailor supervision conditions for their clients to ensure that they reflect the real risks for relapse that offenders will encounter.

Lesson #7: Research Is Needed

No matter the quality of ideas we have developed in this volume, they are largely irrelevant if they cannot be applied. The issue of technology transfer—also called *translational criminology*—has become an important consideration in the past decade; this "refers to the transmission of scientific knowledge from the producers to the potential consumers of this information" (Cullen & Jonson, 2011, p. 324). In other words, it is important to figure out how to ensure that social science research findings are applied in practice. This has prompted scholars and practitioners to wonder how criminological theories can be developed into programs, and then how those program designs can be translated into criminal justice interventions (Gendreau, Goggin, & Smith, 2001). For environmental corrections to be effective, there must be a focus on "fidelity," ensuring continuity from theory to the design of supervision programs to the implementation of a new model of probation and parole. In their original creation of environmental corrections, Cullen, Eck, and Lowenkamp (2002) outlined several questions that research should address, and we encourage researchers to actively explore these issues. Following these initial recommendations for future research, after outlining opportunity-reduction supervision in more detail, we see that three categories of challenges have emerged that require serious contemplation and then empirical investigation.

First, there are *theoretical* challenges. Crime science has contributed a great deal to our understanding of crime opportunities and how to prevent them, but much less work has been dedicated to applying these ideas to community corrections. The theory of opportunity-reduction supervision must be fleshed out to develop day-to-day operations. What this model of community corrections actually looks like once applied will likely require some revisions to the framework itself. For example, organizational considerations (such as administrator and officer cooperation, large caseloads, and resource constraints) may not allow the full implementation of environmental corrections as envisioned in this book. While part of the solution to this problem is to have less offenders in the system (see Chapter 3 for the importance of earned discharge), another resolution to these difficulties is to revise the theory of opportunity-reduction supervision

Second, there are *methodological* challenges. Ideally, probationers' and parolees' case plans would be designed to account for the crime opportunities of each individual offender. To do so, however, requires data. The resources needed to pursue this information may be too few, and the data may be inaccurate or altogether unavailable. Furthermore, community corrections officers must be trained to gather this information, learning the basics of data collection, investigative techniques, and motivational interviewing. These officers would be transformed from their current roles of bureaucrats, pseudo police officers, and service brokers, to problem solvers and change agents. The adoption of a new guiding philosophy of offender supervision would require careful thought about how to transition from the old way of doing business. Early research should explore the processes through which offender assessments are completed. Preliminarily, we can say that it is likely that procedures will vary according to the size of the corrections department and the offender population being supervised.

Third, there are *logistical* challenges. Probation and parole authorities cannot know about and eliminate all crime opportunities. Rather (to be most effective, at least), officers require the cooperation of courts, police partners, community organizations, offenders' social networks, and third-party crime controllers. It is unclear how willing and able these groups are to participate in the goals of opportunity-reduction supervision. Additionally, it is possible that environmental corrections may be more or less effective with certain categories of community-supervised offenders (e.g., low-risk vs. high-risk, community-integrated vs. socially isolated, property offenders vs. violent offenders). Although we have made a number of speculations about when opportunity-reduction supervision will be most effective, these are ultimately questions that require empirical exploration.

These challenges can likely be overcome with proper research, which should be accomplished in developmental stages. Initially, small-scale studies will be needed. These studies can include focus groups, piecemeal implementation of the different components of environmental corrections, and instrument validation. Next, pilot studies should be conducted. These studies may be small at first (e.g., one officer's caseload or a few clients from each officer in a department), but must eventually be implemented using a larger sample. These department-wide adoptions will allow for randomized experimental trials. Finally, evaluation research will be needed. In addition to outcome assessments, researchers should also perform process evaluations in order to determine what portions of environmental corrections are effective and which components require revision.

Lesson #8: Opportunity-Reduction Supervision Can Work

With millions of offenders under community correctional supervision, we must ask ourselves: Is it worth it? Is it working? Although some research evidence indicates that offender supervision is moderately effective (especially compared to alternative sanctions), it is clear that there is room for improvement. In this context, we have advocated for a transformation in community corrections, involving a shift from scaring offenders away from generic causes of crime and toward carefully designed case plans that knife off specific opportunities for offending. Although we are only at the conceptual stages of development, this new framework holds significant promise to orient offender supervision around the principles of crime science that are effective in reducing crime.

Environmental corrections supposes that probation and parole can be dramatically improved by having officers work as problem solvers. The sources of offending should be addressed if we wish to disrupt the environments that breed crime. This approach would entail working in and with the communities that encourage recidivism, creating additional offender handlers, target guardians, and place managers to reduce available crime opportunities. In working with offenders, supervisors can limit re-offending by expanding mechanisms of informal social control, making it more difficult for offenders to access opportunities to commit crime, and creating prosocial routine activities for supervisees. By using knowledge from environmental criminology, probation and parole authorities can reduce recidivism by minimizing chances for offending to occur. With this strong theoretical footing, opportunity-reduction supervision has the potential to substantially enhance public safety and improve offender outcomes. It should, therefore, be pursued as a new guiding philosophy for probation and parole.

References

Adler, F. (1975). *Sisters in crime: The rise of the new female criminal.* New York, NY: McGraw-Hill.

Agnew, R. (2006). *Pressured into crime: An overview of general strain theory.* Los Angeles, CA: Roxbury.

Agnew, R., Brezina, T., Wright, J. P., & Cullen, F. T. (2002). Strain, personality traits, and delinquency: Extending general strain theory. *Criminology, 40,* 43–71.

Agnew, R. S. (1992). Foundation for a general strain theory of crime and delinquency. *Criminology, 30,* 47–87.

Akers, R. L. (1998). *Social learning and social structure: A general theory of crime and deviance.* Boston, MA: Northeastern University Press.

Alarid, L. F., & Wright, E. M. (2015). Becoming a felony offender. In F. T. Cullen, P. Wilcox, J. L. Lux, & C. L. Jonson (Eds.). *Sisters in Crime revisited: Bringing gender into criminology* (pp. 103–122). New York, NY: Oxford University Press.

Allen, H. E., Carlson, E. W., & Parks, E. C. (1979). *Critical issues in probation.* Washington, DC: U.S. Government Printing Office.

Allen, H. E., Latessa, E. J., & Ponder, B. S. (2013). *Corrections in America: An introduction* (13th ed.). Upper Saddle River, NJ: Prentice Hall.

Anderson, E. (1999). *Code of the street: Decency, violence, and the moral life of the inner city.* New York, NY: W. W. Norton.

Andrews, D. A. (1989). Recidivism is predictable and can be influenced: Using risk assessments to reduce recidivism. *Forum on Corrections Research, 1,* 11–17.

Andrews, D. A. (1995). The psychology of criminal conduct and effective treatment. In J. McGuire (Ed.), *What works: Reducing reoffending—Guidelines from research and practice* (pp. 35–62). New York, NY: Wiley.

Andrews, D. A., & Bonta, J. (1995). *The Level of Supervision Inventory-Revised (LSI-R).* North Tonawanda, NY: Multi-Health Systems.

Andrews, D. A., & Bonta, J. (2010). *The psychology of criminal conduct* (5th ed.). New Providence, NJ: Anderson/LexisNexis.

Andrews, D. A., Bonta, J., & Hoge, R. D. (1990). Classification for effective rehabilitation: Rediscovering psychology. *Criminal Justice and Behavior, 17,* 19–52.

Andrews, D. A., Bonta, J., & Wormith, J. S. (2006). The recent past and near future of risk and/or need assessment. *Crime and Delinquency, 52,* 7–27.

Andrews, D. A., & Dowden, C. (2007). Risk-need-responsivity model of assessment and human service in prevention and corrections: Crime-prevention jurisprudence. *Canadian Journal of Criminology and Criminal Justice, 49,* 439–464.

Andrews, D. A., Zinger, I., Hoge, R. D., Bonta, J., Gendreau, P., & Cullen, F. T. (1990). Does correctional treatment work? A clinically-relevant and psychologically-informed meta-analysis. *Criminology, 28,* 369–404.

Anselin, L., Griffiths, E., & Tita, G. (2008). Crime mapping and hot spot analysis. In R. Wortley & L. Mazerolle (Eds.), *Environmental criminology and crime analysis* (pp. 97–116). Cullompton, UK: Willan.

Antonowicz, D. H., & Ross, R. R. (1994). Essential components of successful rehabilitation programs for offenders. *International Journal of Offender Therapy and Comparative Criminology, 38,* 97–104.

Aos, S., Phipps, P., Barnoski, R., & Lieb, R. (2001). *The comparative costs and benefits of programs to reduce crime: A review of national research findings with implications for Washington state.* Olympia, WA: Washington State Institute for Public Policy.

Auburn, T. (2005). Narrative reflexivity as a repair device for discounting "cognitive distortions" in sex offender treatment. *Discourse and Society, 16,* 697–718.

Augustus, J. (1972). *John Augustus: First probation officer.* Montclair, NJ: Patterson Smith. (Original work published 1852)

Baird, C. (2009). *A question of evidence: A critique of risk assessment models used in the criminal justice system.* Madison, WI: National Council on Crime and Delinquency.

Balbi, A., & Guerry, A.-M. (1829). *Statistique comparée de l'état de l'instruction et du nombre des crimes dans les divers arrondissements des académies et des cours royales de France* [Compared statistics of the state of the instruction and number of crimes in the various districts of the academies and royal courses of France]. Paris, France: Jules Renouard.

Bandura, A. (1986). *Social foundations of thoughts and action: A social cognitive theory.* Englewood Cliffs, NJ: Prentice Hall.

Bandura, A. (1997). *Self-efficacy: The exercise of control.* New York, NY: W. H. Freeman.

Barkdull, W. (1976). Probation: Call it control and mean it. *Federal Probation, 40*(4), 3–8.

Barnes, G. C., Hyatt, J. M., Ahlman, L. C., & Kent, D. T. L. (2012). Effects of low-intensity supervision for lower-risk probationers: Updated results from a randomized controlled trial. *Journal of Crime and Justice, 35,* 200–220.

Barnes, H. E., & Teeters, N. D. (1959). *New horizons in criminology.* Englewood Cliffs, NJ: Prentice Hall.

Beccaria, C. (1963). *On crimes and punishment* (H. Paolucci, trans.). Indianapolis, IN: Bobbs-Merrill. (Original work published 1764)

Beck, A. T. (1976). *Cognitive therapies and emotional disorders.* New York, NY: New American Library.

Beck, A. T., & Clark, D. A. (1997). An information processing model of anxiety: Automatic and strategic processes. *Behaviour Research and Therapy, 35,* 49–58.

Bentham, J. (1948). *An introduction to the principles of morals and legislation.* Oxford, UK: Basil Blackwell. (Original work published 1789)

Bernstein, G. A., Farrington, D. P., & Leschied, A. W. (2001). *Offender rehabilitation in practice: Implementing and evaluating effective programs.* New York, NY: Wiley.

Biglan, A., & Hayes, S. C. (1996). Should the behavioral sciences become more pragmatic? The case for functional contextualism in research on human behavior. *Applied and Preventive Psychology, 5,* 47–57.

Blomberg, T. G., & Lucken, K. (2010). *American penology: A history of control.* New Brunswick, NJ: Transaction.

Bonczar, T. P. (1997). *Characteristics of adults on probation.* Washington, DC: Bureau of Justice Statistics.

Bonta, J. (2002). Offender risk assessment: Guidelines for selection and use. *Criminal Justice and Behavior, 29*, 355–379.

Bonta, J., Bourgon, G., Rugge, T., Scott, T.-L., Yessine, A., Gutierrez, L., & Li, J. (2011). An experimental demonstration of training probation officers in evidence-based community supervision. *Criminal Justice and Behavior, 38*, 1127–1148.

Bonta, J., Rugge, T., Scott, T.-L., Bourgon, C., & Yessine, A. K. (2008). Exploring the black box of community supervision. *Journal of Offender Rehabilitation, 47*, 248–270.

Bonta, J., Wallace-Capretta, S., & Rooney, J. (2000). A quasi-experimental evaluation of an intensive rehabilitation supervision program. *Criminal Justice and Behavior, 27*, 312–329.

Boone, H. N., & Fulton, B. A. (1996). *Implementing performance-based measures in community corrections*. Washington, DC: National Institute of Justice, Office of Justice Programs.

Bottoms, A. (2001). Compliance with community penalties. In A. Bottoms, L. Gelsthorpe, & S. Rex (Eds.), *Community penalties: Change and challenges* (pp. 87–116). Cullompton, UK: Willan.

Bottoms, A., Shapland, J., Costello, A., Holmes, D., & Muir, G. (2004). Towards desistance: Theoretical underpinnings for an empirical study. *The Howard Journal, 43*, 368–389.

Bourgon, G., Gutierrez, L., & Ashton, J. (2011). The evolution of community supervision practice: The transformation from case manager to change agent. *Irish Probation Journal, 8*, 28–48.

Bowers, K. J., & Johnson, S. D. (2004). Who commits near repeats? A test of the boost explanation. *Western Criminology Review, 5*(3), 12–24.

Braga, A. A. (2002). *Problem-oriented policing and crime prevention*. Monsey, NY: Criminal Justice Press.

Braga, A. A., & Bond, B. J. (2008). Policing crime and disorder hot spots: A randomized controlled trial. *Criminology, 46*, 577–607.

Braga, A. A., Papachristos, A., & Hureau, D. (2012). Hot spots policing effects on crime. *Campbell Systematic Reviews, 8*(8), 1–97.

Braga, A. A., Papachristos, A., & Hureau, D. (2014). The effects of hot spots policing on crime: An updated systematic review and meta-analysis. *Justice Quarterly, 31*, 633–663.

Braga, A. A., & Weisburd, D. L. (2010). *Policing problem places: Crime hot spots and effective prevention*. New York, NY: Oxford University Press.

Braga, A. A., & Weisburd, D. L. (2012). The effects of "pulling levers" focused deterrence strategies on crime. *Campbell Systematic Reviews, 8*(6), 1–91.

Brantingham, P., & Brantingham, P. (2008). Crime pattern theory. In R. Wortley & L. Mazerolle (Eds.), *Environmental criminology and crime analysis* (pp. 78–93). Cullompton, UK: Willan.

Brantingham, P. J., & Brantingham, P. L. (1981). *Environmental criminology*. Prospect Heights, IL: Waveland Press.

Brantingham, P. L., & Brantingham, P. J. (1993). Nodes, paths, and edges: Considerations on the complexity of crime and the physical environment. *Journal of Environmental Psychology, 13*, 3–28.

Brezina, T., Agnew, R., Cullen, F., & Wright, J. P. (2004). The code of the street: A quantitative assessment of Elijah Anderson's subculture of violence thesis and its contribution to youth violence research. *Youth Violence and Juvenile Justice, 2*, 303–328.

Brockway, Z. R. (1926). Character of reformatory prisoners. In F. C. Allen (Ed.), *Extracts from penological reports and lectures written by members of the management and staff of the New York State Reformatory, Elmira, N.Y.* (pp. 110–118). Elmira, NY: Summary Press.

Browning, C. R., Feinberg, S., & Dietz, R. (2004). The paradox of social organization: Networks, collective efficacy, and violent crime in urban neighborhoods. *Social Forces*, *83*, 503–534.

Buerger, M. E., & Mazerolle, L. G. (1998). Third-party policing: A theoretical analysis of an emerging trend. *Justice Quarterly*, *15*, 301–327.

Burgess, E. W. (1916). Juvenile delinquency in a small city. *Journal of the American Institute of Criminal Law and Criminology*, *6*, 724–728.

Burke, P. B. (1997). *Policy-driven responses to probation and parole violations*. Silver Spring, MD: Center for Effective Public Policy.

Burke, P. B. (2004). *Parole violations revisited: A handbook on strengthening practices for public safety and successful offender transition*. Washington, DC: U.S. National Institute of Corrections, U.S. Department of Justice.

Burke, P. B., & Tonry, M. (2006). *Successful transition and reentry for safer communities: A call to action for parole*. Silver Spring, MD: Center for Effective Public Policy.

Burnett, R., & McNeill, F. (2005). The place of the officer-offender relationship in assisting offenders to desist from crime. *Probation Journal: The Journal of Community and Criminal Justice*, *52*, 221–242.

Burns, D. D. (1989). *The feeling good handbook*. New York, NY: William Morrow.

Burrell, W. D. (1998). Probation and public safety: Using performance measures to demonstrate public value. *Corrections Management Quarterly*, *2*(3), 61–69.

Burrell, W. D. (2012). *Community corrections management: Issues and strategies*. Kingston, NJ: Civic Research Institute.

Byrne, C. F., & Trew, K. J. (2008). Pathways through crime: The development of crime and desistance in the accounts of men and women offenders. *The Howard Journal*, *47*, 238–258.

Byrne, J. M., & Hummer, D. (2004). Examining the role of the police in reentry partnership initiatives. *Federal Probation*, *68*(2), 62–69.

Byrne, J. M., & Pattavina, A. (2013). Technological innovation and offender reentry. In S. Leman-Langlois (Ed.), *Technocrime, policing and surveillance* (pp. 110–132). London, UK: Routledge.

Campbell, N. M. (2008). *Comprehensive framework for paroling authorities in an era of evidence-based practice*. Washington, DC: National Institute of Corrections.

Carr, P. J. (2005). *Clean streets: Controlling crime, maintaining order, and building community activism*. New York, NY: New York University Press.

Carter, P. (2003). *Managing offenders, reducing crime: A new approach*. London, UK: Prime Minister's Strategy Unit.

Caspi, A., Moffitt, T., Silva, P., Stouthamer-Loeber, M., Krueger, R., & Schmutte, P. (1994). Are some people crime-prone? Replications of the personality-crime relationship across countries, genders, races, and methods. *Criminology*, *32*, 163–195.

Chang, E. C., D'Zurilla, T. J., & Sanna, L. J. (2004). *Social problem solving: Theory, research, and training*. Washington, DC: American Psychological Association.

Cherney, A. (2008). Harnessing the crime control capacities of third parties. *Policing: An International Journal of Police Strategies and Management*, *31*, 631–647.

Chesney-Lind, M. (2015). Gendered pathways into delinquency. In F. T. Cullen, P. Wilcox, J. L. Lux, & C. L. Jonson (Eds.). *Sisters in Crime revisited: Bringing gender into criminology* (pp. 83–102). New York, NY: Oxford University Press.

Clark, M. (2006). Entering the business of behavior change: Motivation interviewing for probation. *Perspectives*, *30*(1), 38–45.

Clark, M. D., Walters, S., Gingerich, R., & Meltzer, M. (2006). Motivational interviewing for probation officers: Tipping the balance toward change. *Federal Probation, 70*(1), 38–44.

Clarke, R. V. (1992). *Situational crime prevention: Successful case studies.* Albany, NY: Harrow and Heston.

Clarke, R. V. (1995). Situational crime prevention. In M. H. Tonry & D. Farrington (Eds.), *Building a safer society: Strategic approaches to crime prevention* (pp. 91–150). Chicago, IL: University of Chicago Press.

Clarke, R. V. (1997). Introduction. In R. V. Clarke (Ed.), *Situational crime prevention: Successful case studies* (2nd ed., pp. 2–43). Albany, NY: Harrow and Heston.

Clarke, R. V. (1999). *Hot products: Understanding, anticipating and reducing demand for stolen goods.* London, UK: Policing and Reducing Crime Unit, Home Office.

Clarke, R. V. (2005). Seven misconceptions of situational crime prevention. In N. Tilley (Ed.), *Handbook of crime prevention and community safety* (pp. 39–70). Cullompton, UK: Willan.

Clarke, R. V. (2008). Situational crime prevention. In R. Wortley & L. Mazerolle (Eds.), *Environmental criminology and crime analysis* (pp. 178–194). Cullompton, UK: Willan.

Clarke, R. V. (2010). Crime science. In E. McLaughlin & T. Newburn (Eds.), *The SAGE handbook of criminological theory* (pp. 272–283). Thousand Oaks, CA: Sage.

Clarke, R. V., & Cornish, D. B. (1985). Modeling offenders' decisions: A framework for research and policy. In M. Tonry & N. Morris (Eds.), *Crime and justice: An annual review of research* (Vol. 6, pp. 147–185). Chicago, IL: University of Chicago Press.

Clarke, R. V., & Eck, J. E. (2005). *Crime analysis for problem solvers in 60 small steps.* Washington, DC: Office of Community Oriented Policing Services, U.S. Department of Justice.

Clawson, E., & Guevara, M. (2011). *Putting the pieces together: Practical strategies for implementing evidence-based practices.* Washington, DC: National Institute of Corrections, U.S. Department of Justice.

Clear, T. R. (1992). Punishment and control in community supervision. In C. A. Hartjen & E. E. Rhine (Eds.), *Correctional theory and practice* (pp. 31–42). Chicago, IL: Nelson-Hall.

Clear, T. R. (1996). Toward a corrections of "place": The challenge of "community" in corrections. *National Institute of Justice Journal, 231,* 52–56.

Clear, T. R. (2000). How to make broken windows theory really work in community corrections. *Community Corrections Report, 8*(1), 3–15.

Clear, T. R., Cole, G. F., & Reisig, M. D. (2009). *American corrections.* Belmont, CA: Thomson Wadsworth.

Clear, T. R., & Corbett, R. P. (1999). Community corrections of place. *Perspectives, 23*(1), 24–31.

Clear, T. R., & Frost, N. A. (2014). *The punishment imperative: The rise and failure of mass incarceration in America.* New York, NY: New York University Press.

Cohen, L. E., & Felson, M. (1979). Social change and crime rate trends: A routine activity approach. *American Sociological Review, 44,* 588–608.

Community Policing Consortium. (1994). *Understanding community policing: A framework for action:* Washington, DC: Bureau of Justice Assistance.

Corbett, R. P., Jr. (2002). Reinventing probation and reducing youth violence. In D. R. Karp & T. R. Clear (Eds.), *What is community justice? Case studies of restorative justice and community supervision* (pp. 111–134). Thousand Oaks, CA: Sage.

Cordner, G. (1999). Elements of community policing. In L. K. Gaines & G. W. Cordner (Eds.), *Policing perspectives: An anthology* (pp. 137–149). Los Angeles, CA: Roxbury.

Cordner, G., & Biebel, E. P. (2005). Problem-oriented policing in practice. *Criminology and Public Policy, 4*, 155–180.

Cornish, D. B., & Clarke, R. V. (Eds.). (1986). *The reasoning criminal: Rational choice perspectives on criminal offending.* New York, NY: Springer-Verlag.

Cornish, D. B., & Clarke, R. V. (2003). Opportunities, precipitators and criminal decisions: A reply to Wortley's critique of situational crime prevention. *Crime Prevention Studies, 16*, 41–96.

Cornish, D. B., & Clarke, R. V. (2008). The rational choice perspective. In R. Wortley & L. Mazerolle (Eds.), *Environmental criminology and crime analysis* (pp. 21–47). Cullompton, UK: Willan.

Craig, L. A., Dixon, L., & Gannon, T. A. (Eds.). (2013). *What works in offender rehabilitation: An evidence-based approach to assessment and treatment.* Chichester, UK: Wiley-Blackwell.

Crime and Justice Institute at Community Resources for Justice. (2009). *Implementing evidence-based policy and practice in community corrections* (2nd ed.). Washington, DC: National Institute of Corrections, U.S. Department of Justice.

Cromwell, P., & Birzer, M. L. (2014). *In their own words: Criminals on crime.* New York, NY: Oxford University Press.

Crowe, A. H. (1998). Restorative justice and offender rehabilitation: A meeting of the minds. *Perspectives, 22*(3), 28–40.

Cullen, F. T. (2002). Rehabilitation and treatment programs. In J. Q. Wilson & J. Petersilia (Eds.), *Crime: Public policies for crime control* (2nd ed.; pp. 253–289). San Francisco, CA: ICS Press.

Cullen, F. T., Blevins, K. R., Trager, J. S., & Gendreau, P. (2005). The rise and fall of boot camps: A case study in common-sense corrections. *Journal of Offender Rehabilitation, 40*(3), 53–70.

Cullen, F. T., Eck, J. E., & Lowenkamp, C. T. (2002). Environmental corrections: A new paradigm for effective probation and parole supervision. *Federal Probation, 66*(2), 28–37.

Cullen, F. T., Fisher, B. S., & Applegate, B. K. (2000). Public opinion about punishment and corrections. In M. Tonry (Ed.), *Crime and justice: A review of research* (Vol. 27, pp. 1–79). Chicago, IL: University of Chicago Press.

Cullen, F. T., & Gendreau, P. (2000). Assessing correctional rehabilitation: Policy, practice, and prospects. In J. Horney (Ed.), *Criminal justice 2000: Volume 3. Policies, processes, and decisions of the criminal justice system* (pp. 109–175). Washington, DC: U.S. Department of Justice, National Institute of Justice.

Cullen, F. T., & Gendreau, P. (2001). From nothing works to what works: Changing professional ideology in the 21st century. *The Prison Journal, 81*, 313–338.

Cullen, F. T., & Gilbert, K. E. (1982). *Reaffirming rehabilitation.* Cincinnati, OH: Anderson.

Cullen, F. T., & Gilbert, K. E. (2013). *Reaffirming rehabilitation* (2nd ed.). Waltham, MA: Anderson.

Cullen, F. T., & Jonson, C. L. (2011). Rehabilitation and treatment programs. In J. Q. Wilson & J. Petersilia (Eds.), *Crime and public policy* (pp. 293–344). New York, NY: Oxford University Press.

Cullen, F. T., & Jonson, C. L. (2012). *Correctional theory: Context and consequences.* Thousand Oaks, CA: Sage.

Cullen, F. T., Jonson, C. L., & Mears, D. P. (2015, November). *Reinventing community corrections: Ten recommendations.* Paper presented at the annual meeting of the American Society of Criminology, Washington, DC.

Cullen, F. T., Jonson, C. T., & Nagin, D. S. (2011). Prisons do not reduce recidivism: The high cost of ignoring science. *The Prison Journal, 91,* 48S–65S.

Cullen, F. T., Myer, A. J., & Latessa, E. J. (2009). Eight lessons from *Moneyball*: The high cost of ignoring evidence-based corrections. *Victims and Offenders, 4,* 197–213.

Cullen, F. T., Pratt, T. C., Micelli, S. L., & Moon, M. M. (2002). Dangerous liaison? Rational choice theory as the basis for correctional intervention. In A. R. Piquero & S. G. Tibbetts (Eds.), *Rational choice and criminal behavior* (pp. 279–296). New Brunswick, NJ: Transaction.

Cullen, F. T., & Smith, P. (2011). Treatment and rehabilitation. In M. Tonry (Ed.), *The Oxford handbook of crime and criminal justice.* New York, NY: Oxford University Press.

Cullen, F. T., Wright, J. P., & Applegate, B. K. (1996). Control in the community: The limits of reform? In A. T. Harland (Ed.), *Choosing correctional interventions that work: Defining the demand and evaluating the supply* (pp. 69–116). Newbury Park, CA: Sage.

Cullen, F. T., Wright, J. P., Gendreau, P., & Andrews, D. A. (2003). What correctional treatment can tell us about criminological theory: Implications for social learning theory. In R. L. Akers & G. F. Jensen (Eds.), *Social learning theory and the explanation of crime: A guide for the new century* (pp. 339–362). New Brunswick, NJ: Transaction.

Daigle, L. E., Cullen, F. T., & Wright, J. P. (2007). Gender differences in the predictors of juvenile delinquency: Assessing the generality-specificity debate. *Youth Violence and Juvenile Justice, 5,* 254–286.

Davidson, R. J., Putnam, K. M., & Larson, C. L. (2000). Dysfunction in the neural circuitry of emotion regulation: A possible prelude to violence. *Science, 289,* 591–594.

Day, A. (2009). Offender emotion and self-regulation: Implications for offender rehabilitation programming. *Psychology, Crime, and Law, 15,* 119–130.

De Haan, W., & Loader, I. (2002). On the emotions of crime, punishment and social control. *Theoretical Criminology, 6,* 243–253.

DeMichele, M. T. (2007). *Probation and parole's growing caseloads and workload allocation: Strategies for managerial decision making.* Lexington, KY: American Probation and Parole Association.

Dickey, W. J., & Klingele, C. (2004, May 12–13). Promoting public safety: A problem-oriented approach to prisoner reentry. In *Prisoner reentry and community policing: Strategies for enhancing public safety* (Working Papers, Reentry Roundtable Meeting, pp. 54–75). Washington, DC: Justice Policy Center, Urban Institute.

Dickey, W. J., & Smith, M. E. (1998). *Dangerous opportunity: Five futures for community corrections.* Washington, DC: National Institute of Justice, Office of Justice Programs.

Dowden, C., & Andrews, D. A. (1999). What works in young offender treatment: A meta-analysis. *Forum on Corrections Research, 11,* 21–24.

Dowden, C., & Andrews, D. A. (2004). The importance of staff practice in delivering effective correctional treatment: A meta-analytic review of core correctional practice. *International Journal of Offender Therapy and Comparative Criminology, 48,* 203–214.

Dowden, C,. Antonowicz, D., & Andrews, D. A. (2000). The effectiveness of relapse prevention with offenders: A meta-analysis. *International Journal of Offender Therapy and Comparative Criminology, 47,* 516–528.

Dressler, D. (1962). *Practice and theory of probation and parole.* New York, NY: Columbia University Press.

Duriez, S. A., Cullen, F. T., & Manchak, S. M. (2014). Is Project HOPE creating a false sense of hope? A case study in correctional philosophy. *Federal Probation, 78*(2), 57–70.

Durlauf, S., & Nagin, D. (2011). Imprisonment and crime: Can both be reduced? *Criminology and Public Policy, 10,* 13–54.

Durose, M. R., Cooper, A. D., & Snyder, H. N. (2014). *Recidivism of prisoners released in 30 states in 2005: Patterns from 2005 to 2010.* Washington, DC: U.S. Department of Justice, Office of Justice Programs, Bureau of Justice Statistics.

D'Zurilla, T. J., & Nezu, A. M. (2007). *Problem-solving therapy: A social competence approach to clinical intervention* (3rd ed.). New York, NY: Springer.

Eck, J. E. (1994). *Drug markets and drug places: A case-control study of the spatial structure of illicit drug dealing.* Unpublished doctoral dissertation, University of Maryland, College Park.

Eck, J. E. (2003). Police problems: The complexity of problem theory, research and evaluation. *Crime Prevention Studies, 15,* 67–102.

Eck, J. E. (2005). Crime hot spots: What they are, why we have them, and how to map them. In National Institute of Justice, *Mapping crime: Understanding hot spots* (pp. 1–14). Washington, DC: U.S. Department of Justice, Office of Justice Programs, National Institute of Justice.

Eck, J. E., Clarke, R. V., & Guerette, R. T. (2007). Risky facilities: Crime concentration in homogeneous sets of establishments and facilities. *Crime Prevention Studies, 21,* 225–264.

Eck, J. E., & Spelman, W. (1987a). *Problem-solving: Problem-oriented policing in Newport News.* Washington, DC: National Institute of Justice.

Eck, J. E., & Spelman, W. (1987b). Who ya gonna call? The police as problem-busters. *Crime and Delinquency, 33,* 31–52.

Eck, J. E., & Weisburd, D. (1995). Crime places in crime theory. *Crime Prevention Studies, 4,* 1–33.

Ekblom, P. (1997). Gearing up against crime: A dynamic framework to help designers keep up with the adaptive criminal in a changing world. *International Journal of Risk, Security, and Crime Prevention, 2,* 249–265.

Ekblom, P. (2005). How to police the future: Scanning for scientific and technological innovations which generate potential threats and opportunities in crime, policing and crime reduction. In M. J. Smith & N. Tilley (Eds.), *Crime science: New approaches to preventing and detecting crime* (pp. 27–55). Cullompton, UK: Willan.

Engel, L., & Atkisson, J. (2010). *Priorities and public safety I: Reentry and the rising costs of our corrections system.* Boston, MA: Crime and Justice Institute.

Eriksson, T. (1976). *The reformers: An historical survey of pioneer experiments in the treatment of criminals.* New York, NY: Elsevier.

Evans, D. (2001). Project Spotlight—Partnership in supervision. *Corrections Today, 63,* 110–111.

Farrall, S. (2002). *Rethinking what works with offenders: Probation, social context and desistance from crime.* Cullompton, UK: Willan.

Farrall, S. (2004). Social capital and offender reintegration: Making probation desistance focused. In S. Maruna & R. Immarigeon (Eds.), *After crime and punishment: Pathways to offender reintegration* (pp. 57–82). Portland, OR: Willan.

Farrall, S. (2005). On the existential aspects of desistance of crime. *Symbolic Interaction, 28,* 367–386.

Farrell, G., Tilley, N., Tseloni, A., & Mailley, J. (2010). Explaining and sustaining the crime drop: Clarifying the role of opportunity-related theories. *Crime Prevention and Community Safety*, *12*, 24–41.

Feeley, M. M., & Simon, J. (1992). The new penology: Notes on the emerging strategy of corrections and its implications. *Criminology*, *30*, 449–474.

Felson, M. (1986). Linking criminal choices, routine activities, informal control, and criminal outcomes. In D. B. Cornish & R. V. Clarke (Eds.), *The reasoning criminal: Rational choice perspectives on offending* (pp. 119–128). New York, NY: Springer-Verlag.

Felson, M. (1995). Those who discourage crime. In J. E. Eck & D. Weisburd (Eds.), *Crime and place* (pp. 53–66). Monsey, NY: Criminal Justice Press.

Felson, M., & Boba, R. (2010). *Crime and everyday life* (4th ed.). Thousand Oaks, CA: Sage.

Felson, M., & Clarke, R. V. (1998). *Opportunity makes the thief: Practical theory for crime prevention*. London, UK: Policing and Reducing Crime Unit, Home Office.

Fogg, B. J., & Eckles. D. (Eds.). (2007). *Mobile persuasion: 20 perspectives on the future of behavior change*. Stanford, CA: Stanford Captology Media.

Friestad, C. (2012). Making sense, making good, or making meaning? Cognitive distortions as targets of change in offender treatment. *International Journal of Offender Therapy and Comparative Criminology*, *56*, 465–482.

Fulton, B., Latessa, E. J., Stichman, A., & Travis, L. F. (1997). The state of ISP: Research and policy implications. *Federal Probation*, *61*(4), 65–75.

Fulton, B., Stichman, A., Travis, L., & Latessa, E. (1997). Moderating probation and parole officer attitudes to achieve desired outcomes. *The Prison Journal*, *77*, 295–312.

Garland, D. (2001). *The culture of control: Crime and social order in contemporary society*. Chicago, IL: University of Chicago Press.

Gendreau, P. (1996). The principles of effective intervention with offenders. In A. T. Harland (Ed.), *Choosing correctional interventions that work: Defining the demand and evaluating the supply* (pp. 117–130). Newbury Park, CA: Sage.

Gendreau, P., & Andrews, D. (2001). *Correctional Program Assessment Inventory – 2000 (CPAI-2000)*. Saint Johns, New Brunswick, Canada: Authors.

Gendreau, P., Cullen, F. T., & Bonta, J. (1994). Intensive rehabilitation supervision: The next generation in community corrections? *Federal Probation*, *58*(1), 72–78.

Gendreau, P., Goggin, C., Cullen, F. T., & Andrews, D. A. (2000). The effects of community sanctions and incarceration on recidivism. *Forum on Corrections Research*, *12*(2), 10–13.

Gendreau, P., Goggin, C., & Fulton, B. (2000). Intensive supervision in probation and parole settings. In C. Hollin (Ed.), *Handbook of offender assessment and treatment* (pp. 195–204). Chichester, UK: Wiley.

Gendreau, P., Goggin, C., & Smith, P. (1999). The forgotten issue in effective correctional intervention: Program implementation. *International Journal of Offender Therapy and Comparative Criminology*, *43*, 180–187.

Gendreau, P., Goggin, C., & Smith, P. (2001). Implementation guidelines for correctional programs in the "real world." In G. A. Bernfeld, D. P. Farrington, & A. W. Leschied (Eds.), *Offender rehabilitation in practice: Implementing and evaluating effective programs* (pp. 247–268). New York, NY: Wiley.

Gendreau, P., Little, T., & Goggin, C. (1996). A meta-analysis of the predictors of adult offender recidivism: What works! *Criminology*, *34*, 575–607.

Gendreau, P., & Ross, B. (1979). Effective correctional treatment: Bibliotherapy for cynics. *Crime and Delinquency*, *25*, 463–489.

Gendreau, P., Smith, P., & French, S. (2006). The theory of effective correctional intervention: Empirical status and future directions. In F. T. Cullen, J. P. Wright, & K. R. Blevins (Eds.), *Taking stock: The status of criminological theory* (Advances in Criminological Theory, Vol. 15, pp. 419–446). New Brunswick, NJ: Transaction.

Gentile, J. R. (1995, July–August). Community policing: A philosophy, not a program. *Community Policing Exchange*, (6), article 4.

Gibbons, D. C. (2000). The limits of punishment as social policy. In B. W. Hancock & P. M. Sharp (Eds.), *Public policy, crime, and criminal justice* (pp. 280–294). Upper Saddle River, NJ: Prentice Hall.

Gifford, E. V., & Hayes, S. C. (1999). Functional contextualism: A pragmatic philosophy for behavioral science. In W. O'Donohue & R. Kitchener (Eds.), *Handbook of behaviorism* (pp. 285–327). San Diego, CA: Academic Press.

Ginsburg, J. D., Mann, R. E., Rotgers, F., & Weekes, J. R. (2002). Motivational interviewing with criminal justice populations. In W. R. Miller & S. Rollnick (Eds.), *Motivational interviewing: Preparing people to change addictive behavior* (2nd ed.; pp. 333–346). New York, NY: Guilford.

Giordano, P. C., Cernkovich, S. A., & Rudolph, J. L. (2002). Gender, crime, and desistance: Toward a theory of cognitive transformation. *American Journal of Sociology*, *107*, 990–1064.

Glaze, L. E., & Bonczar, T. P. (2011). *Probation and parole in the United States, 2010*. Washington, DC: Bureau of Justice Statistics, U.S. Department of Justice.

Glaze, L. E., Bonczar, T. P., & Zhang, F. (2010). *Probation and parole in the United States, 2009*. Washington, DC: Bureau of Justice Statistics, U.S. Department of Justice.

Glaze, L. E., & Herberman, E. J. (2013). *Correctional populations in the United States, 2012*. Washington, DC: Bureau of Justice Statistics, U.S. Department of Justice.

Gleicher, L., Manchak, S. M., & Cullen, F. T. (2013). Creating a supervision toolkit: How to improve probation and parole. *Federal Probation*, *77*(1), 22–27.

Glick, B. (2006). *Cognitive behavioral interventions for at-risk youth*. Kingston, NJ: Civic Research Institute.

Glueck, S., & Glueck, E. (1950). *Unraveling juvenile delinquency*. Cambridge, MA: Harvard University Press.

Glueck, S., & Glueck, E. (1968). *Delinquents and nondelinquents in perspective*. Cambridge, MA: Harvard University Press.

Glueck, S., & Glueck, E. (1974). *Of delinquency and crime*. Springfield, IL: Charles C. Thomas.

Glyde, J. (1856). Localities of crime in Suffolk. *Journal of the Statistical Society of London*, *19*, 102–106.

Goldsmith, A. (2005). Police reform and the problem of trust. *Theoretical Criminology*, *9*, 443–470.

Goldstein, H. (1979). Improving policing: A problem-oriented approach. *Crime and Delinquency*, *25*, 236–258.

Goldstein, H. (1990). *Problem-oriented policing*. Philadelphia, PA: Temple University Press.

Gottfredson, M. R. (2006). The empirical status of control theory in criminology. In F. T. Cullen, J. P. Wright, & K. R. Blevins (Eds.), *Taking stock: The status of criminological theory* (Advances in Criminological Theory, Vol. 15, pp. 77–100). New Brunswick, NJ: Transaction.

Gottfredson, M. R., & Hirschi, T. (1990). *A general theory of crime*. Stanford, CA: Stanford University Press.

Gottschalk, M. (2006). *The prison and the gallows: The politics of mass incarceration in America*. New York, NY: Cambridge University Press.

Greene, J. R. (2000). Community policing in America: Changing the nature, structure, and function of the police. In J. Horney (Ed.), *Criminal justice 2000: Vol. 3. Policies, processes, and decisions of the criminal justice system* (pp. 299–370). Washington, DC: U.S. Department of Justice, National Institute of Justice.

Griffin, M., Hepburn, J., & Webb, V. (2004). *Combining police and probation information resources to reduce burglary: Testing a crime analysis problem-solving approach.* Washington, DC: National Institute of Justice.

Gross, J. J. (1998). Antecedent- and response-focused emotion regulation: Divergent consequences for experience, expression, and physiology. *Journal of Personality and Social Psychology, 74*, 224–237.

Guastaferro, W. P., & Daigle, L. E. (2012). Linking noncompliant behaviors and programmatic responses: The use of graduated sanctions in a felony-level drug court. *Journal of Drug Issues, 42*, 396–419.

Hagenbucher, G. (2003). PROGRESS: An enhanced supervision program for high-risk criminal offenders. *Law Enforcement Bulletin, 72*(9), 20–24.

Harcourt, B. E. (2001). *Illusion of order: The false promise of broken windows policing.* Cambridge, MA: Harvard University Press.

Harland, A. T. (Ed.). (1996). *Choosing correctional options that work: Defining the demand and evaluating the supply.* Thousand Oaks, CA: Sage.

Harper, G., & Chitty, C. (2005). *The impact of corrections on re-offending: A review of "what works"* (3rd ed.). London, UK: Home Research Office, Development and Statistics Directorate.

Harries, K. D. (1974). *The geography of crime and justice.* New York, NY: McGraw-Hill.

Harries, K. D. (1999). *Mapping crime: Principle and practice.* Washington, DC: National Institute of Justice, U.S. Department of Justice.

Harris, P. M., Gingerich, R., & Whittaker, T. A. (2004). The "effectiveness" of differential supervision. *Crime and Delinquency, 50*, 235–271.

Harris, P. M., Petersen, R. D., & Rapoza, S. (2001). Between probation and revocation: A study of intermediate sanctions decision-making. *Journal of Criminal Justice, 29*, 307–318.

Healey, K. M. (1999). *Case management in the criminal justice system.* Washington, DC: National Institute of Justice, U.S. Department of Justice.

Higgins, S. T., & Silverman, K. (1999). *Motivating illicit drug abusers to change their behavior: Research on contingency management interventions.* Washington, DC: American Psychological Association.

Hirschi, T. (1969). *Causes of delinquency.* Berkley: University of California Press.

Hollis-Peel, M. E., Reynald, D. M., van Bavel, M., Elffers, H., & Welsh, B. C. (2011). Guardianship for crime prevention: A critical review of the literature. *Crime, Law, and Social Change, 56*, 53–70.

Hope, D. A., Burns, J. A., Hayes, S. A., Herbert, J. D., & Warner, M. D. (2010). Automatic thoughts and cognitive restructuring in cognitive behavioral group therapy for social anxiety disorder. *Cognitive Therapy and Research, 34*, 1–12.

Hughes, R. (1987). *The fatal shore: The epic of Australia's founding.* New York, NY: Knopf.

International Association of Chiefs of Police. (2007). *Police-corrections partnerships: Collaborating for strategic crime control.* Washington, DC: Bureau of Justice Assistance, U.S. Department of Justice.

Jacobs, B. A., & Wright, R. (2009). Bounded rationality, retaliation, and the spread of urban violence. *Journal of Interpersonal Violence, 25*, 1739–1766.

Jalbert, S. K., Rhodes, W., Flygare, C., & Kane, M. (2010). Testing probation outcomes in an evidence-based practice setting: Reduced caseload size and intensive supervision effectiveness. *Journal of Offender Rehabilitation, 49*, 233–253.

Jannetta, J., Elderbroom, B., Solomon, A., Cahill, M., Parthasarathy, B., & Burrell, W. (2009). *An evolving field: Findings from the 2008 Parole Practices Survey.* Washington, DC: Urban Institute.

Jannetta, J., & Lachman, P. (2011). *Promoting partnerships between police and community supervision agencies.* Washington, DC: Office of Community Oriented Policing Services, U.S. Department of Justice.

Jeffery, C. R. (1971). *Crime prevention through environmental design.* Beverly Hills, CA: Sage.

Jolls, C., Sunstein, C. R., & Thaler, R. (1998). A behavioral approach to law and economics. *Stanford Law Review, 50*, 1471–1550.

Jordan, J. T. (1998). Boston's Operation Night Light: New roles, new rules. *Law Enforcement Bulletin, 67*(8), 1–5.

Karoly, P. (2012). Self-regulation. In W. O'Donohue & J. E. Fisher (Eds.), *Cognitive behavior therapy: Core principles for practice* (pp. 183–213). Hoboken, NJ: Wiley.

Karp, D. R., & Clear, T. R. (2000). Community justice: A conceptual framework. In C. M. Friel (Ed.), *Criminal justice 2000: Vol. 2. Boundary changes in criminal justice organizations* (pp. 323–368). Washington, DC: U.S. Department of Justice, Office of Justice Programs.

Karr-Morse, R., & Wiley, M. S. (1997). *Ghosts from the nursery: Tracing the roots of violent behavior.* New York, NY: Atlantic Monthly.

Katz, J. (1988). *The seductions of crime: Moral and sensual attractions of doing evil.* New York, NY: Basic Books.

Kazemian, L. (2007). Desistance from crime: Theoretical, empirical, methodological, and policy considerations. *Journal of Contemporary Criminal Justice, 23*, 5–27.

Kennedy, D. (1998). Pulling levers: Getting deterrence right. *National Institute of Justice Journal, 236*, 2–8.

Kim, B., Gerber, J., & Beto, D. R. (2010). Listening to law enforcement officers: The promises and problems of police-adult probation partnerships. *Journal of Criminal Justice, 38*, 625–632.

Klockars, C. B., Jr. (1972). A theory of probation supervision. *Journal of Criminal Law, Criminology, and Police Science, 63*, 550–557.

Klofas, J., Hipple, N. K., & McGarrell, E. (Eds.). (2010). *The new criminal justice: American communities and the changing world of crime control.* New York, NY: Routledge.

Kornhauser, R. R. (1978). *Social sources of delinquency: An appraisal of analytic models.* Chicago, IL: University of Chicago Press.

Kubrin, C. E., & Weitzer, R. (2003). New directions in social disorganization theory. *Journal of Research in Crime and Delinquency, 40*, 374–402.

Kyckelhahn, T. (2012). *State corrections expenditures, FY 1982–2010.* Washington, DC: U.S. Department of Justice, Office of Justice Programs, Bureau of Justice Statistics.

Landenberger, N. A., & Lipsey, M. W. (2005). The positive effects of cognitive-behavioral programs for offenders: A meta-analysis of factors associated with effective treatment. *Journal of Experimental Criminology, 1*, 451–476.

Langan, P. A., & Levin, D. J. (2002). *Recidivism of prisoners released in 1994.* Washington, DC: Bureau of Justice Statistics, U.S. Department of Justice.

Latessa, E. J. (Ed.). (1999). *Strategic solutions: The International Community Corrections Association examines substance abusers.* Lanham, MD: American Correctional Association.

Latessa, E. J., Cullen, F. T., & Gendreau, P. (2002). Beyond correctional quackery: Professionalism and the possibility of effective treatment. *Federal Probation, 66*(2), 43–49.

Latessa, E. J., & Holsinger, A. (1998). The importance of evaluating correctional programs: Assessing outcome and quality. *Corrections Management Quarterly, 2*(4), 22–29.

Latessa, E. J., & Lowenkamp, C. (2006). What works in reducing recidivism. *University of St. Thomas Law Journal, 3*, 521–535.

Laub, J. H., & Sampson, R. J. (2001). Understanding desistance from crime. In M. Tonry (Ed.), *Crime and justice: A review of research* (Vol. 28, pp. 1–69). Chicago, IL: University of Chicago Press.

Laub, J. H., & Sampson, R. J. (2003). *Shared beginnings, divergent lives: Delinquent boys to age 70.* Cambridge, MA: Harvard University Press.

Laub, J. H., Sampson, R. J., & Allen, L. C. (2001). Explaining crime over the life course: Toward a theory of age-graded informal social control. In R. Paternoster & R. Bachman (Eds.), *Explaining criminals and crime: Essays in contemporary criminological theory* (pp. 97–112). Los Angeles, CA: Roxbury.

La Vigne, N. (2008). *Mapping for community-based prisoner reentry efforts: A guidebook for law enforcement agencies and their partners.* Washington, DC: U.S. Department of Justice, Office of Community Oriented Policing Services.

La Vigne, N., Solomon, A., Beckman, K., & Dedel, K. (2006). *Prisoner reentry and community policing: Strategies for enhancing public safety.* Washington, DC: U.S. Department of Justice, Office of Community Oriented Policing Services.

Leahy, R. L., & Rego, S. A. (2012). Cognitive restructuring. In W. O'Donohue & J. E. Fisher (Eds.), *Cognitive behavior therapy: Core principles for practice* (pp. 133–158). Hoboken, NJ: Wiley.

LeBel, T. P., Burnett, R., Maruna, S., & Bushway, S. (2008). The "chicken and the egg" of subjective and social factors in desistance from crime. *European Journal of Criminology, 5*, 131–159.

Leitenberger, D., Semenyna, P., & Spelman, J. B. (2003). Community corrections and community policing: A perfect match. *FBI Law Enforcement Bulletin, 72*(11), 20–23.

Levenson, R. W. (1999). The intrapersonal functions of emotion. *Cognition and Emotion, 13*, 481–504.

Lilly, J. R., Cullen, F. T., & Ball, R. A. (2015). *Criminological theory: Context and consequences.* Thousand Oaks, CA: Sage.

Lindner, C. (1994). The police contribution to the development of probation: An historical account. *Journal of Offender Rehabilitation, 20*, 61–84.

Lindquist, C. H., Krebs, C. P., & Lattimore, P. K. (2006). Sanctions and rewards in drug court programs: Implementation, perceived efficacy, and decision making. *Journal of Drug Issues, 36*, 119–146.

Lipsey, M. (1999). Can intervention rehabilitate serious delinquents. *Annals of the American Academy of Political and Social Science, 564*, 142–166.

Lipsey, M. W. (2009). The primary factors that characterize effective interventions with juvenile offenders: A meta-analytic overview. *Victims and Offenders, 4*, 124–147.

Lipsey, M. W., Chapman, G. L., & Landenberger, N. A. (2001). Cognitive-behavioral programs for offenders. *Annals of the American Academy of Political and Social Science, 578*, 144–157.

Lipsey, M. W., Landenberger, N. A., & Wilson, S. J. (2007). Effects of cognitive-behavioral programs for criminal offenders. *Campbell Systematic Reviews, 6*, 1–27.

Lipsey, M. W., & Wilson, D. B. (1998). Effective intervention for serious juvenile offenders: A synthesis of research. In R. Loeber & D. P. Farrington (Eds.), *Serious and violent juvenile offenders: Risk factors and successful interventions* (pp. 313–345). Thousand Oaks, CA: Sage.

Lipsky, M. (1980). *Street-level bureaucracy: Dilemmas of the individual in public service.* New York, NY: Russell Sage.

Lipton, D., Martinson, R., & Wilks, J. (1975). *The effectiveness of correctional treatment: A survey of treatment evaluation studies.* New York, NY: Praeger.

Loeber, R., & Hay, D. (1997). Key issues in the development of aggression and violence from childhood to early adulthood. *Annual Review of Psychology, 48,* 371–410.

Lowenkamp, C. T., & Bechtel, K. (2007). The predictive validity of the LSI-R on a sample of offenders drawn from the records of the Iowa Department of Corrections data management system. *Federal Probation, 71*(3), 25–29.

Lowenkamp, C. T., Cullen, F. T., & Pratt, T. C. (2003). Replicating Sampson and Groves's test of social disorganization theory: Revisiting a criminological classic. *Journal of Research in Crime and Delinquency, 40,* 351–373.

Lowenkamp, C. T., & Latessa, E. J. (2004). Understanding the risk principle: How and why correctional interventions can harm low-risk offenders. In *Topics in community corrections* (pp. 3–8). Washington, DC: National Institute of Corrections, U.S. Department of Justice.

Lowenkamp, C. T., & Latessa, E. J. (2005). Increasing the effectiveness of correctional programming through the risk principle: Identifying offenders for residential placement. *Criminology and Public Policy, 4,* 263–290.

Lowenkamp, C., Latessa, E. J., & Holsinger, A. (2006). The risk principle in action: What have we learned from 13,676 offenders and 97 correctional programs? *Crime and Delinquency, 52,* 77–93.

Lowenkamp, C. T., Latessa, E. J., & Smith, P. (2006). Does correctional program quality really matter? The impact of adhering to the principles of effective intervention. *Criminology and Public Policy, 5,* 575–594.

Lucht, J., La Vigne, N., Brazzell, D., & Denver, M. (2011). *Enhancing supervision and support for released prisoners: A documentation and evaluation of the community supervision mapping system.* Washington, DC: Urban Institute, Justice Policy Center.

Luong, D., & Wormith, J. S. (2011). Applying risk/need assessment to probation practice and its impact on the recidivism of young offenders. *Criminal Justice and Behavior, 38,* 1177–1199.

MacKenzie, D. L. (2000). Evidence-based corrections: Identifying what works. *Crime and Delinquency, 46,* 457–471.

MacKenzie, D. L. (2006). *What works in corrections: Reducing the criminal activities of offenders and delinquents.* New York, NY: Cambridge University Press.

MacKenzie, D. L., Browning, K., Skroban, S. B., & Smith, D. A. (1999). The impact of probation on the criminal activities of offenders. *Journal of Research in Crime and Delinquency, 36,* 423–453.

MacKenzie, D. L., & Li, S. (2002). The impact of formal and informal social controls on the criminal activities of probationers. *Journal of Research in Crime and Delinquency, 39,* 243–276.

Maguire, M., & Hopkins, M. (2003). Data and analysis for problem-solving: Alcohol-related crime in pubs, clubs and the street. In K. Bullock & N. Tilley (Eds.), *Crime reduction and problem-oriented policing* (pp. 126–153). Cullompton, UK: Willan.

Maltz, M. D. (1984). *Recidivism*. Orlando, FL: Academic Press.

Martinson, R. (1974). What works? Questions and answers about prison reform. *Public Interest, 35*, 22–54.

Maruna, S. (2001). *Making good: How ex-convicts reform and rebuild their lives*. Washington, DC: American Psychological Association.

Maruna, S., & Immarigeon, R. (2004). *After crime and punishment: Pathways to offender reintegration*. Portland, OR: Willan.

Maruna, S., & LeBel, T. (2003). Welcome home? Examining the "reentry court" concept from a strengths-based perspective. *Western Criminology Review, 4*(2), 91–107.

Maruna, S., LeBel, T. P., Mitchell, N., & Naples, M. (2004). Pygmalion in the reintegration process: Desistance from crime through the looking glass. *Psychology, Crime and Law, 10*, 271–281.

Maruna, S., & Ramsden, D. (2004). Living to tell the tale: Redemption narratives, shame management, and offender rehabilitation. In A. Lieblich, D. P. McAdams, & R. Josselson (Eds.), *Healing plots: The narrative basis of psychotherapy* (Narrative Study of Lives Series, pp. 129–149). Washington, DC: American Psychological Association.

Maruna, S., & Roy, K. (2007). Amputation or reconstruction? Notes on the concept of "knifing off" and desistance from crime. *Journal of Contemporary Criminal Justice, 23*, 104–124.

Matthews, B., Jones Hubbard, D., & Latessa, E. (2001). Making the next step: Using evaluability assessment to improve correctional programming. *The Prison Journal, 81*, 454–472.

Matza, D. (1964). *Delinquency and drift*. New York, NY: Wiley.

May, D. C., & Wood, P. B. (2010). *Ranking correctional punishments: Views from offenders, practitioners, and the public*. Durham, NC: Carolina Academic Press.

Mazerolle, L., & Ransley, J. (2005). *Third party policing*. New York, NY: Cambridge University Press.

McCleary, R. (1978). *Dangerous men: The sociology of parole*. Beverly Hills, CA: Sage.

McGuire, J. (2002). Integrating findings from research reviews. In J. McGuire (Ed.), *Offender rehabilitation and treatment: Effective programmes and policies to reduce reoffending* (pp. 3–38). West Sussex, UK: Wiley.

McKay, B., & Paris, B. (1998). Forging a police-probation alliance. *FBI Law Enforcement Bulletin, 67*(11), 27–32.

McMurran, M. (2009). Motivational interviewing with offenders: A systematic review. *Legal and Criminological Psychology, 14*, 83–100.

McNeill, F. (2006). A desistance paradigm for offender management. *Criminology and Criminal Justice, 6*, 39–62.

McNeill, F., Farrall, S., Lightowler, C., & Maruna, S. (2012). Reexamining evidence-based practice in community corrections: Beyond "a confined view" of what works. *Justice Research and Policy, 14*, 35–60.

McNeill, F., & Weaver, B. (2010). *Changing lives? Desistance research and offender management*. Glasgow, UK: The Scottish Centre for Crime and Justice Research.

Merton, R. K. (1973). *The sociology of science: Theoretical and empirical investigations*. Chicago, IL: University of Chicago Press.

Miller, H. J. (2005). A measurement theory for time geography. *Geographic Analysis, 37*, 17–45.

Miller, J. (2012). Probation supervision and the control of crime opportunities: An empirical assessment. *Crime and Delinquency*, 1–23.

Miller, J., & Mullins, C. W. (2006). The status of feminist theories in criminology. In
    F. T. Cullen, J. P. Wright, & K. R. Blevins (Eds.), *Taking stock: The status of crimino-
    logical theory* (Advances in Criminological Theory, Vol. 15, pp. 217–249). New
    Brunswick, NJ: Transaction.

Miller, W. R., & Rollnick, S. (2013). *Motivational interviewing: Helping people change*
    (3rd ed.). New York, NY: Guilford.

Mischel, W., & Shoda, Y. (1995). A cognitive-affective system theory of personality:
    Reconceptualizing situations, dispositions, dynamics, and invariance in personality
    structure. *Psychological Review, 102*, 246–268.

Mitchell, D., & Tafrate, R. C. (2012). Conceptualization and measurement of criminal
    thinking: Initial validation of the Criminogenic Thinking Profile. *International Journal
    of Offender Therapy and Comparative Criminology, 56*, 1080–1102.

Moffitt, T. E. (1993). Adolescence-limited and life-course-persistent antisocial behavior: A
    developmental taxonomy. *Psychological Review, 100*, 674–701.

Moffitt, T. E., Capsi, A., Rutter, M., & Silva, P. A. (2001). *Sex differences in antisocial behav-
    ior: Conduct disorder, delinquency, and violence in the Dunedin Longitudinal Study.*
    Cambridge, UK: Cambridge University Press.

Moore, M. H. (1992). Problem-solving and community policing. In M. Tonry & N. Morris
    (Eds.), *Modern policing* (Crime and Justice: A Review of Research, Vol. 15,
    pp. 99–158). Chicago, IL: University of Chicago Press.

Moore, R., Gray, E., Roberts, C., Taylor, E., & Merrington, S. (2006). *Managing persistent
    and serious offenders in the community: Intensive community programmes in theory
    and practice.* Cullompton, UK: Willan.

Moran, R., & Guglielmi, A. (2001). Parole enhanced policing program has statewide support.
    In R. Faulkner (Ed.), *Topics in community corrections: Annual issue 2001* (pp. 28–33).
    Washington, DC: National Institute of Corrections.

Morris, N., & Tonry, M. (1990). *Between prison and probation: Intermediate punishments in
    a rational sentencing system.* New York, NY: Oxford University Press.

Murphy, D. (2005). *Making police-probation partnerships work.* El Paso, TX: LFB Scholarly
    Publishing.

Murphy, D., & Lutze, F. (2009). Police-probation partnerships: Professional identity and the
    sharing of coercive power. *Journal of Criminal Justice, 37*, 65–76.

Murphy, D., & Worrall, J. (2007). The threat of mission distortion in police-probation partner-
    ships. *Policing: An International Journal of Police Strategies and Management, 30*, 132–149.

Nagin, D. S., Cullen, F. T., & Jonson, C. L. (2009). Imprisonment and reoffending. In
    M. Tonry (Ed.), *Crime and justice: A review of research* (Vol. 38, pp. 115–200). Chicago,
    IL: University of Chicago Press.

National Research Council of the National Academies. (2008). *Parole, desistance from
    crime, and community integration.* Washington, DC: National Academies Press.

Nee, C. (2004). The offender's perspective on crime: Methods and principles in data collec-
    tion. In A. Needs & G. Towl (Eds.), *Applying psychology to forensic practice* (pp. 3–17).
    Oxford, UK: Blackwell.

Nezu, A. M., & Nezu, C. M. (2012). Problem solving. In W. O'Donohue & J. E. Fisher (Eds.),
    Cognitive behavior therapy: Core principles for practice. Hoboken, NJ: Wiley.

O'Donohue, W., & Fisher, J. E. (2012). *Cognitive behavior therapy: Core principles for prac-
    tice.* Hoboken, NJ: Wiley.

Ohlin, L., Piven, H., & Pappenfort, M. (1956). Major dilemmas of the social worker in pro-
    bation and parole. *National Probation and Parole Association Journal, 2*, 211–225.

Oliver, W. M., & Bartgis, E. (1998). Community policing: A conceptual framework. *Policing: An International Journal of Police Strategies and Management, 21*, 490–509.

Palmer, T. (1975). Martinson revisited. *Journal of Research in Crime and Delinquency, 12*, 133–152.

Palmer, T. (1991). The effectiveness of intervention: Recent trends and current issues. *Crime and Delinquency, 37*, 330–346.

Papa, A., Boland, M., & Sewell, M. T. (2012). Emotion regulation and CBT. In W. O'Donohue & J. E. Fisher (Eds.), *Cognitive behavior therapy: Core principles for practice* (pp. 273–323). Hoboken, NJ: Wiley.

Paparozzi, M., & Gendreau, P. (2005). An intensive supervision program that worked: Service delivery, professional orientation, and organizational supportiveness. *The Prison Journal, 85*, 445–466.

Parent, D., & Snyder, B. (1999). *Police-corrections partnerships*. Washington, DC: National Institute of Justice, Office of Justice Programs.

Park, R., & Burgess, E. W. (1925). *The city: Suggestions for investigation of human behavior in the urban environment*. Chicago, IL: University of Chicago Press.

Paternoster, R., & Bushway, S. (2009). Desistance and the "feared self": Toward an identity theory of criminal desistance. *Journal of Criminal Law and Criminology, 99*, 1103–1156.

Peak, K. J., & Glensor, R. W. (2012). *Community policing and problem solving: Strategies and practices* (6th ed.). Upper Saddle River, NJ: Pearson.

Pearson, F. S., & Lipton, D. S. (1999). A meta-analytic review of the effectiveness of corrections-based treatments for drug abuse. *The Prison Journal, 79*, 384–410.

Pearson, F. S., Lipton, D. S., Cleland, C. M., & Yee, D. S. (2002). The effects of behavioral/cognitive-behavioral programs on recidivism. *Crime and Delinquency, 48*, 476–496.

Petersilia, J. (1999). A decade of experimenting with intermediate sanctions: What have we learned? *Justice Research and Policy, 1*, 9–23.

Petersilia, J. (2003). *When prisoners come home: Parole and prisoner reentry*. New York, NY: Oxford University Press.

Petersilia, J. (2004). What works in prisoner reentry? Reviewing and questioning the evidence. *Federal Probation, 68*(2), 4–8.

Petersilia, J. (2007). Employ behavioral contracting for "earned discharge" parole. *Criminology and Public Policy, 6*, 807–814.

Petersilia, J., & Turner, S. (1993). Intensive probation and parole. In M. Tonry (Ed.), *Crime and justice: A review of research* (Vol. 17, pp. 281–335). Chicago, IL: University of Chicago Press.

Pew Center on the States. (2008a). *One in 100: Behind bars in America 2008*. Washington, DC: The Pew Charitable Trusts.

Pew Center on the States. (2008b). *Putting public safety first: 13 strategies for successful supervision and reentry*. Washington, DC: The Pew Charitable Trusts.

Pew Center on the States. (2010). *Prison count 2010: State population declines for the first time in 38 years*. Washington, DC: The Pew Charitable Trusts.

Pierce-Danford, K., & Guevara, M. (2010). *Commonwealth of Virginia: Roadmap for evidence-based practices in community corrections*. Boston, MA: Crime and Justice Institute.

Piquero, N. (2003). A recidivism analysis of Maryland's community probation program. *Journal of Criminal Justice, 31*, 295–307.

Pisciotta, A. W. (1994). *Benevolent repression: Social control and the American reformatory-prison movement*. New York, NY: New York University Press.

Police Executive Research Forum. (2008). *Violent crime in America: What we know about hot spots enforcement.* Washington, DC: Police Executive Research Forum.

Pratt, T. C. (2009). *Addicted to incarceration: Corrections policy and the politics of misinformation in the United States.* Thousand Oaks, CA: Sage.

Pratt, T. C., & Cullen, F. T. (2000). The empirical status of Gottfredson and Hirschi's general theory of crime: A meta-analysis. *Criminology, 38,* 931–964.

Pratt, T. C., & Cullen, F. T. (2005). Assessing macro-level predictors and theories of crime: A meta-analysis. In M. Tonry (Ed.), *Crime and justice: A review of research* (Vol. 32, pp. 373–450). Chicago, IL: University of Chicago Press.

Quetelet, L. A. J. (1842). *A treatise on man and the development of his faculties.* Edinburgh, UK: W. and R. Chambers.

Ratcliffe, J. H. (2006). A temporal constraint theory to explain opportunity-based spatial offending patterns. *Journal of Research in Crime and Delinquency, 43,* 261–291.

Ratcliffe, J. H. (2008). *Intelligence-led policing.* Cullompton, UK: Willan.

Ratcliffe, J. H. (2010). Crime mapping: Spatial and temporal challenges. In A. R. Piquero & D. Weisburd (Eds.), *Handbook of quantitative criminology* (pp. 5–24). New York, NY: Springer.

Raynor, P., Ugwudike, P., & Vanstone, M. (2014). The impact of skills in probation work: A reconviction study. *Criminology and Criminal Justice, 14,* 235–249.

Raynor, P., & Vanstone, M. (2015). Moving away from social work and half way back again: New research on skills in probation. *British Journal of Social Work,* (published online February 12), 1–17.

Reentry Policy Council. (2005). *Report of the Re-Entry Policy Council: Charting the safe and successful return of prisoners to the community.* New York, NY: Council of State Governments.

Reinventing Probation Council. (2000). *Transforming probation through leadership: The "broken windows" model.* New York, NY: Center for Civic Innovation at the Manhattan Institute.

Reisig, M. D. (2010). Community and problem-oriented policing. In M. Tonry (Ed.), *Crime and justice: A review of research* (Vol. 39, pp. 1–53). Chicago, IL: University of Chicago Press.

Reiss, A. (1988). Co-offending and criminal careers. In M. Tonry & N. Morris (Eds.), *Crime and justice: A review of research* (Vol. 10, pp. 117–170). Chicago, IL: University of Chicago Press.

Reynald, D. M. (2011). *Guarding against crime: Measuring guardianship within routine activity theory.* Burlington, VT: Ashgate.

Rhine, E. E. (2002). Why "what works" matters under the "broken windows" model of supervision. *Federal Probation, 66*(2), 38–42.

Rhine, E. E., Mawhorr, T. L., & Parks, E. C. (2006). Implementation: The bane of effective correctional programs. *Criminology and Public Policy, 5,* 347–358.

Rhine, E. E., & Paparozzi, M. (1999). Reinventing probation and parole: A matter of consequence. *Corrections Management Quarterly, 3*(2), 47–52.

Rich, T. (1999). Mapping the path to problem solving. *National Institute of Justice Journal, 241,* 1–9.

Robinson, C. R., Lowenkamp, C. T., Holsinger, A. M., VanBenschoten, S., Alexander, M., & Oleson, J. C. (2012). A random study of Staff Training Aimed at Reducing Re-arrest (STARR): Using core correctional practices in probation interactions. *Journal of Crime and Justice, 35,* 167–188.

Robinson, C. R., VanBenschoten, S., Alexander, M., & Lowenkamp, C. (2011). A random (almost) study of Staff Training Aimed at Reducing Re-arrest (STARR): Reducing recidivism through intentional design. *Federal Probation, 75*(2), 57–63.

Robinson, G., & McNeill, F. (2010). The dynamics of compliance with offender supervision. In F. McNeill, P. Raynor, & C. Trotter (Eds.), *Offender supervision: New directions in theory, research and practice* (pp. 367–383). New York, NY: Willan/Routledge.

Rothman, D. J. (1980). *Conscience and convenience: The asylum and its alternatives in progressive America*. Boston, MA: Little, Brown.

Rueda, M. R., Posner, M. I., & Rothbart, M. K. (2004). Attentional control and self-regulation. In R. F. Baumeister & K. D. Vohs (Eds.), *Handbook of self-regulation: Research, theory, and applications* (pp. 283–300). New York, NY: Guilford.

Sampson, R., Eck, J. E., & Dunham, J. (2010). Super controllers and crime prevention: A routine activity explanation of crime prevention success and failure. *Security Journal, 23*, 37–51.

Sampson, R. J. (2004). Neighborhood and community: Collective efficacy and community safety. *New Economy, 11*, 106–113.

Sampson, R. J. (2011). The community. In J. Q. Wilson & J. Petersilia (Eds.), *Crime and public policy* (pp. 210–236). New York, NY: Oxford University Press.

Sampson, R. J., & Groves, W. B. (1989). Community structure and crime: Testing social-disorganization theory. *American Journal of Sociology, 94*, 774–802.

Sampson, R. J., & Laub, J. H. (1993). *Crime in the making: Pathways and turning points through life*. Cambridge, MA: Harvard University Press.

Sampson, R. J., & Laub, J. H. (2005). A life-course view of the development of crime. *Annals of the American Academy of Political and Social Science, 602*, 12–45.

Sampson, R. J., Raudenbush, S. W., & Earls, F. (1997). Neighborhoods and violent crime: A multilevel study of collective efficacy. *Science, 277*, 916–924.

Schaefer, L., Eck, J. E., & Cullen, F. T. (2014). *Monitoring offenders on conditional release*. (Problem-Oriented Guides for Police, Response Guide Series, No. 12). Washington, DC: Office of Community-Oriented Policing, U.S. Department of Justice.

Schlager, M. D., & Pacheco, D. (2011). An examination of changes in LSI-R scores over time: Making the case for needs-based case management. *Criminal Justice and Behavior, 38*, 541–553.

Schwalbe, C. S. (2012). Toward an integrated theory of probation. *Criminal Justice and Behavior, 39*, 185–201.

Scott, M., Eck, J., Knutsson, J., & Goldstein, H. (2008). Problem-oriented policing and environmental criminology. In R. Wortley & L. Mazerolle (Eds.), *Environmental criminology and crime analysis* (pp. 221–246). Cullompton, UK: Willan.

Scott, M. S. (2006). Implementing crime prevention: Lessons learned from problem-oriented policing projects. *Crime Prevention Studies, 20*, 9–35.

Shaw, C. R., & McKay, H. D. (1942). *Juvenile delinquency and urban areas: A study of rates of delinquency in relation to differential characteristics of local communities in American cities*. Chicago, IL: University of Chicago Press.

Sherman, L. W. (1992). Attacking crime: Police and crime control. In M. Tonry & N. Morris (Eds.), *Modern policing* (Crime and Justice: A Review of Research, Vol. 15, pp. 159–230). Chicago, IL: University of Chicago Press.

Sherman, L. W. (1993). Defiance, deterrence, and irrelevance: A theory of the criminal sanction. *Journal of Research in Crime and Delinquency, 30*, 445–473.

Sherman, L. W. (2011a). Criminology as invention. In C. Hoyle & L. Bosworth (Eds.), *What is criminology?* (pp. 423–439). Oxford, UK: Oxford University Press.

Sherman, L. W. (2011b). Offender desistance policing (ODP): Less prison and more evidence in rehabilitating offenders. In T. Bliesner, A. Beelman, & M. Stemmler (Eds.), *Antisocial behavior and crime: Contributions of developmental and evaluation research to prevention and intervention* (pp. 199–218). Cambridge, MA: Hogrefe.

Silver, E., & Miller, L. L. (2002). A cautionary note on the use of actuarial risk assessment tools for social control. *Crime and Delinquency, 48*, 138–161.

Simon, H. A. (1957). *Models of man—Social and rational.* New York, NY: Wiley.

Simon, J. (1993). *Poor discipline.* Chicago, IL: University of Chicago Press.

Skeem, J. L., & Manchak, S. (2008). Back to the future: From Klockars' model of effective supervision to evidence-based practice in probation. *Journal of Offender Rehabilitation, 47*, 220–247.

Smith, M. E., & Dickey, W. (1998). What if corrections were serious about public safety? *Corrections Management Quarterly, 2*(3), 12–30.

Smith, M. J. (2003). Exploring target attractiveness in vandalism: An experimental approach. In M. J. Smith & D. B. Cornish (Eds.), *Theory for practice in situational crime prevention* (Vol. 16, pp. 197–236). Monsey, NY: Criminal Justice Press.

Smith, P., Cullen, F. T., & Latessa, E. J. (2009). Can 14,737 women be wrong? A meta-analysis of the LSI-R and recidivism for female offenders. *Criminology and Public Policy, 8*, 183–208.

Smith, P., Gendreau, P., & Goggin, C. (2009). Correctional treatment: Accomplishments and realities. In P. Van Voorhis, M. Braswell, & D. Lester (Eds.), *Correctional counseling and rehabilitation* (7th ed., pp. 271–280). New Providence, NJ: Anderson/NexisLexis.

Smith, P., Gendreau, P., & Swartz, K. (2009). Validating the principles of effective intervention: A systematic review of the contributions of meta-analysis in the field of corrections. *Victims and Offenders, 4*, 148–169.

Smith, P., & Manchak, S. M. (2015). A gendered theory of offender rehabilitation. In F. T. Cullen, P. Wilcox, J. L. Lux, & C. L. Jonson (Eds.), *Sisters in Crime revisited: Bringing gender into criminology* (pp. 371–395). New York, NY: Oxford University Press.

Smith, P., Schweitzer, M., Labrecque, R. M., & Latessa, E. J. (2012). Improving probation officers' supervision skills: An evaluation of the EPICS model. *Journal of Crime and Justice, 35*, 189–199.

Solomon, A. L. (2006). Does parole supervision work? Research findings and policy opportunities. *Perspectives, 30*(2), 26–37.

Solomon, A. L., Kachnowski, V., & Bhati, A. (2005). *Does parole work? Analyzing the impact of postprison supervision on rearrest outcomes.* Washington, DC: Justice Policy Center, Urban Institute.

Solomon, A. L., Osborne, J., Winterfield, L., Elderbroom, B., Burke, P., Stroker, R., Rhine, E., & Burrell, W. (2008). *Putting public safety first: 13 parole supervision strategies to enhance reentry outcomes.* Washington, DC: Urban Institute.

Solomon, A. L., Waul, M., Van Ness, A., & Travis, J. (2004). *Outside the walls: A national snapshot of community-based prisoner reentry programs.* Washington, DC: Urban Institute.

Sousa, W. H. (2010). Paying attention to minor offenses: Order maintenance policing in practice. *Police Practice and Research, 11*, 45–59.

Sousa, W. H., & Kelling, G. L. (2006). Of broken windows, criminology, and criminal justice. In D. Weisburd & A. Braga (Eds.), *Police innovation: Contrasting perspectives* (pp. 77–97). New York, NY: Cambridge University Press.

Spiegler, M. D., & Guevremont, D. C. (2009). *Contemporary behavior therapy* (5th ed.). Belmont, CA: Wadsworth.

Stanley, D. (1976). *Prisoners among us: The problem of parole.* Washington, DC: Brookings Institute.

Steffensmeier, D. J. (1983). Organization properties and sex-segregation in the underworld: Building a sociological theory of sex differences in crime. *Social Forces, 61*, 1010–1032.

Steffensmeier, D. J., & Allan, E. (1996). Gender and crime: Toward a gendered theory of female offending. *Annual Review of Sociology, 22*, 459–487.

Stewart, E., & Simons, R. L. (2010). Race, code of the street, and violent delinquency: A multilevel investigation of neighborhood street culture and individual norms of violence. *Criminology, 48*, 569–605.

Stohr, M. K., & Walsh, A. (2011). *Corrections: The essentials*. Thousand Oaks, CA: Sage.

Sullivan, T. N., Helms, S. W., Kliewer, W., & Goodman, K. L. (2010). Associations between sadness and anger regulation coping, emotional expression, and physical and relational aggression among urban adolescents. *Social Development, 19*, 30–51.

Sykes, G. M., & Matza, D. (1957). Techniques of neutralization. *American Sociological Review, 22*, 664–260.

Tangney, J. P., Stuewig, J., Furukawa, E., Kopelovich, S., Meyer, P. J., & Cosby, B. (2012). Reliability, validity, and predictive utility of the 25-item Criminogenic Cognitions Scale (CCS). *Criminal Justice and Behavior, 39*, 1340–1360.

Taxman, F. S. (1999). Unraveling "what works" for offenders in substance abuse treatment services. *National Drug Court Institute Review, 2*, 93–134.

Taxman, F. S. (2002). Supervision: Exploring the dimensions of effectiveness. *Federal Probation, 66*(2), 14–27.

Taxman, F. S. (2006). What should we expect from parole (and probation) under a behavioral management approach? *Perspectives, 30*(2), 38–45.

Taxman, F. S. (2008). No illusions: Offender and organizational change in Maryland's proactive community supervision efforts. *Criminology and Public Policy, 7*, 275–302.

Taxman, F. S. (2011). Parole: Moving the field forward through a new model of behavioral management. In L. Gideon & H.-E. Sung (Eds.), *Rethinking corrections: Rehabilitation, reentry, and reintegration* (pp. 307–328). Thousand Oaks, CA: Sage.

Taxman, F. S. (2012). Crime control in the twenty-first century: Science-based supervision (SBS). *Journal of Crime and Justice, 35*, 135–144.

Taxman, F. S., & Byrne, J. (2001). Fixing broken windows probation. *Perspectives, 25*(2), 22–30.

Taxman, F. S., Henderson, C., & Lerch, J. (2010). The socio-political context of reforms in probation agencies: Impact on adoption of evidence-based practices. In F. McNeill, P. Raynor, & C. Trotter (Eds.), *Offender supervision: New directions in theory, research and practice* (pp. 409–429). New York, NY: Willan/Routledge.

Taxman, F. S., Shepardson, E. S., & Byrne, J. M. (2004). *Tools of the trade: A guide to incorporating science into practice*. Washington, DC: National Institute of Corrections, U.S. Department of Justice.

Taxman, F. S., Soule, D., & Gelb, A. (1999). Graduated sanctions: Stepping into accountable systems and offenders. *The Prison Journal, 79*, 182–204.

Taxman, F. S., & Thanner, M. (2006). Risk, need, and responsivity (RNR): It all depends. *Crime and Delinquency, 52*, 28–51.

Taxman, F. S., Yancey, C., & Bilanin, J. (2006). *Proactive community supervision in Maryland: Changing offender outcomes*. Baltimore: University of Maryland.

Taxman, F. S., Young, D., & Byrne, J. (2003). Transforming offender reentry into public safety: Lessons from OJP's Reentry Partnership Initiative. *Justice Research and Policy, 5*, 101–128.

Taxman, F. S., Young, D., & Byrne, J. M. (2004). With eyes wide open: Formalizing community and social control intervention in offender reintegration programmes. In S. Maruna & R. Immarigeon (Eds.), *After crime and punishment: Pathways to offender reintegration* (pp. 233–260). Portland, OR: Willan.

Taylor, M., & Nee, C. (1988). The role of cues in simulated residential burglary. *British Journal of Criminology, 28,* 396–401.

Taylor, R. B. (1997). Social order and disorder of street blocks and neighborhoods: Ecology, microecology, and the systemic model of social organization. *Journal of Research in Crime and Delinquency, 34,* 113–155.

Taylor, R. B., & Harrell, A. V. (1996). *Physical environment and crime.* Washington, DC: U.S. Department of Justice, Office of Justice Programs, National Institute of Justice.

Teague, M. (2011). Probation in America: Armed, private and unaffordable? *Probation Journal, 58,* 317–332.

Thacher, D. (2004). Order maintenance reconsidered: Moving beyond strong causal reasoning. *Journal of Criminal Law and Criminology, 94,* 381–413.

Tonry, M. (2004). *Thinking about crime: Sense and sensibility in American penal culture.* New York, NY: Oxford University Press.

Topalli, V. (2005). When being good is bad: An expansion of neutralization theory. *Criminology, 43,* 797–836.

Townsley, M., & Pease, K. (2003). Two go wild in Knowsley: Analysis for evidence-led crime reduction. In K. Bullock & N. Tilley (Eds.), *Crime reduction and problem-oriented policing* (pp. 20–37). Cullompton, UK: Willan/Routledge.

Travis, J., & Waul, M. (2002). *Reflections on the crime decline: Lessons for the future?* Washington, DC: Urban Institute.

Trotter, C. (1996). The impact of different supervision practices in community corrections: Cause for optimism. *Australian and New Zealand Journal of Criminology, 29,* 1–18.

Turner, S. (2010). Case management in corrections: Evidence, issues and challenges. In F. McNeill, P. Raynor, & C. Trotter (Eds.), *Offender supervision: New directions in theory, research and practice* (pp. 344–366). New York, NY: Willan/Routledge.

van Gelder, J.-L., Elffers, H., Nagin, D., & Reynald, D. (2013). *Affect and cognition in criminal decision making: Between rational choices and lapses of self-control.* New York, NY: Routledge.

Van Voorhis, P., Braswell, M., & Lester, D. (2009). *Correctional counseling and rehabilitation* (7th ed.). New Providence, NJ: Anderson/NexisLexis.

Vose, B., Cullen, F. T., & Smith, P. (2008). The empirical status of the Level of Service Inventory. *Federal Probation, 72*(3), 22–29.

Wagers, M., Sousa, W., & Kelling, G. (2008). Broken windows. In R. Wortley & L. Mazerolle (Eds.), *Environmental criminology and crime analysis* (pp. 247–262). Cullompton, UK: Willan.

Walker, S. (1984). "Broken windows" and fractured history: The use and misuse of history in recent police patrol analysis. *Justice Quarterly, 1,* 75–90.

Walters, S. T., Clark, M. D., Gingerich, R., & Meltzer, M. L. (2007). *A guide for probation and parole: Motivating offenders to change.* Washington, DC: National Institute of Corrections, U.S. Department of Justice.

Ward, T., & Marshall, B. (2007). Narrative identity and offender rehabilitation. *International Journal of Offender Therapy and Comparative Criminology, 51,* 279–297.

Ward, T., Melser, J., & Yates, P. M. (2007). Reconstructing the risk-need-responsivity model: A theoretical elaboration and evaluation. *Aggression and Violent Behavior, 12,* 208–228.

Warner, B. D. (2007). Directly intervene or call the authorities? A study of forms of neighborhood social control within a social disorganization framework. *Criminology, 45,* 99–129.

Warr, M. (1998). Life-course transitions and desistance from crime. *Criminology, 36,* 183–216.

Warr, M. (2002). *Companions in crime: The social aspects of criminal conduct.* New York, NY: Cambridge University Press.

Watson, D. L., & Tharp, R. G. (2002). *Self-directed behavior: Self-modification for personal adjustment.* Belmont, CA: Thomson Wadsworth.

Weisburd, D., & Eck, J. (2004). What can police do to reduce crime, disorder, and fear? *Annals of the American Academy of Political and Social Science, 593,* 43–65.

Weisburd, D., Groff, E. R., & Yang, S.-M. (2013). Understanding and controlling hot spots of crime: The importance of formal and informal social controls. *Prevention Science,* 1–13.

Weisel, D. L. (2003). The sequence of analysis in solving problems. *Crime Prevention Studies, 15,* 115–146.

Wells, W. (2007). Type of contact and evaluations of police officers: The effects of procedural justice across three types of police-citizen contacts. *Journal of Criminal Justice, 35,* 612–621.

West, A. D., & Seiter, R. P. (2004). Social worker or cop? Measuring the supervision styles of probation & parole officers in Kentucky and Missouri. *Journal of Crime and Justice, 27,* 27–57.

Whitworth, A. (2009). Strategies for effective parole supervision: Ohio's graduated sanction guidelines. *Corrections Today, 71,* 106–107.

Wilkinson, D. L. (2007). Local social ties and willingness to intervene: Textured views among violent urban youth of neighborhood social control dynamics and situations. *Justice Quarterly, 24,* 185–220.

Wilkinson, R. (Ed.). (2004). *Reentry best practices: Directors' perspectives.* Middletown, CT: Association of State Correctional Administrators.

Wilson, D. B., Bouffard, L. A., & MacKenzie, D. L. (2005). A quantitative review of structured, group-oriented, cognitive-behavioral programs for offenders. *Criminal Justice and Behavior, 32,* 172–204.

Wines, F. H. (1919). *Punishment and reformation: A study of the penitentiary system.* New York, NY: Thomas Y. Crowell.

Winstone, J., & Pakes, F. (2005). *Community justice: Issues for probation and criminal justice.* Cullompton, UK: Willan.

Wood, J., & Kemshall, H. (2007). *The operation and experience of Multi-Agency Public Protection Arrangements (MAPPA).* London, UK: Home Office.

Worrall, A., & Hoy, C. (2005). *Punishment in the community: Managing offenders, making choices* (2nd ed.). Cullompton, UK: Willan.

Worrall, J. L., & Gaines, L. K. (2006). Effect of police-probation partnerships on juvenile arrests. *Journal of Criminal Justice, 34,* 579–589.

Wortley, R. (1997). Reconsidering the role of opportunity in situational crime prevention. In G. Newman, R. V. Clarke, & S. G. Shohan (Eds.), *Rational choice and situational crime prevention* (pp. 65–81). Aldershot, UK: Ashgate.

Wortley, R. (1998). A two-stage model of situational crime prevention. *Studies on Crime and Crime Prevention, 7,* 173–188.

Wortley, R. (2001). A classification of techniques for controlling situational precipitators of crime. *Security Journal, 14*(4), 63–82.

Wortley, R. (2008). Situational precipitators of crime. In R. Wortley & L. Mazerolle (Eds.), *Environmental criminology and crime analysis* (pp. 48–69). Cullompton, UK: Willan.

Wortley, R., & Mazerolle, L. (Eds.). (2008). *Environmental criminology and crime analysis.* Cullompton, UK: Willan.

Wright, J. P., & Cullen, F. T. (2004). Employment, peers, and life-course transitions. *Justice Quarterly*, *31*, 183–205.

Wright, R., & Bennett, T. (1990). Exploring the offender's perspective: Observing and interviewing offenders. In K. L. Kempf (Ed.), *Measurement issues in criminology* (pp. 138–151). New York, NY: Springer-Verlag.

Wright, R. T., & Decker, S. (1994). *Burglars on the job: Streetlife and residential break-ins.* Boston, MA: Northeastern University Press.

Yochelson, S., & Samenow, S. (1976). *The criminal personality: Vol. 1. A profile for change.* New York, NY: Jason Aronson.

Zimring, F. E., & Hawkins, G. (1995). *Incapacitation: Penal confinement and the restraint of crime.* New York, NY: Oxford University Press.

Index

About the Authors

Lacey Schaefer is Lecturer in the School of Criminology and Criminal Justice at Griffith University. She received her Ph.D. in Criminal Justice from the University of Cincinnati. She previously worked as a Research Fellow for the University of Cincinnati Policing Institute and in the Australian Research Council's Centre of Excellence in Policing and Security, exploring the impact of community efforts on crime-reduction interventions and the disruption of offending pathways. Professor Schaefer's publications apply criminological theory to community and correctional interventions, examining the intersection of research and practice. In 2013, she coauthored *Monitoring Offenders on Conditional Release* in the Problem-Oriented Guides for Police series. Among other forums, her writings have appeared in the *Journal of Research in Crime and Delinquency* and *The Prison Journal*. Her current research explores the individual and community predictors of crime-controller actions, outlining the processes associated with crime-opportunity reduction.

Francis T. Cullen is Distinguished Research Professor Emeritus and Senior Research Associate in the School of Criminal Justice at the University of Cincinnati. He received his Ph.D. in Sociology and Education from Columbia University. Professor Cullen has published over 300 works in the areas of criminological theory, corrections, white-collar crime, public opinion, and the measurement of sexual victimization. He is author of *Rethinking Crime and Deviance Theory: The Emergence of a Structuring Tradition* and is coauthor of *Reaffirming Rehabilitation, Corporate Crime Under Attack: The Ford Pinto Case and Beyond, Criminology, Combating Corporate Crime: Local Prosecutors at Work, Criminological Theory: Context and Consequences, Unsafe in the Ivory Tower: The Sexual Victimization of College Women*, and *Correctional Theory: Context and Consequences*. He has coedited a number of volumes, including most recently *Criminological Theory: Past to Present, The Oxford Handbook of Criminological Theory, Challenging Criminological Theory: The Legacy of Ruth Rosner Kornhauser, Sisters in Crime Revisited: Bringing Gender into Criminology,* and *The American Prison: Imagining a Different Future*. Professor Cullen is a Past President of the American Society of Criminology and of the Academy of Criminal Justice Sciences. He was the recipient of the 2010 ASC Edwin H. Sutherland Award. In 2013, he was given an honorary Doctorate in Public Service from Bridgewater State University, his undergraduate alma mater.

John E. Eck is Professor of Criminal Justice at the University of Cincinnati, where he teaches police effectiveness and crime prevention. He received his bachelor's and master's degrees from the University of Michigan, and his doctorate from the University of Maryland's Department of Criminology. Professor Eck has conducted research into police operations since 1977, and served as the Research Director for the Police Executive Research Forum (PERF). At PERF, he spearheaded the development of problem-oriented policing throughout the United States. He was also the Evaluation Coordinator for Law Enforcement at the Washington/Baltimore High Intensity Drug Trafficking Area, and a consultant to the London Metropolitan Police, Royal Canadian Mounted Police, Police Foundation, and other organizations. His research has focused on the development of problem-oriented policing, police effectiveness, crime patterns, and crime prevention. He is particularly interested in concentrations of crime in very small areas, how these form, and what can be done to prevent crime at these places. Professor Eck was a member of the National Academy of Science's Committee to Review Research on Police Policy and Practices. He is the coauthor (with Ronald Clarke) of *Crime Analysis for Problem-Solvers: In 60 Small Steps*, as well as the coauthor of many publications on problem-oriented policing, crime mapping, crime prevention, and problem places. He is a coauthor of the forthcoming *Place Matters: Criminology for the 21st Century* (Cambridge University Press).